This book is dedicated to
Joe Crump

contents

high tech · high touch

ALSO BY JOHN NAISBITT

High Tech

BROADWAY BOOKS

New York

High Touch

*Technology and Our Search
for Meaning*

John Naisbitt

with Nana Naisbitt and Douglas Philips

BROADWAY

Broadway Books titles may be purchased for business or promotional use or for special sales.
For information, please write to: Special Markets Department, Random House, Inc.,
1540 Broadway, New York, NY 10036.

BROADWAY BOOKS and its logo, a letter B bisected on the diagonal, are trademarks
of Broadway Books, a division of Random House, Inc.

Visit our website at www.broadwaybooks.com

Library of Congress Cataloging-in-Publication Data
Naisbitt, John.
   High tech/high touch : technology and our search for meaning/
John Naisbitt, with Nana Naisbitt and Douglas Philips.
      p.   cm.
   ISBN 0-7679-0383-8
   1. High technology—Social aspects.   I. Naisbitt, Nana, 1957–   .
II. Philips, Douglas.   III. Title.
   T14.5.N33   1999
   303.48'3—dc21   99-37766
                                                                   CIP

Endnotes, the index and the catalogue of images can be found at
www.hightechhightouch.com

FIRST EDITION

Designed by Lee Fukui

99 00 01 02 03   10 9 8 7 6 5 4 3 2 1

introduction
our Technologically intoxicated zone

AMERICA'S STORY

Softened by the comforts technology brings to our lives, fascinated by its gadgetry, reliant on its constant companionship, addicted to its steady delivery of entertainment, seduced by its promises, awed by its power and speed, Americans are intoxicated by technology. Technology feeds our pleasure centers physically and mentally, but its intoxication is squeezing out our human spirit, intensifying our search for meaning.

Today technology is America's story. America has had a steady stream of stories: religious freedom, go west young man, the Underground Railroad, cowboys and Indians, rugged individualism, land of the free and home of the brave, land rush, gold rush, pull yourself up by your bootstraps, baseball, the melting pot, surviving the Great Depression, making the world safe for democracy, split-ting the atom and dropping the bomb, containing communism, I have a dream, rock and roll, first on the moon, make love not war, black power, the unknown soldier, Hollywood, information econo-my, the richest and strongest nation on earth, and the world's global superpower.

As a young nation, the quest for survival and comfort inspired entrepreneurs and inventors to create new technologies that alleviat-ed human suffering and lessened daily drudgery, and by the 1950s the boom of affordable "labor-saving" household appliances and cars allowed most Americans to live in comfort. Technological innovation and its cultural acceptance have since snowballed, but not without consequences. Over time, America has transformed from a techno-logically comfortable place into a Technologically Intoxicated Zone.

America is the most technologically advanced country in the world, from the military to the media. And we are intoxicated by its overpowering excitement. We talk of little else. Listen to any ordi-nary conversation. We rant and rave about the technology with which we surround ourselves. We love technology when it works. We hate it when it looms like an owner's manual we're never going to read. We love technology when it feels like a brand-new toy, but we hate it when it breaks. We talk about television shows, media events, and Internet jokes as if they were our own personal stories. Fear or worship of technology is often the subject of the films we watch, books we read, magazine stories, news headlines, and it fuels the conversations that follow.

Advertising messages in print, on billboards and television, are saturated with technology's promises. Technology offers an endless supply of quick fixes. It pledges to make us better, to make us smarter, to increase our performance, and to make us happy. It promises to be faster, cheaper, and easier than whatever came before. Technology vows to provide us with security, stability, pri-vacy, and control while it brings us peace of mind and keeps us worry free. Technology promises to connect us to the world at large and keep us close to our beloved friends and family. It records and reminds us of life's precious moments. Technology promises to become the basis of the new world economy and the great equalizer. It promises to make us rich.

Technology's promises are music to our ears. We want to believe that any given solution is only a purchase away.

Intoxicated by technology's seductive pleasures and promises, we turn our backs to technology's consequences and wonder why the future seems unpredictable. Few of us have a clear understanding of what place technology has in our lives (or should have), what place it should have in society, and most fundamentally of all, what it is. We grant technology a special status, as if it's a natural law, an inalienable right that our daily lives, our formative experiences, even the natural world are destined to be "managed" by increasingly sophisticated software. Technology marches to the beat of our economy, while we are left to plug in, get online, motor on, take off, and ultimately pick up the pieces. We feel that something is not quite right but we can't put our finger on it. The Intoxicated Zone is spiritually empty, dissatisfying and dangerous, and impossible to climb out of *unless* we recognize that we're in it. As Marshall McLuhan liked to say, he didn't know who discovered water, but he was sure it wasn't a fish. When you're in something so deep it's hard to see it.

Fortunately we are not fish. Some artists, theologians, scientists, and members of the military, among others, are recognizing and publicly acknowledging that, at its best, technology supports and improves human life, and warning that, at its worst, it alienates, isolates, distorts, and destroys. Fringe voices raise flags, blaze trails, and give perspective. They warn, they amuse, they cajole, often with wisdom. If we listen carefully to the voices that seem extreme today, we may glean what it would be like to live as peaceful human beings in a technologically dominated time.

With a conscious awareness of technology, we can evaluate the relevance of existing technologies with clarity and build an appropriate relationship with technology. We can begin to anticipate the development of new technologies and debate the merits and the consequences in advance of the application of those technologies, and in doing so we will become less anxious about the future. There are signs that we are beginning to do this.

John Selover, vice chairman of the Christian Science Church, offers a fresh perspective. "It's important to love progress, to love being part of it and not to fear it. Out of that love for progress, there can come the skills that are needed." To love technological progress means that we would cherish it, see its faults and triumphs, heed warning signals, admit mistakes, be open and compassionate, watch, listen, face problems squarely, get philosophical, set standards, question standards, review standards, be informed, and welcome opinions from all professions and denominations. If we love technology we will be careful with it. We won't be reckless. We can enter aware and receptive into a dialogue about technology. We will begin to *nurture* the power of technology instead of rejecting it (as do so-called technophobes) or blindly embracing it (as do technophiles).

"Awake" is how Buddha described his state of being. And it would serve us all well to be awake to the consequences of technology, both good and bad. We should not shut our eyes, or close our ears, or silence a dialogue, or be seduced by technology.

We hope this book will give you a conscious awareness of your relationship with technology so you can see and feel the Technologically Intoxicated Zone—and help yourself, your family, your community and business. Informed by this conscious awareness, our society can collectively begin to anticipate the consequences of new technologies and apply them responsibly, not mindlessly or foolishly. In doing so, we may consume less conspicuously, engage in more intelligent discussions about technology, more fully learn to respect human differences and the human spirit, become a nation more at peace with itself.

Self-help books, twelve-step programs, quick-fix solutions abound in America, but usually they serve only as stop-gap measures. This book is a primer for detoxifying our relationship with technology, not a list of coping skills.

SYMPTOMS OF HIGH TECH INTOXICATION

After all the research we conducted, after scores of interviews with cultural leaders in business and the arts, with academics and theologians, and after careful examination of our own lives, we discovered a handful of clear symptoms that indicate an unsettling diagnosis of our way of life. These symptoms reveal our society to be a Technologically Intoxicated Zone, one defined by the complicated and often paradoxical relationship between technology and our search for meaning.

The symptoms of a Technologically Intoxicated Zone are:

1. We favor the quick fix, from religion to nutrition.

2. We fear and worship technology.

3. We blur the distinction between real and fake.

4. We accept violence as normal.

5. We love technology as a toy.

6. We live our lives distanced and distracted.

By being aware of these symptoms and how they manifest themselves, we can better understand the role technology has or could have in our lives. We urge the reader to look for signs of these symptoms in the four chapters of this book as well as in our culture.

Symptom Number One: We Favor the Quick Fix, from Religion to Nutrition

Feeling a recurring void, we blindly search for something to fill it and ambiguously call it meaning.

Some Americans join book clubs, poetry groups, and martial arts classes or pursue quiet interests like bird watching, gardening, or Feng Shui. But in the United States the most common venue of the pursuit of meaning is religion. Today more Americans belong to a church, synagogue, temple, or mosque (70 percent today compared to 17 percent in 1776) than at any other time in history.

Americans are eager to embrace the security and sanctity of religion and spirituality. Archbishop Randolph W. Sly of the Charismatic Episcopal Church believes that "we are living in an age where not only are people returning to more ancient faiths, but people are becoming more mystical. People are trying to find something higher, deeper, greater, more profound. Something that unites them with something bigger than just who they are."

America is in the midst of a religious revival. We are seeking and welcoming a religious or spiritual context in nearly all aspects of our lives—on television and film, in the workplace, in hospitals, in books, in advertisements, on campuses, in mega-churches. "All over the place there are more visible evidences of religion in public life," said Martin Marty, the popular professor of comparative religion at the University of Chicago. "All across the spectrum of public life, people are more at ease with expressions of religion."

Religious experimentation and exploration is popular in America. More than 1,000 nondenominational churches are formed every year, and more than 1 million native-born Americans have converted to Buddhism during the past decade. The number of religious denominations in America has doubled in the last thirty-five years, from 800 to more than 1,600.

Yet, despite all our seeking, we still feel a spiritual void. Something's not quite right.

Religious book sales have skyrocketed (150 percent increase from 1991 to 1997 compared to 35 percent for the rest of the publishing industry), outpacing every other category. Even secular "soul books" and simple guides to daily happiness like *Don't Sweat the Small Stuff,* the *Chicken Soup* series (the most successful book series in publishing history, with over 30 million copies in print), and *Simple Abundance* are topping the national bestseller lists as if a quick read will ease a spiritual void.

In an Intoxicated Zone, spiritual "supplements" are big business. The equivalent of a quick hit of caffeine, they take the form of books, New Age magazines, relaxation tapes, chimes, candles, crystals, incense, essential oils, prime-time religious shows, astrology, numerology, aromatherapy, rock fountains, magnetic therapy, and meditation. These detox supplements promise to make us more centered, rejuvenated, relaxed, peaceful, connected, fulfilled, and reflective while giving us inspiration, happiness, harmony, visions, vitality, clarity, self-discovery, depth, enlightenment, subtle energy, and balance.

Ironically, technology promises to detoxify us—from massage chairs to canned sounds of nature—while it intoxicates. Advertisements are loaded with technology's promises to simplify our complex lives, relieve our stress, and calm our nerves.

As traditional links between generations have been broken and links within nuclear families have weakened, the traditional couriers of values and practical wisdom—extended family, the church, the community—have increasingly been replaced by popular culture. En masse, we are turning to information technologies, TV, videos, magazines, and how-to books for answers to fundamental questions: "How to pick a mate," "How to express heartfelt commitment," "How to be happy in eight minutes," "How to date out of your league."

Instead of long talks or mentorship, we look to quick fixes to solve everything life throws at us, big or small. And popular culture delivers in the form of step-by-step programs, self-help books, and advice columns: "Nine Vital Food Commandments," "Twenty-three Fat-Burning Shortcuts," "Seven Secrets of Hot Sex," "Four Marriage Savers," "Eight Signs It's Over," "Thirty-five Symptoms Cured Instantly," "Two-Minute Health Check," "Eleven Genetic Keys to Spiritual Awakening," "Five Steps to Knowing God's Will," "The Seven Habits of Highly Effective Families," "The Seven Spiritual Laws of Success," "Seven Paths to God," "The Seven Stages of Power and Healing," "Seven Steps to Bible Skills." (Seven seems to be the winning number.)

What began as advertising slogans—"One a Day" and "Twelve Ways to Build Strong Bones"—have become cultural solutions. Television delivers in large doses, serving as surrogate minister, mother, and father: In 1996 there were 257 religious TV channels, up from 9 in 1974; the second-fastest-growing cable channel is the Food Network, whose audience grew 53 percent in 1997 and reached into 27 million homes; and the fastest-growing cable channel, Home & Garden Television, has more than 40 million subscribers in the United States alone.

We have become an over-the-counter society with an across-the-board supplement mentality—everything from religion to nutrition. Since the 1960s we have been dismantling traditions, leaving deficiencies for which supplements are viewed as correctives or antidotes.

For decades, doctors have pushed the quick fix of medication, and patients have come to expect instant relief from a pill. Americans spent a disproportionate $85 billion on prescription drugs in the 1996 global drug market of $180 billion and an additional $20 billion on over-the-counter drugs. By 1997 one in eight Americans were on (or had been on) Prozac. Viagra broke all previous sales records in the history of the pharmaceutical industry with close to $1 billion in sales its first year on the market.

Dietary supplements take the form of shakes, pills, drops, and powders, promising to make us smarter, more beautiful, healthier, sexier, slimmer, less stressed, less toxic, more youthful and energetic. There is even a supplement's supplement, AbsorbAid, which claims to enhance the body's absorption of all the other supplements. In an unconscious effort to escape the Technologically Intoxicated Zone, Americans are self-supplementing to the tune of 10 billion pills a year. Americans spend more than $700 million a year on quick-fix vitamins but on average eat less than one piece of fruit a day. And french fries account for 25 percent of all the vegetables we consume.

Cosmetic surgery is another form of a quick fix. More than 2 million cosmetic surgeries were performed in America in 1997. Led by California, Texas, and New York, cosmetic surgery is gaining national cultural acceptance: 52 percent more face-lifts were performed in 1997 than in 1992; almost 25 percent of cosmetic surgeries are performed on people between the ages of twenty and thirty-nine; the number of breast implant surgeries performed in 1997 was up 375 percent over 1992; and liposuction operations have increased 215 percent since 1992. Laser surgery, butt tucks, lip implants, and penile enlargements are all becoming more commonplace.

The Band-Aid culture of the quick fix is ultimately an empty one. Something doesn't feel quite right and we don't know why, so we grab for the fix. It's easy to be seduced by the promise of technology in a land intoxicated by it.

Symptom Number Two: We Fear and Worship Technology

Will technology save humankind or destroy it? Regularly, passionately, the debate resurfaces and it has changed little since the Luddites were executed for smashing textile factories at the beginning of the Industrial Revolution. Put so starkly, the debate seems almost absurdly polarized, yet the extreme positions of technology as savior or technology as destroyer point to the blind faith and fear we project onto technology and to its cultural deification.

One thousand years ago, as we approached the end of the first millennium, human beings feared God's wrath visiting death and destruction upon the earth. With the new millennium, that fear has been rechanneled into a technological Armageddon called Y2K. Like God's all-powerful wrath, some fear that computer technology gone awry threatens to shower mayhem upon humankind—planes dropping out of the sky, missiles firing uncontrollably, the global economy crashing, massive technological failure. Some people have even prepared well-stocked bomb shelters or off-the-grid survival homes, as if technology itself is an uncontrollable force capable of creating pandemonium and mass destruction.

Others believe technology offers a cure for society's ills. They bestow tremendous faith in technological solutions: The Internet in every classroom will make schools better, genetic engineering of humans will eradicate disease, bioengineering of crops will feed the world.

One of the most public deifiers of technology today is Nicholas Negroponte, founding director of the Media Lab at the

Massachusetts Institute of Technology (MIT). Few people have as much faith in technology as he and his son, Dimitri, who have declared it their mission to secure a laptop computer with Internet access for every one of the world's 1 billion children through a foundation they formed called 2B1 (To Be One). They believe that universal Internet access is tantamount to creating world peace, securing the fate of humanity, ensuring the health of the planet and the global economy. (Electronic game maker Sega Enterprises was the first significant donor to the foundation.)

Esther Dyson, owner of Edventure Holdings, Inc., which publishes the newsletter *Release 1.0,* is another technophile. She promotes the Net as a potential home for us all and envisions a future in which students are diligent, employers judicious, consumers well informed, and citizens exercise freedom of speech. Double helix discoverer James Watson has complete faith in the new genetic sciences. He sees no need to hesitate before altering human evolution through genetic engineering and in fact thinks it's silly to discuss any humanistic issues it might raise. Chief executive officer (CEO) Bob Shapiro of Monsanto, a giant in the emerging life sciences industry, claims that genetic engineering of crops by his company and others will save the planet from starvation.

On the other end of the spectrum, educational psychologists such as author Jane Healy warn that extended computer use is capable of harmfully altering the physiology of a child's brain and causing a pandemic of attention deficit disorder (ADD) and depression in children. Healy believes that computer use by small children is "brain training"—but not of the sort suggested by software developers. Computer games, she argues, are antagonistic to any kind of reflective, future-oriented thinking or inner speech. She believes we are at risk of developing a whole generation of impulsive, stimulus-driven, nonreflective people who later have difficulty with moral behavior.

Technology critic Jeremy Rifkin vehemently warns against letting the biotechnology genie out of the bottle, and he rallied 200 theologians to take a stance against genetic patenting. The most extreme warnings against the evils of technology are sounded by paranoid loners like Ted Kaczynski, the Unabomber. Kaczynski, who wrote a 35,000-word treatise against the dehumanizing nature of technology and machines, asserted, among other things, that modern technology trivializes the ancient quests for food, water, and shelter.

Some people automatically turn to technology for a solution. Others never turn to technology for a solution. Some people draw a line in the sand and reject only new technology. The Amish draw the line at about the year 1900. The Neo-Luddites draw a line at the end of World War II. The Catholic Church took its stand against the pill and abortion in the 1960s and hasn't budged. But most of us have a relationship with technology that rebounds from one extreme to another. One moment we are afraid of it, one moment inspired by its power. One day we begrudgingly accept it for fear of falling behind our competitors or co-workers, the next day embracing it enthusiastically as something that will make our lives or businesses better, then feeling frustrated and annoyed when it fails to deliver. For most of us, technology is far from neutral. It shapes our choices; it directs our actions. We have a largely unexamined relationship with technology that consists to some degree of both fear and worship.

Symptom Number Three:
We Blur the Distinction Between Real and Fake

In a world where technology can transform nature as never before, it is no wonder that we repeatedly ask, "Is that real?" "Is that fake?" Authentic or simulated? Genuine or imitation? Original or copy? In a time when technology can create the surrogate, the ersatz, the virtual, the cyber, we are increasingly confused about what is real and what is fake.

Are her breasts fake? Is that his real hair? Were the pictures from the Mars Pathfinder really taken in Arizona? Is his Rolex fake? Is that a real Armani? Is Celebration, Florida, a real community? Are those fights on Jerry Springer staged, or did she really hit him? If you climb Mount Everest with supplemental oxygen, have you really climbed it by "fair means," or did technology give you an edge? If a runner with a prosthetic flex foot beats the all-time record for the 100-yard-dash, does it count? Or did technology make him a bionic man? The discourse, the argument, the stories seem endless in our effort to make sense of this world.

Nowhere is this confusion more damaging than in America's relationships with the "screens" that pervade our lives: movie screens, TV screens, computer screens, Gameboy screens, personal electronic organizer screens, beeper screens, cell phone screens, call-screening screens, microwave oven screens, heart monitor screens, and whatever screen will be dreamed up by tomorrow's technologists. Screens are everywhere, in every setting, directing us, informing us, amusing us. And without our conscious awareness, they are shaping us. The screens that entertain us—TV, movies, the Web, electronic games—are explained away as "virtual," and we don't take them seriously. We easily dismiss egregious content. We believe that what is projected on the screen is fantasy, a kind of idealized story as unreal as the family sitcoms in the 1950s. But the consequences are very real.

The number-one entertainment in America today is media, and the number-one genre of content is violence. Yet we don't take it seriously. The specter of violence on our screens seeps into our memories, our dreams, and our conversations, and we insist it is benign, even educational. Jokingly we dismiss violent content on screens as unreal. It's only a cartoon . . . an electronic game . . . a movie . . . or the news. . . . By denying the screen's content as real, we give ourselves and our children permission to thoughtlessly consume thrilling violence regularly and then feel shocked and bewildered when a child opens fire on classmates at school.

It is a radical idea to suggest that screens and their content are real. But the consequence of thinking of them as fantasy, as virtual, as benign, is devastating. The surfaces of the screens are flat, the images appear three-dimensional, and the medium is compelling whether the story is or not. Blue glowing boxes, flat movie screens, dizzying electronic games suck us in and spit us out happier, sadder, more in love, more pumped than when we went in. We tell each other the screens are inconsequential and merely entertainment.

People who witness "real" acts of violence have a hard time erasing the terrifying images from their minds. Most parents would shield their children from the sight of a "real" brutal crime, and it is unthinkable to invite a child to curl up on the couch and witness a "real" death. But we do it all the time with such top-rated television shows as *X-Files, NYPD Blue, ER,* and *Cops* and blockbuster movies like *Armageddon, Saving Private Ryan, Men in Black,* and *Matrix,* and megaselling electronic games like Quake, Doom, Golden Eye, and Tomb Raider.

Screen images can sear one's memory as deeply as "real" trauma: the mean lady speeding down the dirt road on the bicycle with Toto in the basket who suddenly becomes the Wicked Witch of the West; Marion, the woman in the shower in *Psycho;* Mike and Nick in *The Deer Hunter,* waiting to play Russian roulette; the skinnydipper in the dark ocean, like a hooked bobber as the shark attacks in *Jaws.* We all have our own unforgettable, burning images; more than a few we wish we could erase.

Increasingly, even the story lines on our screens are becoming less fake, more real.

Television and film changed forever as video cameras became readily available to the average consumer (along came Rodney King and the LAPD), whetting our voyeuristic appetite for live drama. Then followed *America's Funniest Home Videos, Geraldo,* the white Bronco, real TV, Road Rules, the President and the Intern, and JennyCam, real-time sex changes, Internet, brain surgery and childbirth along with the regular lives of countless people who post them for public consumption. Our screens are very real indeed.

In an era of near-perfect special effects, what is simulation? Are you rowing a boat if you're going nowhere? Are you climbing stairs if you never ascend? Are you really in New York if you're a guest in Las Vegas's New York, New York hotel? Or in Venice if you ride the gondola at the Bellagio? Is a vacation to Disney World's Animal Kingdom as good as a safari? Better than one? Do Keanu Reeves and

Laurence Fishburne even know kung fu? Or does the movie *The Matrix* just have a great programmer?

In a time when it is difficult to distinguish the real from the fake, businesses are latching onto authenticity. Authenticity can be commercially very successful. It is no longer viable for companies to get their product ideas from a middle market, such as designers, hence the new profession of "cool hunters." They're out in the streets seeking inspiration closer to the source — from artists, hipsters, rappers, urban teens, or the traditions of other cultures. In a world where information is transmitted instantaneously and people are transported almost as quickly, the climate is right for mass imitation, fakes, copies, and simulations. The raw authentic is hunted down by cool hunters, snatched up, stripped clean, and mass marketed. It is no wonder we question what is genuine.

Our obsession with the real has marched forward unobstructed. We crave memoirs, biographies, documentaries, and talk shows, but not simply because we like gossip. In a time when technology is obscuring the real while simultaneously exaggerating it, we are reassured by the authentic.

Symptom Number Four: We Accept Violence as Normal

Small Soldiers, a 1998 movie made for children, is typical of the violence marketed as "action-packed" and rated PG-13.

In the film, by DreamWorks Studios, a high-tech munitions conglomerate, Globotech, buys Heartland, an old-fashioned toy manufacturer, to "introduce advanced battle technology into consumer products for the whole family." In the opening sequence, the hard-edged CEO of Globotech scolds his toy designers for not understanding the basic concept of good versus evil in play. "What do soldiers need?" he asks, referring to the prototype foot-tall toy soldier on the conference table. "Enemies, sir," replies his assistant. "Our guys have to vaporize them," roars the CEO, referring to the cardboard prototypes of mutant monsters. One of the two toy designers asks, "Don't you think that's a bit violent?" The CEO answers coolly, "Exactly. So don't call it violence. Call it action. Kids love action. It sells." Like Hollywood, he is loath to say "Kids love violence," preferring the industry's code-word, "action."

By combining military technology and toys, the aggressive Commando Elite soldiers and their peaceful monster enemies, the Gorgonites, are able to walk, talk, think, and learn. The smart soldiers quickly employ household items as weapons. The garbage disposal is a torture chamber, the medicine cabinet a source for "chemical warfare," and with fresh perspective, the soldiers see the garage not as a storage place or woodworking shop but as a weapons arsenal. The small soldiers ogle a girl's collection of Barbie-like dolls as "fully poseable" sex toys but then see them as "reinforcements" and transform them into living violent freaks in camouflage-patterned bikinis with the proportions of electronic game warrior Laura Croft.

Hundreds of determined "toy" soldiers, with names like Butch Meathook, Nick Nitro, and Kip Killagin, ruthlessly wage war against their toy enemies (who are programmed to hide) and nine human beings. The motto of the Commando Elite is "There will be no mercy." The feckless adults in the film are rather useless in their fight for survival, but the teenagers gleefully maim, kill, and destroy the soldiers, after being repeatedly victimized and attacked by the Commando Elite with nail guns, fire, chainsaws, bombs, and mini-choppers (attacking to the music of the movie *Apocalypse Now*).

The scenes in *Small Soldiers* are not "action-packed," but packed with violence. Violence is also packaged in the form of merchandise, usually spinoffs from film and television, and targeted at children, whatever the rating. Merchandise spin-offs from electronic games, films, and television shows often target children even if the film or game's rating is adult. Hasbro toy company released twelve Small Soldiers movie theme toys at the same time as the film. Sony PlayStation issued a Small Soldiers video game, and Burger King gave away miniaturized Commando Elite and Gorgonites.

But a moral issue loomed for the local Burger King franchisees in Springfield, Oregon. The name of one Small Soldiers' character, Kip Killigan (kill-again), sounds almost identical to the name of a fifteen-year-old boy who two months before the film's release on July 10, 1998, killed his parents, then shot and killed two classmates at school, wounding twenty-four others. The Springfield Burger Kings pulled the Kip Killigan action figure because his name might be a sad reminder to their customers and, because like the student, he was a gun-toting killer. Although the Springfield shooting was a national story, Burger King and Toys "R" Us continued to merchandise the entire collection nationwide, pushing sales to the top ten among all toys.

Two weeks after the release of *Small Soldiers*, DreamWorks released another film, *Saving Private Ryan*, which brought home the message "war is hell." Steven Spielberg refused to sell any toy merchandising rights to his serious film. Meanwhile his company is making millions merchandising *Small Soldiers* to children, suggesting "war is fun."

Tragedies, such as the Springfield and Littleton school shootings, momentarily highlight what has become a daily diet of violence in America. Rock concerts, National Rifle Association (NRA) conventions, television shows, or films may be canceled temporarily or moved to a new time slot "out of respect," but violence is pervasive.

Symptom Number Five: We Love Technology as a Toy

Affluence finances play. Americans recently listed "having fun" as their top priority, followed by losing weight and getting organized.

In America today, leisure tends toward diversion—something to fill time—like so many movies. But trying to relax or slow down in America is like trying to take a nap in a video arcade. In a culture dominated by consumer technology, leisure is largely undemanding and passively received. We busy ourselves with electronic distractions as if we can't find anything more worthwhile to do with our time. In a Technologically Intoxicated Zone, we think television is relaxing.

We want, we need, we desire this year's top-of-the-line

Cannondale mountain bike, or a Nokia cellular phone with interchangeable slipcovers to match our wardrobe, or a transparent tangerine iMac. The need for a Christmas-like fix on a regular basis, in a culture steeped in high-tech toys, entrenches us in the never-ending upgrade cycle. Gadgets that marry the imagination of a child with powerful new technologies will roll out month after month to tempt us. Most new high-tech toys don't satisfy us for very long though. There is always something better and more enticing, and at a lower price.

Nicholas Negroponte, head of the MIT Media Lab, perceptively noted the similarity of the toy industry and the electronic industry: "Every year, 75 percent of all toys are new, meaning newly designed that year. The toy industry lives and dies on invention. Toys gush into homes every Christmas and Hanukkah, every birthday, and lots of other days besides. This tremendous churn rate means that toys are well matched to the pace of change in the digital world." Not surprisingly, MIT's new business partners include Lego, Disney, Mattel, Hasbro, and Toys "R" Us. "Many people accuse the MIT Media Lab of being a giant playpen," says Negroponte. "Well, they're right. It is a digital wonderland, overflowing with outrageous toys. Staying a child isn't easy, but a continuous stream of new toys helps."

We are unashamedly comfortable with adult toys because consumer technologies have evolved from *luxury* to *necessity* to *toy*.

In the early part of the twentieth century, a car, for example, was an enviable luxury. By the 1950s America was mobile, and our culture was shaped by the automobile. Suburbia, shopping malls, and commuting made the car a necessity. Today we buy cars as if they were toys: a new Volkswagen Beetle for nostalgia, a Smart Car for fun, and a Humvee for attention. Nicholas G. Hayek, founder and CEO of the Swatch Group and coproducer of the playful, original Smart Car, told us, "If you combine powerful technology with the fantasy of a six-year-old kid, you can create miracles."

Adult toys are ubiquitous. Childhood memories are awakened

by "new and improved" high-tech variations of favorite childhood playthings. For $8,000, you can buy a go-cart that exceeds 100 miles an hour, accelerates from zero to 60 in four seconds, and generates two Gs of force. If you prefer less risk, try an adult-size 13 mile-per-hour electric-powered scooter designed conveniently to fit in your car. Or relive the days you ran around your neighborhood playing "I Spy" with a crackling walkie-talkie. Motorola's TalkAbouts allow high-quality communication you only wished for as a kid, and the colors are better. All for $200 to $400 a pair.

The toy indulgence doesn't begin and end with "boy toys." Playing house is no longer only the realm of young girls with an Easy Bake Oven or Suzy Home Maker. Adults can now toast a panda bear's face on a piece of bread using a bright-yellow Sanyo toaster emblazoned with panda decals. And adults can clean house with a vacuum cleaner that resembles a Play Skool toy for babies yet sells for more than $400. Kenmore encourages playfulness through its appliance advertisements: "Get a load of our shiny new toys . . . playing in the kitchen is a whole lot of fun."

And where are we buying our toys? We shop at complexes like Minnesota's Mall of America, which are ingenious at making "people feel like children," according to James Farrell, a history professor at nearby St. Olaf's College. Mall of America's slogan is "There's a place for fun in your life." Or in cities like Chicago, which promotes its lakefront Ferris wheel, gliding riverboats, bike paths, sailboat harbors, and downtown Loop with the slogan, "Live, Work, Play." Or in stores, like REI's 80,000-square-foot-store in Seattle, where adults can play at a giant water table (just like at nursery school) testing water filters and purifiers, or scramble up the largest free-standing climbing wall in the world, or stomp through an in-store "forest" in high-tech boots, or try out the latest in waterproof gear in a rain chamber. With Disney at the helm, simulated experiences abound. At Nike shoot basketballs with Michael Jordan's visage. View real-time videos at Sony or enjoy a full-scale musical production at American Girl.

We bring home bags and bags of fun stuff from these entertaining stores or order things online. Then we have to organize it all and ditch what we no longer need. And what we don't throw away, we store. The mini-warehouse storage business has grown to an astonishing $9 billion a year to house the overflow of stuff we can no longer fit in our homes.

As children we absorbed new toys, found places for them in our rooms, and became accustomed to the thrill of a new diversion. As adults we quickly absorb new consumer products—increasingly high-tech ones—and we find places for them in our homes, which have grown to match our consumption. Home offices have sprung up from our dens, and we fill them with computers, speakers, faxes, printers, scanners, and CD-ROMs. Our living rooms, once quiet havens with comfortable armchairs and fireplaces, now resemble arcades with high-tech televisions, VCRs, stereos, and Nintendo systems. Our garages are filled with outdoor gear and garden toys.

America's current obsession with play is visible and palpable, though most of our ancestors cherished few playthings as children. Nana's grandmother Lillian, born in 1906, had only one doll as a child and no books. John, born in 1929, had a fistful of toy soldiers and a favorite picture book of mighty ships that sailed the Atlantic. Nana, born in 1957, got presents only at Christmas and on her birthday. With her siblings, she had shelves of books to read, rows of dolls to dress, blocks to build, balls to throw, and a pair of metal roller skates.

Douglas's toy lineage is much the same, but Douglas, born in 1964, received toys year-round. By the age of twelve he had his own stereo, a banana bike with a sissy bar, GI Joe and Big Jim action figures, an Evel Knievel motorcycle man, electric race cars, a Creepy Crawler maker, a chemistry set, and Rembrandt oil paints. The family had motorcycles, sailboats, motor boats, water skis, and trick skis, among other toys. And while affluence and location obviously affect the types of toys parents buy for their children, the mind-set of the American toy culture has become clearly entrenched in our society. Today over half the children in America have a television in their bedroom, and one in five has his own VCR or video game player attached to that T V. The average American girl has eight Barbie dolls. Eighty percent of American boys play video games on a regular basis. Toy rooms have replaced toy boxes.

Two recent ads sum up our obsession with technology toys. A Zenith advertisement for a big-screen television reads: "Big fun. That's the point, isn't it?" And a Mercedes magazine ad with a photograph of two little kids in the midst of a whopping pillow fight in pajamas on a bed in a room with no car or road or adult in sight simply reads "Fun."

John Adams, our second president, almost anticipated the proliferation of play. In 1780 he wrote to his wife, Abigail, "I must study politics and war, that my sons may have the liberty to study mathematics and philosophy. My sons ought to study mathematics and philosophy . . . in order to give their children a right to study painting, poetry, music, architecture, statuary, tapestry and porcelain." Adams might have concluded, and "their children ought to study painting, poetry and music, so that their children might create the business of play."

Electronic toys are intoxicatingly fun, but they distract us from play's important relative, leisure. A decade ago British philosophy professor Cyril Barrett wrote, "Leisure is not a trivial pursuit; not a poor relation of work; not a gap or vacuum in the turmoil of life to be filled somehow. Leisure is life lived at its fullest, richest, most complete." In its most profound sense, leisure allows questions of life's meaning and purpose to surface. Leisure requires tranquility, patience, attentiveness, and an open heart. Leisure is not based on the desire to consume, or upon passive relaxation, or upon entertainment.

Silence nourishes thought, reflection develops wisdom, listening begets humanity. When there's no silence, there's no room for thought. We've become so accustomed to the noise, we no longer hear it. In a beeping, ringing, flashing world it is no wonder 77 million baby boomers are searching for meaning.

Symptom Number Six:
We Live Our Lives Distanced and Distracted

British Artist Damien Hirst's book title, *I Want to Spend the Rest of My Life Everywhere, with Everyone. One to One. Always. Forever.*

Now. is an almost perfect metaphor for the Internet and for how most of us feel as we stay connected through cell phones, e-mail, and modems. The Internet is full of millions of personal websites, people sharing their private lives with everyone, everywhere, now and forever.

We're even extending our reach into the universe. A company called Encounter 2001 will send anyone's DNA on a spacecraft zooming past Pluto and out of the solar system for $49.95. Timothy Leary and others, the first to arrange for their ashes to orbit the earth, will reenter our atmosphere in about eight years. New customers of Celestis Inc. 2001 will orbit the earth for 240 years.

The Internet and cell phones promise to connect us to the world. But when is it appropriate and when is it a distraction? Sitting alone in a room "talking" in a chat room on the Internet is a new social phenomenon, but it does not constitute community. E-mail in the office connects employees, but many people e-mail their co-worker down the hall and complain about the number of their own messages. A cell phone or Walkman on the beach makes hearing the waves a sidebar. A laptop on vacation connects you to work but distracts you from the experience of being away from work. Banking by computer, you never have talk to a teller. Purchasing by e-commerce, you never have to talk to a salesperson. The noise of these technologies, both literally and figuratively, can actually isolate humans from each other, from nature, and from ourselves. Technology can create physical and emotional distance and distract us from our lives. Is isolation the reward of technology?

Technology's bells and whistles are seductive, but we are not fully aware of how they distance and distract us from our own lives. Few of us have stopped to ask what cell phones, electronic games, television, or cameras add to or detract from the quality of our human experience.

Technology distracts us with its promise to document. The camera was invented in the late 1830s, and today inexpensive, sophisticated cameras and cheap processing allow us to record and document life's magic moments. (Americans take more than 17 billion photographs a year.) At graduations, school plays, high school basketball games, violin recitals, and little league baseball games, automatic cameras click and rewind loudly (shzzzzzzzzzz) and parents with techno-gadget faces are ubiquitous. But what do the children see? The eye of a camera trained on them. Do cameras document life's most important events, or do they distract us from experiencing the emotions, the sights, the sounds of the occasion? Perhaps they actually cause us to miss the moment rather than capture it. Just owning a camcorder or a camera may make us feel compelled to use it, then archive the images. We have become a documentary society, but to what end?

Technology also distracts with its promise to entertain. Big screens of dazzling pixilated color and surround sound deliver up-to-the-minute information and "action-packed" drama. The metaphor of the TV as the modern "family hearth" is optimistic. Family members scatter to different rooms of the house to watch their own favorite shows or listen to their own music. Today many Americans are living together in isolation.

what is
High Tech·
High Touch?

Because of the intrusive pace of technological change, High Tech · high touch is far more crucial today than it was in 1982 when John first introduced the idea in the smallest chapter of *Megatrends*. Echoes of its increasing relevance led Douglas to suggest that John's next book be a reexamination of High Tech·high touch, now considered by many to be the most important concept of that book. John agreed and welcomed the idea of a high touch collaboration among himself, his daughter Nana, and Douglas, both artists, writers, and entrepreneurs.

The first struggle was to come to an agreement about what the terms meant exactly—a task easier said than done, and one that evolved the more we learned. We began by asking, conceptually, what exactly is technology.

WHAT IS TECHNOLOGY?

The changing definition of the word is revealing. In 1967, in the *Random House Dictionary*, technology was defined as a thing, an object, material and physical and clearly separate from human beings. By 1987, when Random House released its completely updated unabridged dictionary, the word grew to include technology's "interrelation with life, society, and the environment." Technology no longer existed in a vacuum.

WHAT IS HIGH TECH?

Even more revealing is the 1998 Tech Encyclopedia online definition of high technology, which expands the power of technology to include its "consequences." From thing to interrelationship to *consequence*. We now understand that powerful technologies have powerful consequences. Technology embodies its consequences, both good and bad. It is not neutral.

What is high tech? Menu. Mouse, bug, spider. Web, Net. Cookies, vanilla, apple, java, spam. Spew. Pilot, pirate, doctor, director, agent, server, provider, nanny. Chat. Domain, community, home, room, window, mailbox. Access. Boot, footprint. Glove, thumbnail. Navigate, browse, search, scan, zip, go. Location, address. Click. Bulletin board, desktop, briefcase, file, folder, document, notepads, page, bookmark. Smart. Scripting, scrolling, clustering, linking. Save, trash, recycle. Memory. Trojan horse, Orphan Annie, Mae West. Wildcard. Shortcut, overload, shut down. Log, link, surf. Keyboard. Tools, hardware, bits. Engine, backup. Virus. Wired, surge, connected, merge, purge. Crash. Shockwave, flame, ram, hit. Holy War.

What is high tech? www.technology.com. 3D, HDTV, HTML, HTTP, CD, DVD. MCI, IBM, AOL, Intel, Inspiron, OptiPlax, Omimax, Connectix, Teledesic, Xircon, Inprise. FYI, TBD, IPO, ROI, IT. IV, MRI, EKG.

What is high tech? Fire? Wheel, well, spear, loom, printing press, indoor plumbing, electricity, stoves, refrigerators, air conditioning, washers and dryers, cell phones, faxes, organizers, cars, high-speed trains, hydroplanes, bridges, tunnels, skyscrapers, supertankers, Mars Pathfinder, AWACs, JSTARS, space shuttles, particle colliders, nanotechnology, bioengineering, cloning, genetic engineering.

What is high tech? Ones and twos. Smaller, cheaper, faster. Real time. Quick time. Virtual, simulated, cyber. Interactive. Digital. Networked. Connected. Hardware. Software. Pixels. Resolution. Bandwidth. Convergence. Killer apps. Tech-ccssorize. Voice recognition. Space tourism.

What is high tech? Future advancements, innovations, progress—control.

WHAT IS HIGH TOUCH?

What is high touch? It's the look of an unknown three-year-old girl who turns suddenly to show you her sweet fresh face and flashes a smile that belies her stubborn personality, it's the love of your own child, it's panting for breath because the view was worth the climb, it's wanting to help your father because you notice that bending is now difficult for him, it's listening to the ever-constant rush of a creek, it's forgiving your friend who was mad at you for having a baby before she married, it's smelling a wide bowl of soup, it's longing for a lover, it's feeling god in your throat, it's sitting quietly, it's a lick on your face by a dog you once disliked, it's an idea that tickles your soul, it's a cold wind that burns your face, it's recognizing when you're wrong, it's crying at the beauty of a painting, it's a rhythm that beats in your bones, it's doodling and liking what you've drawn, it's gazing into the eyes of a nursing baby, it's feeling empathy, it's forgoing power to do what's right, it's acknowledging another person's place in this world, it's being respectful of a waitress, it's honoring a mother's depth of understanding, it's honoring a father's steadfastness, it's honoring a child's space to grow without fear, it's delighting in watching a thirteen-year-old boy find his way in a new community, it's giving of oneself to nature, to human emotions, to family, to the universe, to a higher power. High touch is embracing the primeval forces of life and death. High touch is embracing that which acknowledges all that is greater than we.

WHAT IS HIGH TECH•HIGH TOUCH?

It is a human lens.

It is embracing technology that preserves our humanness and rejecting technology that intrudes upon it. It is recognizing that technology is an integral part of the evolution of culture, the creative product of our imaginations, our dreams and aspirations—and that the desire to create new technologies is fundamentally instinctive. But is also recognizing that art, story, play, religion, nature, and time are equal partners in the evolution of technology because they nourish the soul and fulfill its yearnings. It is expressing what it means to be human and employing technology fruitfully in that expression. It's appreciating life and accepting death. It is knowing when we should push back on technology, in our work and our lives, to affirm our humanity. It is understanding that technology zealots are as shortsighted as technology bashers. It is creating significant paths for our lives, without fear of new technology or fear of falling behind it. It is recognizing that at its best, technology supports and improves human life; at its worse, it alienates, isolates, distorts, and destroys. It is questioning what place technology should have in our lives and what place it should have in society. It is consciously choosing to employ technology when it adds value to human lives. It is learning how to live as human beings in a technologically dominated time. It is knowing when simulated experiences add value to human life. It is recognizing when to avoid the layers of distractions and distance technology affords us. It is recognizing when technology is not neutral. It is knowing when to unplug and when to plug in. It is appropriate human scale.

High Tech • high touch is enjoying the fruits of technological advancements and having it truly sit well with our god, our church, or our spiritual beliefs. It is understanding technology through the human lens of play, time, religion, and art.

FROM HIGH TECH TO HIGH TOUCH

When does high tech become low tech, and, more dramatically, when does high tech become high touch? High tech becomes high touch with longevity and cultural familiarity. Today a wooden shuttle loom warped with yarn is high touch. Four thousand years ago in Assyria and Egypt, the loom was the latest advancement in technology. The spear, the wheel, the wedge, the pulley were all once high tech. In the 1920s, a radio encased in plastic Bakelite was considered high tech. Today it is high-touch nostalgia. Eight-track players (a '70s technology) are now collectibles, as are phonographs and the accompanying collection of great 45s, LPs, or cassettes. Older technologies become nostalgic more quickly as new technologies are introduced more rapidly.

Old-fashioned technologies become reference points for us all. They mark a certain time in our lives, triggering memories. They evoke emotion. High tech has no reference point—yet. High tech holds the hope of an easier life but it does not provoke memory. High-tech consumer goods are only new toys to be explored. They are not yet evocative. The technologies and inventions of the American Industrial Revolution have aged enough now to be considered quaint—no longer obsolete, outdated, old-fashioned, or a symbol of bygone drudgery. Today we romanticize outdated technologies.

The imperfections of old technologies—double exposures, sputtering engines, electric shocks—are clearly discernible today, yet the imperfections of today's technologies will be clear only in the face of tomorrow's advancements.

PART ONE

TODAY:
UNDERSTANDING
CONSUMER TECHNOLOGY
THROUGH TIME
AND PLAY

Technology is the currency of our lives

The two biggest markets in the $8-trillion-a-year economy of the United States are 1) consumer technology and 2) the escape from consumer technology.

Consumer technology is changing the way we understand time—collapsing, crunching, compressing it. Today technology is a self-perpetuating engine run by upgrades, add-ons, and refills. It accelerates our lives and fosters dependence, which necessitates relief, for which we all too often turn back to technology for the most accessible, immediate solution. Stressed out? Buy a massager. Life's disorganized? Buy a personal electronic organizer. Traveling with children? Buy a Gameboy. Neighborhood unsafe? Buy a security system.

Your PowerBook sits on your desk at home beside a stack of

important unread articles, but you choose a cold beer and a little TV to unwind. The evening passes quickly, and you retire to bed after the nightly news and an earful of office voice-mail. You lie awake while your spouse talks on an Internet chat room, and inventory the events of your day. You feel ashamed about losing your temper with a new co-worker; you realize that the repairman didn't return your call as promised even when you beeped him; you wish you had read your son a bedtime story despite being tired; you feel proud of holding the real estate deal to a 4 percent commission. Your mind skips ahead as you fall asleep while making a mental check list of things that need to get done tomorrow. You wake at 6:30 A.M. with no memory of dreaming. You rise immediately to a pot of hot coffee and e-mail. You then head to the car with a bagel in your hand for a twenty-minute commute during which you listen to the first installment of a popular business book because you're falling behind in your professional reading. The cell phone rings, and your colleague reminds you a client is due for a meeting in fifteen minutes. Your thoughts drift past the noisy narrator to an overwhelming desire to get out of town.

HIGH-TOUCH TIME

The way we live in time has changed steadily in the last hundred years and drastically in the last ten. Our modern lives restrict our connection to nature's rhythms and sounds. A little more than a century ago, before electricity, cell phones, and e-mail, most Americans woke when the sun rose, went to bed when the sun set, ate home-grown meals, and worked close to home. People spoke of moments as fleeting, memories as lasting, and admonished their children with such phrases as "haste makes waste." Stories began with "Once upon a time," and we actually had a sense of what that meant. Days were based more on light than hours and years more on seasons than calendars. It took weeks for a letter to cross the country and more than that for a response.

Time was set by nature's rhythms: tides, lunar cycles, seasons, stars, sunrise, sunset, shadows, plants. As early as 4 B.C., sources note, a scribe of Alexander the Great observed that the leaves of certain trees opened during the day and closed during the night. In the eighteenth century, natural scientist Carolus Linnaeus discovered that petals of certain flowers opened and closed at regular times. He created a garden so that he could tell the time of day by looking at his plants.

That kind of subtle awareness is lost when we have a clock, a watch, an appointment, a deadline, a favorite 7:00 television show.

HIGH-TECH TIME

Since the advent of the wind-up clock (1876) and the battery-operated watch (1956), there has been a shift from living in high-touch time to high-tech time. In contrast to the language of high-touch time, phrases today reveal a sense of urgency about time: lack of time, quick time, real time, face time, deadline, check list, multitask, behind, finding time, making time, losing time, filling time, killing time, spending time, wasting time, on time, out of time, time frame, fast-forward.

Consumer technology traditionally has promised to save time and labor, freeing us to pursue activities that really matter, and few would deny that consumer technologies have made our lives easier during the past century. We no longer have to do laundry by hand, calculate figures in our head, or make bread from scratch. "Do things quickly, leaving more time for happy," in the words of a Microsoft ad. Consumer products lure us with a wide spectrum of promises then crank up our lives, rev up our expectations. Over the years we have consumed those promises as fast as affluence would allow.

More and more, what promises to save us time consumes our time. Consumer technology requires prioritizing needs, selecting brands, buying, installing, maintaining, upgrading.

Consumer technologies have reached a point of diminishing returns. Our homes are filled with labor-saving devices, yet our use of time is not the beneficiary. One study has shown that the amount of labor-saving, simplifying, time-reducing, promise-making technology we have in our homes actually does little to reduce the amount of time we spend doing household chores. But we remain obsessed with productivity and efficiency. How much can we accomplish in a day, an hour, in ten minutes?

America's best-known documentary filmmaker, Ken Burns, who spends years creating a single film, is concerned about a sort of mass attention deficit disorder. "When you're bombarded with so many images—not just television, but all around—you really speed up. You need so much, so quickly—food, impressions, everything— that the opposite has begun to happen: Instead of enriching ourselves, as you might imagine you would if you get more of something, we've actually created a kind of poverty. And that poverty, first and foremost, can be measured in a loss of attention."

The car, still considered our most expedient piece of consumer technology, offers a case in point. In addition to moving from one location to another, we expect to stay connected and entertained. We conduct business on the cell phone, read at stop lights, and scribble notes on pads of paper suction-cupped to the windshield. Other "productivity tools" for cars include factory-installed, voice-activated computers capable of sending and receiving e-mail and faxes. GM's OnStar system will do everything from dispatch a tow truck to recommend a nearby restaurant, all while you're behind the wheel.

Seeking to maximize the time we spend commuting, we also consume entire meals on the road, for which we buy specialized foods, cups, and traveling bibs. Kellogg's, manufacturer of the world's first mass-produced convenience food, is now concentrating on portable breakfast foods because 13 percent of Americans eat breakfast in the car and Kellogg's says it wants "to be in those cars." McDonald's now does most of its business through the drive-through rather than over the counter.

As we increasingly behave in our cars as we do in our homes, businesses are rushing to provide us with additional "solutions" for the road. Portable car offices designed to fit in the front passenger seats are available. At least one minivan on the market comes equipped with a built-in entertainment system, including a flip-down color monitor for viewing movies or playing electronic games. The kids in the back can wear headphones and play Nintendo while the driver listens to his or her choice of music. (Conversation is no longer necessary, squabbling temporarily averted.)

In a society saturated with consumer technologies, how are we spending our time? We live in our cars, talk on the phone, write e-mail, watch TV, work on the computer, listen to music, stay tuned, stay connected, stay wired, stay ahead. We're organized (or want to be), efficient (that new software should help), and productive (a faster modem is the answer). I'll buy the new Palm VII. If I get a satellite dish, I'll never have to go to Blockbuster again. Since Amazon.com, how long has it been since I've been to a bookstore?

As we outfit our lives with more sophisticated automated systems, our activities and our very language are changing. Fires are turned on, not lit. Sidewalks are heated, not shoveled. Drapes are no longer pulled but operated by remote control. Foods are zapped, not cooked. We are plugged in, cranked up, and few of us know how to disconnect long enough to reflect on the choices we're making. We are left with a feeling that our lives are run by technology.

Consumer technologies that make us accessible at all times to all others alter our sense of time and well-being. Cell phones fit in our pocket, Palm Pilots in our hand, beepers on our belt. The fax machine and e-mail have collapsed "response time," and along with the mobile phone, these technologies make us available twenty-four hours a day, like a convenience store. What is the effect of surrounding ourselves with technology all day, every day, at home, at work, and in our cars, with no relief?

Zoë Leonard, an artist who was born and raised in New York City but now lives in Alaska, talks about bargaining with time: "I'm such a city kid, and because of that I have this idea that time can be bargained with. Oh, you're running late, take a cab. You need to mail something and you're running late, send it priority. If it's really late, Federal Express it. If the Federal Express office is closed, fax it. You *know* there's always a way to bargain with time. But being up there in Alaska, the elements are so extreme there's no bargaining. You can't argue with a storm; you can't argue with distance."

Tranquility is a word little used today; stress seeds our vocabulary. And we dream of a trip to the country.

THE SIREN'S CALL

The promise of technology is a Siren's call so sweet and melodic we can't resist. Day in and day out, we are surrounded by the promise of technology, delivered through advertisements and packaging, as well as testimonials of salesmen, co-workers, and friends. And as a stressed-out, time-pressed society we are begging for upgraded solutions. We inhale step-by-step programs as fast as they are released and turn to technology for answers: from better to smarter, new to revolutionary, fast to instant, safety to security, easy to effortless, clean to sterile, power to performance. But like the Siren's song, the call of technology can be deceiving. It lures, then ensnares.

Advertisers of new consumer technologies tend to wildly over-promise. In the 1950s the biggest promise of consumer technology was convenience. Today's prevailing advertising theme is the promise to simplify—consumer technology as antidote to complexity, as *the* solution for the 77 percent of Americans polled who felt they "need to take measures to simplify" their lives.

Today consumer technology forms the invisible foundation of our lives. As a personal test, would you be willing to fundamentally change the way you live by eliminating even a few of the most basic consumer technologies? Imagine cooking dinner. From the freezer you take a packet of frozen ravioli and dump the contents into a pot of boiling water on a gas range turned up high. From the refrigerator you take a jar of Paul Newman's Spaghetti Sauce and heat it in the microwave in a Pyrex container. In the broiler you toast crusty Italian bread with Parmesan and basil. Dinner's convenient and tasty. The dishes get loaded into the dishwasher and you set to work on your computer to prepare for tomorrow's meeting. A stove, a refrigerator, a microwave, a dishwasher, a computer, gas, electricity, running water. Do you want to give any of these up?

Our lives are so steeped in technology that the acquisition of more comes naturally.

In the 1960s and 1970s, Ralph Nader encouraged Americans to become "informed consumers," giving rise to ingredient labels and safety regulations. Today it is no longer enough to compare brands, consult *Consumer Reports,* or research the performance and quality of a given product. Today's consumer technologies are far more powerful and intoxicating than they were in Nader's time. In order to transcend the Technologically Intoxicated Zone, we must become Reflective Consumers and begin to consider the consequences of introducing new technology into our lives, begin examining the effect that technology has on time and the value it adds to human experience. Reflective Consumers understand that the promise of technology can be deceiving and often omits the unintended consequences on our community, our business, our children, and ourselves.

Waterford, a village of 250 Reflective Consumers living in about eighty homes in Virginia's Blue Ridge Mountains, made history in the fall of 1995 by becoming the first American community to refuse cable. "People here have time to talk to each other. I'm proud of our bad TV reception," a Waterford townsman said at the Citizens' Association meeting at which cable access was being considered. "It gets us out of our houses, and I'd kind of hate that to change because there's nine different football games to watch. Personally, I'd rather go fishing than watch the fishing channel."

ADVANCED SIMPLICITY

"I live more like the rest of the world than like an American," said thirty-two-year-old writer Karen Metzger as she describes her day-to-day life. Karen is an extreme example of a movement called "voluntary simplicity" that to date has inspired 10 to 12 percent of the American population to scale back. She is articulate, bright, well educated, and resourceful. Nine thousand feet above sea level, in the majestic San Juan mountain range in Colorado, Karen lives in a nine-by-nine-foot cabin with a small sleeping loft. At the base of three storybook peaks, the cabin sits across a dirt road from an old abandoned homestead chosen for its breathtaking scenery as a setting for John Wayne's 1969 film, *True Grit*. Built entirely out of scrap materials, her cabin's tiny frame tilts forward, the windows askew. Dr. Seuss could have made it.

Five years ago she moved from Chicago, population 3 million, to Hastings Mesa, population fifty. Karen, whose father would "blacktop his lawn and paint it green if he could," learned to cook, clean, and survive the extreme mesa winters without plumbing or proper electricity or all the other luxuries that extend from those basic technologies—a toilet, a shower, tap water, a refrigerator. "Luxury camping" is how Karen summarizes a life in which she hauls in her drinking water, hauls out her garbage, heats creek water or snow to wash her dishes, walks fifty feet to the outhouse, bathes twice a week at a nearby town hot springs, keeps a "cute" .22 Winchester rifle that her mother passed down to her, kicks aside carcasses of marmots that her dogs drag home to the front porch, and struggles to negotiate the unplowed snowdrifted country roads in her 1984 Subaru—the one piece of technology she could not live without.

"People can actually convince themselves that they need far more than they do. It's just a mental block. Amenities are actually a pain in the ass. The more things that you have to keep track of and keep running, the more time it takes. I don't have to worry about my pipes freezing."

Why would Karen choose to eschew the basic consumer technologies that have formed the foundation of American life? Because in forgoing the basic comforts that most Americans take for granted, her world has expanded.

A different sense of time orders her days. "The intense wind, intense starry nights, intense sunsets, epic snowfalls" envelop her in a setting undisturbed by development, traffic, or power lines. She has matured into a jack-of-all-trades and gained a sovereign sense that comes, she says, from being able to live without much technology. She derives far more pleasure from each activity she consciously chooses to engage in. Her life is physical and her body is not divorced from daily routine. Rent is a $100 a month and propane $100 a year, so she can choose not to work for long periods of time. An eight-inch-square solar panel powers her CD player and three tiny lights. She reads and writes, and works with her hands. She has become comfortable with solitude and silence. She "rediscovered" her imagination because she has to entertain herself. From her pillow she sees mountaintops, and more wildlife than humans cross her path.

"I would love to have electricity and be able to work on my computer [which she otherwise powers at her more fully equipped neighbor's house or while in town]. I'll return to that some day, but I'll return to it with a consciousness that one acquires from being directly connected to providing everything for oneself."

The Complexities of Simple Living

The decision to simplify one's own life by scaling back on technology is not an easy one to make or to execute, but there are varying degrees to which many people are trying. To some, simplifying might mean moving to a small town or a rural community. (America's rural population grew 6 percent from 1990 to 1996.) It might involve changing jobs or moving to a smaller house. To others it might mean turning on the television less often or locking away the Nintendo set.

"Simple living is really complex," says artist and clothing designer J. Morgan Puett, who in 1998 scaled back her publicity-rich, high-profile life and business (with discreet celebrity retail clients and upscale wholesale clients like Barneys New York). After a long, persistent effort to disentangle herself from her complex business and life in New York City, Puett relocated to ninety acres in rural northeast Pennsylvania with her boyfriend, Mark, and cat, Roadkill. They live without indoor plumbing in handsome shacks heated with woodburning stoves and sometimes surf the 300 television channels they receive via satellite—one of the technologies Puett very consciously chooses not to live without. She communicates with her partner, who runs their one retail store (they no longer wholesale), by fax, computer, and phone, technologies that enable her to live in the country. Time she once spent devoted to her growing clothing business, she now gives to painting. About the move, she quotes a saying her parents permanently push-pinned to the kitchen bulletin board in their home on a bee farm in Georgia: "As long as you're green you grow, but the minute you think you're ripe you begin to rot."

Change is hard. Where do you start? Millions of people are turning to how-to books for simple solutions to coping with the complexities of their lives. Elaine St. James, author of five bestselling *Simplify Your Life* books (2.5 million in print), offers step-by-step ways to scale back and slow down our lives. Another book, *Simple Abundance*, by Sarah Ban Breathnach is a guide to appreciating life's simple pleasures and has more than 3.7 million copies in print. A voluntary simplicity movement is making inroads into American culture and promoting spirituality and environmentalism while discouraging the work-spend cycle. Barbara Brandt, author of *Whole Life Economics: Revaluing Daily Life,* describes the movement "as weaning ourselves from an addiction to high-tech electronic devices, in particular our television addiction." She says that the movement toward simplicity is "about reclaiming your life and getting more from what you truly value."

HIGH-TECH SIMPLICITY

"Simplicity and convenience are the words we hear the most," says Lisa Montgomery, editor of *Electronic House Magazine*, in discussing the opposite end of the simplicity spectrum known as home automation, a growing business serving those people who acquire more technology in an effort to simplify their lives. "Really, the more complex home automation systems are, the simpler it is. The higher tech you go, the easier it is. People want a system that can prepare the house for bed, vacation, work, or whatever with the push of a button."

Home automation systems have come to the public's attention through the publicity surrounding Bill Gates's $53-million home on Puget Sound in Washington State, where everything from the bathtub to video artwork is automated and electronically monitored. Michael Avery of Smart Systems Supply, a company that worked on Gates's 45,000-square-foot home, believes that Gates and his Microsoft cofounder, Paul Allen, "have nurtured and supported an industry that has slowly migrated to the common man. We're at a real transition, a jumping-off point. The key here is that people can electronically customize their house based on their lifestyle."

Wired Homes, a home automation company based in East Brunswick, New Jersey, suggests on its website that if you buy its system, you can tell a box "I'm going to work," and the system will respond by turning off the coffee maker, turning off bathroom outlets (so that no curling irons are left on), dropping the house temperature (to save on electricity and gas), opening or closing the drapes depending on your preference, turning on and off the lights and television at varying times, giving the illusion that someone is home, locking doors, and activating the alarm system.

Jay Lippman of Bennett Homes, a wired community in Redmond, Washington, stresses that "this is common stuff—it's what is going to be installed in everyone's house. It isn't just for the rich and famous."

Mike Bookey, a network architect for a planned community near Puget Sound, estimated that 20 percent of home buyers in the area have inquired about state-of-the-art wiring for high-tech entertainment, security, communications, and energy control equipment. In other more affluent communities, he estimates the figure is closer to 50 percent.

What once existed only in the animated world of *The Jetsons* is now becoming a reality. People are beginning to envision smart homes in which your alarm clock inquires politely if you would care for fresh coffee, then communicates to the pot to start brewing. Or your smart refrigerator responds to your e-mail inquiry from work asking what out-of-stock ingredients are needed to make vegetarian lasagna for dinner that night. The refrigerator talks to the cupboard, then e-mails an online grocery delivery service for the missing ingredients, which are delivered to the front door by 6:00 P.M.

The home automation industry's scope has the potential to extend into your neighborhood, your community, and even your children's school.

TECHNOLOGY AS COMMUNITY

Celebration is a high-tech community located less than a mile from Disney World near Orlando, Florida. Urban planners, designers, and architects, working with Disney Imagineers, developed a community based on five principles: architecture, health, education, community, and technology. Plans call for 15,000 residents.

In the summer of 1996, the first inhabitants moved into this community of grand homes that could almost pass for an old, established neighborhood—except for the odd juxtaposition of the turn-of-the-century style homes and newly planted saplings. A hundred years hence majestic elm trees may spread their sheltering canopies over lanes and buckle sidewalks with their billowing roots, but not today. Currently 2,000 residents live in homes that boast more front yard than back, old-time columned porches facing central community parks, tall double-sashed windows, and peaked roofs. Main Street is lined with piped-in music and shops with wooden shingles advertising the longevity of their businesses—"Since 1905"—even though in reality they have been in Celebration only since 1996 and were founded elsewhere.

The pleasant, clapboard facades of these homes and this community belie the fact that they are wired to the hilt. Celebration— like the more than 100 other similar communities sprouting up around the United States—is attempting to create more than just a tranquil and picturesque place for families to raise children. The planners hope to create new kinds of links—electronic ones—that connect students and teachers and parents, community groups, retailers and customers, healthcare providers and patients. Ninety-eight percent of the residents own at least one personal computer. Residents get a free e-mail account and access to the Internet when they move to town. A community Intranet allows for discussion groups, bulletin board services, and local e-mail. Closed circuit footage of school and community events is filmed by the town's television crew and posted on the Intranet, like a never-ending documentary.

Even town meetings are conducted electronically, with comments and suggestions sent via e-mail by "attendees." Perry Reader, vice president and general manager of Celebration, said of a recent town meeting, "The question and answer flow was organized and the people didn't have to get dressed and come down and get in the meeting hall and listen to a bunch of conversation. That was very effective."

Founders and residents of Celebration see "technology as a community builder." The "thing that fosters a sense of community is having our own Intranet," says Reader. "Even though it is public to everybody in the community, there is a sense of privacy to it in knowing that just anyone can't just come in from the outside world." Cheryl Cassano, a former elementary school principal who moved to Celebration from Richfield, Connecticut, with her husband and three children, is enthusiastic about the Intranet: "I have been a Cub Scout den mother and I will tell you that in Richfield I would spend an entire evening—or two evenings—calling each boy on the phone every three weeks to explain what we were doing. Here you put up one notice on the Intranet. The ease of relaying information is just fabulous!" Cassano also gave an enthusiastic testimonial about Motorola's TalkAbouts (high-tech two-way radios). "For his birthday my son received a TalkAbout and now his friends are getting them," she continued. "That way you can feel comfortable about letting your child go to the pool or wherever. He calls me after school and says, 'Mom, Adam and I want to go the library for half an hour.' I say fine, and then when a half hour is up I call him."

With Motorola TalkAbouts, children wander farther away from home than a mother's holler out the back door.

Wired Kids

The public school in Celebration, like the homes, is state of the art. "We have no computer labs. Our computers are fully integrated into the instructional process. When you walk into a neighborhood [a term the school uses for classrooms], you see computers and technology everywhere. It isn't isolated in one environment. Technology needs to be where the learner is and where the learning takes place," said Scott Muri, the school's instruction technology specialist.

At the Celebration school, technology is not only ubiquitous, it is powerful and high speed. The school boasts 800 computers for 940 students, 1,800 Ethernet connections, 900 fiber optic cabling connections, 450 two-way coaxial cable connections, and three T-1 lines. The school has its own Intranet, which allows students to publish their work online as well as tap into other students' work for reference. Everything is high tech, high speed. The school has several advisors from Harvard University, Johns Hopkins, Apple Computer, and Sun Microsystems, a privilege afforded the school through its Disney connections.

"We don't lose instructional time by waiting on an Internet page to download or waiting on a document to move over the network," explained Muri. "Our technology philosophy focuses on the Web. We realize that the Internet will offer great connectivity from the school to the home to the outside world."

The Celebration school's full media management system gives teachers and students access to cable, satellite, TV, laser discs, and videos. The school has developed a system that encodes student information into wearable technology, a "Java" ring that communicates information about individual students. The ring carries their name, social security number, which books they've checked out, what assignments are late. Parents program their child's Java ring with money, enabling the child to buy lunch from the lunchroom or snacks from a vending machine simply by inserting the ring into a slot. (What's next, a bar code tattooed on the arm of every school kid?)

The children learn in "neighborhoods" of widely different ages, because some students are capable of using more sophisticated technology than others. "When it comes to teaching technology," Celebration's general manager, Perry Reader, says, "kids teach technology to kids probably better than any other [mentor] relationship we've seen. Show me a kid with a video game and a younger kid who wants to play it; then watch the older kid transfer that wisdom faster than any parent." The school's technology specialist, Muri, recognizes that technology is changing the teaching environment. The problem, he says, "is not bringing kids information. The problem is sorting it, making sense of it, synthesizing it."

The most dangerous promise of technology is that it will make our children smarter. President Bill Clinton's 1996 State of the Union address proclaimed "the Internet in every classroom" to be a noble goal. Access to information will not teach synthesis and analysis. School expenditures on information technology reached $4.34 billion in 1997, yet at the same time programs for music and the arts were defunded.

Community as Theme Park

Celebration promotes itself as a community built on the principles of architecture, health, education, community, and technology. However, one overwhelms the rest. Celebration is a community seduced by technology's promises.

Town meetings occur online, and in a town that boasts of its traditional front porches (that look wooden but are fiberglass and upon which few people sit), the Celebration Intranet has a "Front Porch" community bulletin board as a "resource for communicating with each other." The community also touts cable lines that are "state-of-the-art technology," including "impulse pay-per-view ordering," "optional interactive television guide," "live on-location programming via a two-way network," "Knowledge TV Programming," and the Celebration Community Channel, which airs programming of Celebration events such as Parade of Pride, Celebration Foundation Discovery Series, School Advisory Council Meetings, and Celebration's school graduations, high school basketball games, and Little League games. Community events can be viewed on screens rather than in gyms or on fields or in churches.

Celebration manifests many of the conditions of living in a Technologically Intoxicated Zone. The Java rings children are wearing are indicative of the devout faith the Disney planners and townspeople have in technology. The rings, like the wedding rings nuns wear to symbolize their devotion and marriage to Christ, symbolize the town's worship of technology.

Few communities suffer the real/fake, fake/real confusion as much as Celebration. It is built by the masters of simulation. Disney, which created the facade of an idealized community, is a little defensive about its authenticity. "Celebration is an innovative, real town," declares its promotional literature. Resident Kelly Wrisley also finds it necessary to declare her town as genuine. "People here have their joys and sorrows just like everyplace. It's real life and the real world." But Disney World visitors view it as just one more attraction, not unlike the safari Animal Kingdom. The occupants and their dwellings become specimens to observe, like the lion on the rock or the hippos in the mud. Main Street shops serve the same function as retail outlets at all Disney attractions. Innocuous music litters the town square and emanates from the same semihidden speakers strategically placed around Disney World. Celebration is made to look like an historical all-American town, but it is really a theme park extension, and behind the facade of an old-time community, Disney is really selling high-tech real estate.

EXPANDING TIME

High-tech homes, schools, and communities impact the way we live in time and drive the belief that more and more can be accomplished more conveniently in ever shorter periods of time, all the while causing a nostalgic sense that things were somehow better in the past.

Few businesspeople have capitalized more on our vexed sense of time than Martha Stewart. In the last fifteen years, she has built an empire around a particular and (sometimes) contrarian sensibility about time. Every image created for her magazine *Living* is imbued with a sense of nature's time: weathered stone, faded cloth, a tree planted. Every image reflects a time of day and a sense of season, spring buds just opened in the first warm winds and beets recently harvested at sunrise. What is soulful and sensuous and beautiful comes with attentive care or by lingering or by working hands. While consumer technology holds the promise of saving us time and labor, Stewart's aesthetic entices us with a sentiment that implies exactly the opposite: The things most valued in life come from diligent labor and the nurture of time.

"Before cutting the fabric, we scrubbed the kitchen floor and laid down white sheets so the pristine organdy would not get soiled," Stewart remembers the days when she was nineteen, making her wedding dress with her mother. "Mother had the scissors sharpened so the cloth would cut cleanly, and we bought new steel pins so there would be no rust or spotting. Every seam was carefully basted, stitched, and ironed. All went well, but slowly . . . the tiny, fine seams, the even row of minuscule button loops, and the extra-thin piping at the waist. And I'm amazed at how well it has withstood the march of time."

Stewart's use of words and images urges her readers to make room in their lives for more soul-enriching projects. She viscerally reminds them of what used to be and taps into the desire for a slower, more tranquil life. In an era when prewashed lettuce packaged in airtight plastic bags has been called "the most important thing that's happened to grocery stores in the last five years," a recipe in *Living* suggests: "To make your own extract, place one split vanilla bean in a jar with three-quarters cup vodka, and let sit in a cool, dark place, sealed for about six months."

Time and appreciation brand *Living*, and, by extension, Stewart's entire product line. Like Celebration, Stewart guises her brand in an authentic, traditional all-American aesthetic, but at the core of her business is technology.

A HIGH-TOUCH MESSAGE THROUGH HIGH-TECH MEDIA

Most of Stewart's readers are upper-income professional working women, whose everyday lives differ greatly from that portrayed in her magazine, but they like to imagine the life she renders so attractive. She understands the effect of high-tech time and has built a $1-billion-a-year business selling a high-touch world. Part of her brilliance is that she delivers her high-touch message through the very technology that is stripping time of its grace. Her website gets 476,000 hits per week. *Living Weekdays* is broadcast six days a week on CBS. *Living Weekend* appears in more than 200 television markets. The *askMartha* radio program is broadcast from 260 stations nationwide. Subscribers to her magazine number 2.1 million. Her column appears in 220 newspapers. Stewart has published 26 books, more than 4 million copies currently in print, and she now has a mail-order catalog. The bulk of her products sell through mass marketer Kmart. Stewart is also developing *Everyday After School*, tapping into the next generation of followers. She describes the concept of the show as "an interactive TV program for children," designed to utilize both the television and computer to guide them through specific projects. Stewart wants to spend the rest of her life everywhere, with everyone, one to one, always, forever, now.

Few brands so diligently direct its customers from one medium to the other. Shortly after www.marthastewart.com was launched, an article in *Living* guided readers to the website, and on television Stewart took viewers step by step through the Internet to her site. Sixty percent of her readers now correspond with the company by e-mail. *Living* rhetorically asks each month "Where to find Martha . . . ," which it answers in about ten pages of advertising: World Wide Web, Daytime Television, Morning Television, Martha's Bookshelf, Martha by Mail, Martha by Subscription. Like

Cheryl Cassano, the Celebration mother who is in constant connection with her son through the TalkAbout, Stewart is always connected to her surrogate children.

Today Martha is the country's consummate female brand name. Yet she has no physical site to promote her collection of wares. No flagship store to serve as billboard for her brand. "Virtual" Martha is taking the country by storm.

Personally, Stewart may be one of the most wired women in the world. She has six personal fax numbers, fourteen personal phone numbers, seven car phone numbers, two cell phone numbers, and a PowerBook she carries with her at all times. Her Chevy Suburban is equipped with a mini-dictation disc player, a television, noise-canceling headphones, mobile navigational software, and a cell phone. The New York City conference room at her Omnimedia headquarters has an audiovisual teleconferencing system controlled by a touch-panel remote so Stewart can avoid attending board meetings in person. Technology, she believes, should complement a life enriched by nature, hard work, and friends. One of her recent ads declares, "Your mother was wrong. Television's a good thing."

Stewart's experience has taught her that what interests her will interest millions of others. Currently she's obsessed with technology and is looking for a strategic alliance with both a software and a hardware company to provide her customers with a technology that is uniquely Martha. "In ten years every woman in America is going to want to be wired," she says. Stewart will make technology as desirable and unthreatening as a vase of flowers for her readers, her Kmart customers, her television viewers, and her devotees, who will trust that she has solved the technology problem in a practical, methodical, aesthetically pleasing way as she has always done with cookies, hospital corners, and Easter eggs. Her customers and readers trust that Stewart will take them step by step through unfamiliar technology in a friendly, gentle way.

"Today, although our online business is still a tiny percentage of overall revenues, the future of my company lies in cyberspace. Just this year, our weekly e-commerce revenues are up 80 percent; we've doubled our online-store capacity and increased our Web capacity by 33 percent," Stewart wrote in late 1998, adding that conservative estimates for 1999 revenues will double that.

Her message is high touch; her medium is high tech. If the medium is the message, Martha is shifting to high tech.

LABOR OR LEISURE

Although Stewart is the queen of do-it-yourself, affluence and technology grant many Americans the privilege of outsourcing household jobs they find distasteful. We hire rent-a-husbands, dog walkers, professional errand runners, nannies, painters, maids (whichever tasks we hate the most); cooking is the most outsourced household chore in America.

The home meal replacement industry (not including meals eaten in restaurants or made by personal chefs) reached $108 billion in 1996. That's food on the go, ready to eat, ready to heat, or ready to cook. Today the preparation time for a typical meal is fifteen minutes or less. Forty-one percent of carry-out meals consumed at home are fast food, while another 43 percent are restaurant and supermarket takeout. Unlike the days our mothers cooked from scratch, three-quarters of Americans don't know at 4:00 P.M. what they are going to eat for dinner that evening.

"We're almost at the point where boiling water is a lost art," says Warren J. Belasco, an American Studies Professor at the University of Maryland. "Cooking touches a lot of aspects of life, and if you are really going to cook, then you're really going to have to rearrange a lot of the rest of how you live."

The chores we *do* enjoy—the very ones that our ancestors may have considered drudgery, like growing vegetables or making bread—have shifted from chore to leisure activity. Our favorite chores are becoming pleasurable activities, as we outsource those chores we find arduous.

"Accomplishing a task, whether it is as simple as a minor household repair or as complicated as painting a decorative floor, gives us all a feeling of self-worth, satisfaction, reward, and independence," writes Martha Stewart, who step-by-step teaches her readers how *not* to outsource and *why* mundane tasks are pleasurable.

Part of Stewart's appeal is that the language she uses in *Living* is foreign in the world of consumer technology. Fast, convenient, and easy are not in the vocabulary of the magazine that sets the idealized stage for her other mediums:

"To start a compost heap, add a six- to twelve-inch layer of brown materials to a commercial or homemade bin, then . . . in three to twelve months, you will have nutrient-rich, deep dark compost." That's months, not days.

"Garlic is essentially being transplanted every time it is planted, and so it may take a couple of years to acclimate to new soil and weather. . . . Fall is the ideal time to plant. And like asparagus and artichokes, which also test the gardener's patience, garlic is distinguished by its rather slow performance." Years, not months.

"Growing asparagus is a labor of love: The plant needs two full years in the ground before it can be harvested, but the patient gardener will be rewarded. Properly cared for, the plants will send up delicious spears for decades." Decades.

"Among the twenty thousand species of the ethereal flowers called orchids, there is only one that produces a delight for the eyes and for the taste buds as well. From the exquisite celadon blooms of the so-called orchid of commerce come the pods that yield one of the world's great flavors: vanilla. . . . Though we call it a bean, the vanilla pod is actually a fruit whose flower must be pollinated in order for it to be formed. This is no easy feat, for the blossoms of the vanilla orchid, one of nature's most ephemeral creations, open only one day a year." Ephemeral.

High-touch time, Stewart suggests, is the antidote to the invisible but momentous force of high technology, a force that drives us ever faster. But the older, gentler way of living in time that she espouses is a source for censure and sarcasm. Critics charge that no normal person has that kind of time, and they're probably right, considering that the average American spends half of his or her personal time watching television waiting for a vacation.

RECIPE FOR ESCAPE

Needing a reprieve from consumer technology, you board a plane for a three-day escape. Jammed elbow to elbow between a well-dressed businessman with a lap top and a mother with a lap baby, you stare at the phone in the seat ahead as it ticker-tapes a message: "Impatient Boss, Anxious Client—Make That Call." You resist the pressure. Instead you pull out United's *Hemispheres* magazine and thumb past the ads and business articles to read *Three Perfect Days in Vienna* and fantasize about a romantic getaway. The photographs of rural China also catch your eye, as do grainy images of forests and poetry by Thoreau. The escape is appreciated. Next you pull out the in-flight catalog from the seat pocket and wonder if the towel warmer would be a luxury worth purchasing, or the clothes steamer. As a bonus, if you charged it, Mileage Plus VISA will reward you with frequent flier miles. The phone unit delivers another message. This time: "What's the price of not making that call?"

The two magazines carried by United Airlines, the high-tech mail-order catalog *High Street Emporium* and the high-touch *Hemispheres*, reflect America's two biggest markets, consumer technology and the escape from consumer technology. Through an ingenious marketing network, the airline and credit card companies have joined together to create a plan whereby the purchase of consumer technologies feeds the escape from consumer technology. Purchase a Humvee on your MasterCard, for example, and receive 54,975 travel miles. "Get a mortgage, get miles." "Pick up a phone. Pick up miles."

The more consumer technology you purchase, the more you'll need an escape.

Few people make the choice to alter their lives by scaling back on their possessions or moving to a small town, but most Americans are attracted to the temporary escape of travel. On vacation

Americans feel the desire to unplug: Television viewing drops precipitously while time savoring sleep, the pleasure of food, the outdoors, and books expands. On vacation we spend time more like Karen Metzger. "I never go on vacation," declares this woman, whose life is lived with few jacks, wires, or switches and the accompanying buzzes and breakdowns. "I don't need to go away," Metzger genuinely feels. But most of us do.

Packaged Experiences

Travel, a $442-billion-a-year industry in America alone, is our number-one venue for escaping the stress engine of consumer technology. The trend is toward long weekend trips; there is no trend toward longer vacations. Even time off is squeezed in. Weekend trips increased by 70 percent between 1986 and 1996, and 80 percent were for pleasure. An entire industry has grown up around this three-day phenomenon. Every major airline, hotel chain, and rent-a-car company has allied to create inexpensive, no-brainer, getaway packages designed to indulge impulse buys. But what do you do once you get there? How do you avoid feeling like a bumbling tourist, losing precious time getting lost, doing dumb things? How do you have an authentic experience?

Once the territory of guide books like *Fodor's* and magazines like *Travel and Leisure*, savvy marketers are getting smarter and more aggressive at removing all the guesswork from travel, providing one-stop shops for people in a hurry, and they promise authenticity.

As a business response to this long-weekend, quick-escape trend, *Hemispheres* and United Airlines created a savvy recipe for escape: *Three Perfect Days* (in your choice of eighty cities). It packages the transportation and the experience.

"Why *Three Perfect Days?*" Randy Johnson, editor of *Hemispheres*, asks rhetorically. "Three days is exactly a long weekend. It's a travel-window many people are adopting nowadays. When you go away you basically opt out of whatever your normal world is and check into someone else's reality." Begun in 1992, the *Three Perfect*

Days series is now the most requested feature of *Hemispheres.* Much like Martha Stewart's Omnimedia, *Three Perfect Days* is extending its brand through multiple channels and cross-references, all of them for multiple hits.

The premise of *Three Perfect Days* is simple: Americans increasingly seek the services of specialists, outsourcing the work they care not to do or don't have the time to do. Planning a vacation carefully to an unfamiliar destination takes time. So why not outsource the itinerary of long weekends? And for those people with more money than time who have a desire to check off the world's cities like a grocery list, *Three Perfect Days* provides the solution.

"Through the east wing of the hotel," directs a typical *Three Perfect Days'* article, "you will find an entrance to the Mass Transit Railway. Take the train under the harbor to Admiralty; follow the signs to the Pacific Place shopping mall and from there to the High Court." So easy and convenient, you can "plug in" to the itinerary immediately—having just unplugged from a high-tech life.

The pace of the itinerary is very reasonable. "Settle for moving slowly along the cracked bits of sidewalk, watching for tree-root hazards while keeping your eyes on the houses," suggests John DeMers, the local writer of *Three Perfect Days in New Orleans,* about a walk through the city's elegant residential Garden District. He further orchestrates an "unhurried lunch" at Commander's Palace, an old established eatery situated across the street from Cemetery No. 1, where he suggests the reader take a stroll among crumbling tombstones dating back to 1833.

Three Perfect Days, or any weekend getaway, is not a sustained antidote to stress. Transplanting oneself from one city to the next, from one schedule to the next, is not relaxing. Despite a change in architecture, despite a change in food or climate, a city's energy is a city energy, and traveling long distances in a short period of time is disquieting. The typical traveler will take along a laptop, a cell phone, a camera, and possibly a video camera, the very things that create stress-inducing high-tech time.

The weekend is over and you stand crammed in the aisle of the plane, grateful to stretch your legs. Passengers hurry off to the luggage carousel where everyone clusters around the snaking conveyor belt checking the name tags of one black roller bag after another. You've just checked back into your own reality.

ESCAPE THROUGH ADVENTURE TRAVEL

"The ordinary traveler should regard travel as an adventure and take chances," Carolyn Bennett Patterson, former legends editor of *National Geographic,* suggests, describing what many Americans are already doing.

Adventure travel is a $220 billion-a-year industry in the United States alone. What was once the realm of eccentric, trained expeditioners traveling in teams sponsored by *National Geographic* or NASA is now, or soon will be, available to anyone with the will and money to try. Technology has opened the world of adventure travel to amateurs. In the last century alone, with great effort and sacrifice, humans reached for the first time the North Pole, the South Pole, the highest place on earth, the deepest spot in the ocean, and the moon. Now there are high-tech, guided group excursions to the top of Mount Everest, organized voyages to the depths of the ocean floor, and boat tours of ice-encrusted polar waters. Space tourism, well under way, could push the adventure travel market into trillions of dollars as it evolves from suborbital flights, to orbital flights, to moon walks, to space plane taxis, to Mars colonization (predicted as early as 2018). Richard Branson, the always-ahead-of-the-curve entrepreneur, established Virgin Galactic Airways in 1999, which will initially offer two-hour space flights costing $50,000 starting in the year 2007.

What is so *compelling* about adventure travel today?

"Lifestyles are changing," says Chicagoan Bud Davis, who organized the first Adventure Travel and Outdoor Show. "Many people aren't content anymore just to be a beach potato and fry in the sun. They want to do something active. Add to that a genuine concern about our vanishing wilderness and the desire to get out into our magnificent outdoors before it disappears, and you've got the drive behind the [growth in] adventure travel."

Adventure travel encompasses a wide spectrum: from soft to hard, from simulated to real, from comfort to misery, from sunburn to malaria, from safety to death, from souvenirs to survival stories. Imagine a spectrum that begins with a space roller coaster, continues on along to a zero-gravity rocket simulation aboard a Russian IL-76 MDK, and ends with space tourism. Or another spectrum: cultural adventure travel that begins with Epcot Center, continues to a two-week guided cultural tour of Bhutan, and ends with working and living on a small family rice farm in Vietnam for a year.

As Americans, we are far from living in a survival economy. For most of us, our basic needs for food, clothing, and shelter are more than taken care of and we are living in peacetime. Physically, our bodies are transported from place to place by cars, and we exercise our minds while seated in chairs, clicking on computer keyboards. The desire to test the strength of our body outside of a gym, feel our physical presence on the earth itself, and thrive under adversity drives many people voluntarily to put themselves in harsh environments and high-risk conditions to *feel* alive.

"People are now less willing to be shown the world," said Geoffrey Kent, chair of one of the largest adventure travel tour agencies in the world, Abercrombie & Kent. "They want to participate in it—and they expect to get their feet wet, their hands dirty, and their minds stimulated."

Heightening sensory experiences and awakening basic instincts drive adventure travelers. Individuals are escaping to nature through mountain climbing, ice climbing, white-water kayaking, tundra dog-mushing, and distance bicycling. Adventure travel is a booming industry, and your neighbor, your dentist, and your banker are the new breed of expeditioner. A 1998 Travel Industry survey found that 98 million Americans have taken an adventure travel vacation in the past five years.

"American travelers want their vacations to be more thrilling," says the president of Travel Industry Association of America, William S. Norman. "They are looking for new ways to challenge themselves, to push their physical energies to the edge and face nature at its boldest moment."

Adventure travel is so common it's turning into a family event. In 1998 a wealthy Chicago family held their annual family reunion in Kenya. The highlight was summitting Mount Kilimanjaro (19,340 feet) and included children as young as ten. Such family adventures are a far cry from family car trips when the biggest thrill was standing too close to the edge of the Grand Canyon.

A growing multibillion-dollar industry of adventure outfitters— Abercrombie and Kent, Mountain Travel·Sobek, Mountain Madness, Alpine Ascents International—have changed the face of travel for mainstream sojourners. These outfitters appeal to those who prefer to stay on the safe and somewhat comfortable side of adventure travel. Almost 10,000 American tour operators offer adventure trips: from bicycling trips in France, to treks in Nepal, to white-water rafting in Patagonia. The common denominator among these companies is the assurance of capable, experienced guides, knowledge of the area, and a detailed itinerary. All you have to do is show up with the gear they recommend. And what gear it is.

Adventure Technology

Today's style of adventure travel is steeped in consumer technology. High-tech gear is available for every conceivable need, for every conceivable journey: digitally perfect-fit hiking boots, helmets with twenty-seven air vents, hydration packs, portable water purifiers, internal-frame backpacks with fiberglass stays to enable a hiker to haul fifty pounds with little strain, bike shorts with a rubberized back-spray-repelling seat. Adventure travel has done for Power Bars and Cliff Bars what NASA did for Tang in 1957.

Recreational Equipment, Inc. (known as REI), a Seattle-based retail store that specializes in adventure travel and outdoor sports gear, has sales of more than $500 million a year. L.L. Bean's sales top $1 billion, and Eddie Bauer had sales of $1.5 billion in 1997. The terminology these companies use to describe and sell their gear is unmistakably high tech: anodized, alloy, high density, bicarbon, polyethylene, polypro, trillium, hydro-dry, hyper-flex—and that's just for items under $20.

Elite and enterprising adventurers fuel the technological breakthroughs that allow us weekend athletes to become adventure travelers. In 1995, when Goran Kropp decided to ride his bicycle to Katmandu from his native Sweden, climb Mount Everest solo (without supplemental oxygen), and pedal back again, he first approached a Swedish company, Primus. He asked them to design a camping stove that would enable him to use white gas, kerosene, diesel, or whatever type of petroleum fuel he might find on his more than 16,000-mile trip. The company accepted the challenge and produced the world's first multifuel camping stove, which it quickly took to market. The technology produced for, or by, adventurous athletes funnels quickly down to the average consumer, making available technology that is better, cheaper, and far more innovative than it otherwise would be.

"While the media exposure these guys bring us is very important," said bike manufacturer Cannondale's Tom Armstrong about the athletes the company sponsors, "half the battle is taking advantage of their feedback on products and turning that into manufacturing results. If Tinker [Juarez] or Missy [Giove] rides a bike in the morning and decides the top tube is a quarter-inch too long, they can call us, and we'll make a new frame and have it on the UPS truck that afternoon."

Sophisticated technology ultimately is rendered sexy, fun, and simple for the consumer market. All technology tends toward consumer technology.

Carry Nothing and Move Fast

Technological advancements, originally fostered by the needs of elite athletes, result in a market saturated with adventure "stuff." The regular guy, with a desire to feel his pulse race, to challenge himself in nature, is now able to accomplish what was once the exclusive realm of elite athletes, forcing the elite athletes to perform even more extreme stunts in order to remain on top. To do that they often eschew technology. Prestige is earned "by tackling the most unforgiving routes with minimal equipment, in the boldest style imaginable," wrote adventurer and bestselling author Jon Krakauer.

The challenges get ever more difficult to achieve: Climb the seven highest summits on each of the seven continents; climb them in seven months; climb them, then snowboard down; climb the world's fourteen 8,000-plus-meter peaks; climb the fourteen peaks without oxygen; climb the peak's hardest routes; in winter; solo; and on and on. "Probing the edges of what may be possible is the only thing I know how to do," said the legendary mountain climber Reinhold Messner.

Technology allows humans to travel to places on earth never before considered habitable and to accomplish previously unthinkable feats, yet some adventurers work toward eliminating the very technology that allowed men and women to accomplish the act in the first place.

A major case in point is Mount Everest. Fewer than fifty years ago, Sir Edmund Hillary and Tensing Norgay reached its summit using military siege-like tactics and an enormous expedition team. The two men reached the highest point on earth, 29,028 feet above sea level, after decades of failed attempts by other teams and many deaths. Part of their essential equipment was supplemental oxygen. In 1978 Reinhold Messner and Peter Habeler astonished the world of high-altitude mountaineers by climbing Everest "by fair means." Previously, no one believed Everest could be summitted without supplemental oxygen. Messner was credited with reinventing mountaineering by eliminating the military-siege mentality, climbing as quickly as possible, using as little equipment as possible and as small a team as possible, and, most important, without bottled oxygen. Of the roughly 750 people to summit Mount Everest, only about 65 have done so without supplemental oxygen. To be considered among the elite of the elite alpiners today, you must be able to survive the "death zone" (above 26,000 feet) without bottled oxygen.

Austrian Thomas Bubendorfer offers another example of a minimalist adventurer. He climbs mountains without ropes, without what he calls "artificial security." Security lies within himself, he believes. His specialty is free solo climbing, and his personal style is to begin and end a climb—which might be a sheer mountain face 10,000 feet high—in a single day. "Climbing records are a by-product of my style, because I carry nothing and move fast."

Another minimalist sport is B.A.S.E. jumping, an extreme sport that reinvented parachuting by eliminating the airplane. To be a registered B.A.S.E. jumper, one must successfully jump from each of four categories using a small customized parachute: B is for building (e.g., the Empire State Building), A is for antenna (Seattle Space Needle), S is for span (St. Louis Arch), and E is for earth (Mount Rushmore). In 1995 there were only 450 B.A.S.E. jumpers; as of 1999 there were more than 4,000 in the United States alone. They often work in small teams. Many times they work at night, scouting sites, tracking traffic patterns, jumping fences, getting keys for locks, or trading access codes to doors via the Web. They watch the weather and wind currents. They set up get-away vehicles and have incorporated military jargon—such as stealth, strategy, tactics—to describe their sport of risky, sometimes illegal, jumps. B.A.S.E. jumpers stripped away the dominant technology of skydiving (the plane) to achieve a purer test of their skill and courage. They also eliminated all automatic deployment devices. One B.A.S.E. jumper even disrobed, starting a new trend.

Adventure Death

In our effort to feel our own physical, sensory humanity, sometimes we dramatically raise the stakes—and the consequences—by dismissing technological support. Now moderately skilled athletes are rejecting technology and increasing the risks of their adventures. Fran Arsentiev, a resident of Telluride, Colorado, became the first American woman, and the second woman ever, to summit Mount Everest without supplemental oxygen in 1998. She died on the descent, survived by her eleven-year-old son.

In the same year three men died in an attempt to be the first to parachute to the South Pole. They wore no standard life-saving technology. The unusually high altitude, a blinding landscape, and the high speed drop due to thin polar air may have disoriented the team as they attempted a four-way formation. The fourth man on the team, Michael Kearns, wore an automatic activation device that deployed his chute at a predetermined altitude, saving his life.

For these athletes, technology seems to dilute the triumph, as if it dilutes their own humanity.

While extreme adventurers dismiss certain kinds of technology, they have tremendous faith in the technology they choose to keep. The more sophisticated the equipment, the greater the risks they dare. Snowboarders armed with avalanche transceivers venture confidently into backcountry even under the most dangerous conditions. Dirt bikers plunge down steeper hills because their leather suits now sport better padding and their helmets are more protective.

"Technology doesn't fail, humans do" is the typical refrain of the more daring adventure travelers. Most accidents in adventure travel and extreme sports are attributed to human error, not technological failure. This attribution allows the living to continue practicing their sport, despite their peers' fatal accidents. They are sure that the technology won't fail them when they need it, and they assure themselves that they are too experienced, too focused to make tragic, foolish errors.

"When accidents happen, I think it's always human error," former Mount Everest guide Scott Fischer told a reporter about the risks inherent in his sport. "So that's what I want to eliminate. I've had lots of climbing accidents in my youth. You come up with lots of reasons, but ultimately it's human error." Fischer died climbing Everest in 1996.

Eat Potato Chips and Die

The inherent risk of adventure travel reawakens primal instincts and responses, reminding us of what it means to be human. The intensity of adventure travel and extreme sports is in direct contrast to a life dominated by consumer technologies, which promote comfort, safety, and entertainment above all else. Advertisers like Nike tap into this polarity: "You could get mauled by a bear and die.

You could fall off a cliff and die. You could get shot by a hunter and die. Or you could stay home on the couch, eat potato chips and die."

Ads for adventure gear depict climbers hanging by ropes from cliffs, or white-water rafters plunging down rapids, with tag-lines like North Face's: "I am not alive in an office. I am not alive in a taxi cab. I am not alive on a sidewalk." Or New Balance's: "One less person stuck in a meeting. One less person caught in traffic. One less person put on hold. One more human being . . . being more human."

Just what is it about adventure travel that enables us to feel more human?

For one thing, a clearly defined goal, such as a summit, gives purpose, urgency, and meaning to one's life while in the act of pursuing that goal. The goal focuses the mind and body, and everything else seems insignificant by comparison. Ambivalence and ambiguity disappear, as do life's everyday concerns. This intense feeling of focus is shared by B.A.S.E. jumpers, rock climbers, mountain climbers, and backcountry snowboarders.

Second, danger makes us feel alive. It's exhilarating. "I lay face-down on the rock and whimpered," said mountain-climbing instructor Joe Lentini of his first experience. "Then a few days later I couldn't wait to do it again. The fear fades, but you don't forget the exhilaration." Climber Thomas Bubendorfer puts it another way: "What sharpens your senses is danger—it makes you really listen carefully. If you seek out risk voluntarily, if your passion happens to be dangerous, there's a subtle and intricate thing that happens in a human body and soul, that we can't put our thumb on, like instinct that's honed for decades."

Third, adrenaline and an altered sense of time are part of the draw to adventure travel and extreme sports. B.A.S.E. jumper Mario Richard says of his ritualistic daily jumps off a local antenna, "A funny thing happens when the adrenaline hits. Time seems to stretch out. It's so intense that it slows down time." Another accomplished B.A.S.E. jumper, Christian Sewell, agreed: "When I parachute from a plane, I have twenty to thirty seconds before I pull the cord. The free-fall time seems to race by. When I B.A.S.E. jump, I have three to five seconds, maybe less, before I release the chute, but those few moments last hours. When your adrenaline is racing it makes you aware of everything around you. You are alone. You are the only one in control. You have to be completely in your head. You have to be completely there."

Adventure is now the cutting edge of the travel industry, although soon it may become mainstream. "It's what I call the Ken and Barbie syndrome," said B.A.S.E. jumper Mario Richard, who as a manufacturer of highly specialized parachuting rigs has a perspective shaped by his changing clientele. "It's what's happened to skydiving. The typical guy, typical girl [Ken and Barbie], anyone can be a skydiver compared to not long ago when these people were more like marginal people in life. But now you bump into people who don't have an extreme lifestyle. You can be a lawyer. You can be a policeman. Now everybody, every Tom, Dick and Harry, skydives."

Outdoor adventure and gear companies stir our desire to escape consumer technology. A recent L.L. Bean advertisement showed a photo of a happy couple paddling a canoe on a quiet river. The text read:

6 miles to the nearest TV
You've replaced your 27 inch screen with 360 degrees of water and sky.
Now all you need is a favorable current.

But not everyone leaves behind the consumer technologies that drive them to escape in the first place. On the ill-fated 1996 guided trip to Mount Everest in which twelve people died, wealthy New York socialite Sandy Pittman brought along two laptops, a video camera, two tape recorders, a CD-ROM, a printer, solar panels and batteries, and an espresso machine. On another journey, to Antarctica, she brought a TV and a VCR—toys she could not leave behind.

Pittman is an extreme example of taking your cell phone to the beach.

Consumer technology creates a world of high-tech time. High-tech time drives us crazy, giving us a low-grade fever that makes us feel that something is not right. We feel a vague but profound yearning to escape from high-tech time. Without knowing it, we are seeking the relief of high-touch time. Without a conscious awareness of the pervasiveness of consumer technology and the impact it has on our lives, it becomes impossible to escape. Technology is the air we breathe, so we can't leave it behind without extraordinary effort and reflection. We remain tethered to work, to home, to media, and to all the electronic technologies that promise progress but in fact ensure distance and distraction. Like a dog chasing its tail, it is a never-ending cycle and a little ridiculous.

The Military-Nintendo complex

In America, children are being drafted into war at about the age of seven. The Military-Industrial Complex that President Eisenhower warned against is becoming a Military-Nintendo Complex, with insidious consequences for our children and our society. American military actions resemble high-tech electronic games while on our own soil we are witnessing another war: The soldiers are children, the battlegrounds their schools, and their engagements resemble the same violent electronic games that train our military and "entertain" our children.

"Doom will become reality!" wrote one of the two Littleton terrorists before the Columbine High School killings began. Those two student killers won a place in history (for the moment) on April 20, 1999, by committing the worst school massacre in American history: They killed twelve fellow classmates, one teacher, themselves, and wounded twenty-three others in a five-hour siege. "What they did wasn't about anger or hate," said their friend Brooks Brown. "It was about them living in the moment, like they were inside a video game."

The two teenage boys were immersed in America's culture of violence delivered through television, films, the Internet, stereo systems, and electronic games such as Doom, which they played for hours daily, including a personalized version of the game that one of the boys had modified to match the corridors of his high school, Columbine. "You're one of earth's crack soldiers, hard-bitten, tough, and heavily armed," describes the instruction manual of Doom, which has sold about 2.7 million copies. "When the alien invasion struck Mars, you were the first on the scene. By killing, killing, and killing, you've won." The boys had linked their home computers so they could play first-person-shooter "death matches" against each other while sitting alone in their own rooms.

Retired Lieutenant Colonel David Grossman, an expert at desensitizing soldiers to increase their killing efficiency and author of *On Killing: The Psychological Cost of Learning to Kill in War and Society*, says, "Violent video games hardwire young people for shooting at humans. The entertainment industry conditions the young in exactly the same way the military does. Civilian society apes the training and conditioning techniques of the military at its peril." The two students mimicked the game Doom in the Littleton high school massacre. *Time* magazine's diagram of the boys' arsenal of weapons and pipe bombs they used that day looked as if it were copied from the Doom manual.

America is entrenched in a culture of violence. Our reputation in the world as a violent culture is based on crime statistics, but far more prevalent—and damaging—is the steady stream of violence on our screens: film, television, Internet, and electronic games. And many electronic games, which grant the player the privilege of pulling the trigger, are *relentlessly* violent, militaristic, and graphic. Living in a Technologically Intoxicated Zone, we are not troubled by the violence on our screens, yet we are perplexed by the violence committed by our young.

A 1998 advertisement in *Next Generation*, a magazine marketed to children, promoted an electronic game called Vigilance (rated

Teen 13+). The ad encouraged the player to "put your violent nature to good use." Mimicking schoolyard tragedies, the ad pictured a boy's legs from the knees down, in tennis shoes and jeans, the barrel of a shotgun at his side and two dead classmates at his feet. The tag-line read: "You Should Fit Right In."

Left alone in their homes, their bedrooms, in arcades, playing games that we brush off as harmless sport or watching violent shows we insist are not real, many American children are left unprotected in the electronic war zone. Ninety-eight percent of American homes have at least one television set. Movie attendance is at an all-time high. Films are projected on screens in multiplexes that exercise little control over which movies children actually view, and electronic games have been incorporated into the daily routines of 65 percent of all U.S. households, 85 percent of those with male children. Video games are the most dangerous medium of the electronic war zone.

Stephen Kline, a Simon Fraser University communications professor, director of the Media Analysis Lab, and a researcher of electronic games and children, found that few parents understand the nature of these games. "I don't think people are fully aware of either the scope of the industry or the impact video games are having on our kids. Parents don't monitor it. They see it simply as a kind of benign pastime. They have no sense of the scale or the avidity with which their children play the games or the way it disrupts their lives."

HUGE MARKET

The electronic game industry generates $16 billion a year in the United States alone, more than twice that of Hollywood's box office gross of nearly $7 billion and more than 30 percent of the U.S. playthings market. The popularity of electronic games has surpassed that of popular films. Sales of Duke Nukem totaled nearly $150 million, more than Disney's *Hercules* or the *Hunchback of Notre Dame*, which each earned about $100 million.

There are an estimated 27 million casual gamers and 6 million hard-core gamers in America, and the Interactive Digital Software

Association (IDSA) estimates that nearly 45 percent of all interactive gamers are under the age of eighteen.

Doug Lowenstein, president of IDSA, the electronic game industry's trade association, recently said, "There has been a sea change in home entertainment preferences over the last few years as the quality, intensity, and complexity of the video and PC game experience has leapt forward. As a result, video and PC games are changing the way Americans play and are firmly entrenched as the third leg of the American triad," along with television and film.

FROM PING-PONG TO MURDER

Electronic games like basketball, football, and snowboarding are popular, but children prefer violent games, according to a study of seventh and eighth graders by Dr. Jeanne Funk of the Medical College of Ohio's Department of Pediatrics. Almost half the best-selling games are violent, and those twenty titles account for 70 percent of the video game market. Nintendo's electronic game South Park, for example, is an adaptation of the animated television show set in Colorado. The television series includes the violent death of a third grader, named Kenny, in every episode. In the electronic game version, the player gets to kill Kenny.

Well aware of the appeal violence has to young people, the industry uses the language of violence to sell their games: "More fun than shooting your neighbor's cat"; "Act Locally, Kill Globally, Unleash the Beast Within"; "You're serving up massive destruction and road kill is the main course"; "Ever seen a body with 10,000 volts running through it? Want to?"; "Get in touch with your gun-toting testosterone pumping cold-blooded murdering side."

How did the industry go from Pong (a game of electronic Ping-Pong) and Mario Brothers (two plumbers who go through mazes to save a girl) to mayhem? Chris Charla, editor in chief of gaming magazine *Next Generation*, said, "As soon as Doom came out, everyone decided that the way to be successful was to make their games satanic and violent too." The latest games include rape and torture and endless killings. By the time a player reaches the highest level of the game Carmaggedon, he will have run over and killed 33,000 pedestrians.

FROM AUDIO AND VISUALS TO TACTILE

The gaming industry is using all the technology at its disposal to make the games more "real," and soon the image quality will equal that of film. "That is certainly the ultimate objective of the video games category as a whole," says Doug Faust, the publisher of Sony's *PlayStation Magazine*. "The discussion is more and more along the lines of an experience, a graphic experience that is very, very difficult to distinguish from a movie experience."

In an effort to make their products more compelling through realism, the interactive entertainment industry invested approximately $2 billion in research and development of new gaming technology in 1997. The results are such accessories as the new Dual Shock Analog Controller by PlayStation, which is advertised as "a totally intensified gaming experience where you'll feel the action come to life whether its the sweet revving of a car's engine or a warrior's thrusting blow. With total precision and awesome handling, the Dual Shock Analog Controller is as real as it gets."

There are goggles that make a small computer image appear as a giant theater screen to the wearer. Haptic feedback allows a player actually to feel what looks wet and sticky with a special glove, and smart force feedback allows players to feel g-force pulls, vibrations, resistance, and hits. Soon children will be able to sit before a console, with a mind's-eye image the size of a giant movie screen, and feel the backfire of a gun as they shoot, the impact of their punches as they hit, and the dripping blood of their maimed victims while screams of pain and terror fill their ears as they kill hundreds of human beings in a single sitting.

Meanwhile, these games rattle our sense of sanity with increasingly perverse story lines. In the online Internet electronic game called 10Six, for instance, if you log off-line to go to the bathroom, your base can be attacked in your absence. "We have this community based on a paranoia philosophy," says Larry Pacey, executive producer of 10Six. Another psychological thriller, Sanitarium, also toys with a player's sanity. "The premise of the game is, are you crazy? Is the world that you are living in a construct? Is it real, or not? We go to great lengths to confuse you about what is real and what's not," said the game's executive producer, Travis Williams.

"Video game technology is young, changing, and growing," notes Dr. David Walsh, executive director of the National Institute on Media and the Family, an organization that promotes the benefits and warns against the harm media does to children. "The technology has advanced so quickly that it has caught people by surprise. People over thirty aren't familiar with this kind of technology because they didn't grow up with it. Though only about 30 percent of all the games on the market feature violence as a theme, they are made more dangerous with advances in the quality of the graphics and the interactive nature of the games themselves."

As media technologies converge, social scientist Eugene Provenzo raises questions about the influence of electronic games on the omnipresent television (which has already been influenced graphically). "If the video game industry is going to provide the foundation for the development of interactive television, then concerned parents and educators have cause for considerable alarm. During the past decade, the video game industry has developed games whose social content has been overwhelmingly violent, sexist, and even racist."

PACKAGED EMOTIONS

The technology of electronic games is addictive. "Every species is born with the ability to monitor their environment for danger and as soon as they identify danger they stay riveted to it," says Lieutenant Colonel David Grossman, who also is a former professor of psychology at West Point. "They cannot look away from it. That's the addiction. Children, until they are five, six, or seven years of age, cannot tell the difference between fantasy and reality, so when they see someone shot, stabbed, brutalized, or degraded on the screen, for them it is real."

The electronic game industry, which includes interactive games on the TV, Internet, computer, and in arcades, pours money into making electronic games real but consistently denies any impact its games might have on children, insisting that they can distinguish between what is real and fantasy.

"The computer is far more powerful than television," says Jane Healy, educational psychologist and author of three books on media's impact on children. And although nearly all media violence studies to date focus on television programming, Healy warns that computers are more insidious. "The computer is even more engaging. When children are watching television they are frequently playing or doing something else, but computer software is designed to rivet their attention." Unlike television, where the audience passively absorbs the images, in electronic games children inflict the violence themselves.

Professor Stephen Kline worries about what children are learning through playing electronic games: "Play is paradoxical: It subsumes both a connection to reality and imagination by definition. Video game violence is not real violence, but it is an intense simulation of personal conflict. We should think about whether that is something worth encouraging our children to do on a regular basis with high degrees of engagement."

The influence of violent media is both psychological and physical. Kline calls electronic games packaged emotions: "Here we have a form of entertainment that is producing high levels of emotional stress and intensity—the same heart rate acceleration that people experience in either a stressful job or while doing a strenuous physical exercise. This will increasingly be documented."

Kline's research has found that one in four children who play electronic games is addicted. "They constantly refer to this experience of not being able to put it down, not being able to quit in the middle of the game," he said. "The whole structure is an emotional roller coaster which configures itself not unlike other addictive activities."

On the other hand, Arthur Pober, executive director of Entertainment Software Rating Board (ESRB), champions the positive benefits of video games: "Electronic games are a social medium, a social vehicle to talk with other kids." Professor Kline's study found the opposite to be true. Playing video and computer games isolates children rather than providing them opportunities for socialization. Children typically play electronic games by themselves in their own rooms, his study found. "I have looked at the changes of play culture as kids' lives become colonized by technology," says Kline. "They are being drawn into their bedrooms and playing packaged emotion machines."

While Pober suggests that "there are a lot of tremendous positive things that these games do in many ways, whether it is increasing thinking skills, motor coordination, and just sheer enjoyment," Professor Kline thinks otherwise. "I am always asked, 'Surely video games teach eye-hand coordination, right?' My response to this is, yes. For $2,500 you can buy the latest computer that delivers eye-hand coordination. On the other hand, for $1 you can go get them a ball. Put them in the backyard and have a good time with them too. You know, this idea that computers teach eye-hand coordination is such an idiot argument."

Computer simulation trains and conditions our young more like soldiers killing and less like children playing catch.

SIMULATION FOR SOLDIERS

High-tech simulation training and conditioning, along with high-tech sophisticated weaponry, can be credited with creating the most advanced military in the world, the American armed forces.

Technological innovations in training came slowly to the military. General H. Norman Schwarzkopf, the leader of the allied forces in the Gulf War, joined the army in the presimulation days, when soldiers still trained in the field. "I used to win the Medal of Honor regularly under blank fire," Schwarzkopf told us. "Never got hurt one time. But of course the maneuvers were totally unrealistic. The tanks would line up on one side and the other, and you would have your infallible Master Plan. You'd come rolling across hill and dale and in the end there was always a big argument about who had won. We used to do these huge maneuvers and had people running around who were umpires, but they never knew where to look and most of the time they didn't know what the hell was going on."

War games that put thousands of vehicles and soldiers in the field were expensive, and they also ended without any clear winners or better soldiers. In the 1970s the armed forces saw the beginnings of a new training system called Multiple Integrated Laser Engagement Systems (MILES), which changed the nature of U.S. military war games forever. In MILES, soldiers wore vests and shot at each other with blanks that triggered laser pulses. If a soldier's vest was hit, a buzzer went off and his gun was deactivated.

When MILES was first incorporated into training, General Schwarzkopf thought, "This is Mickey Mouse we're creating." But he became a convert. "It was incredible the impact this had on the realism of training," remembered Schwarzkopf. "Suddenly the soldier, a guy who up until now had a rather 'I don't give a damn' attitude, is creeping and crawling on the ground and jumping up and leaping into mud puddles to avoid being hit." The laser system for soldiers was quickly applied to military vehicles for even greater accountability. It became much more difficult "to win the Medal of Honor."

Reminiscent of the film *Small Soldiers*, the military technology of MILES was picked up by the toy industry and spawned a new, successful, commercial toy product, Laser Tag, an example of how war and play industries have begun to commingle their technologies in recent years.

In 1997 sales of Laser Tag guns and accessories reached $175 million, up 35 percent from the previous year, and in 1998 revenues for laser tag totaled more than $245 million. Sixty-one percent of competitors are aged seven to nineteen, and kids can purchase the guns at toy stores or play Laser Tag at Laser Tag centers in malls. Toys "R" Us and FAO Schwartz claim not to sell "realistic" toy guns, but they do sell Laser Tag technology, which requires at least two sets to play and retail for about $75 each. According to the Toy Soldier at FAO Schwartz in Chicago (an employee outfitted in a lipstick-red toy soldier uniform with painted cheeks), the Laser

Challenge was, in the spring of 1998, the "hippest thing and sold out immediately."

In his conversation with us, the Toy Soldier recommended that we buy a back sensor for an additional $15. "Makes it more realistic. If someone runs away you can shoot them." The back sensor plugs into the front vest. It makes a sound when it's hit and sends a signal to the front vest that squirts water—imitating blood—at the victim's face. "If you get hit ten times, a warning siren sounds," said the Toy Soldier. "Twenty times, you're dead."

SERIOUS WAR GAMES

Although Laser Tag has taken off commercially, its use waned in the military in the early 1980s, for it still required transporting troops and equipment into the field. In the mid-1980s, according to Schwarzkopf, the military turned instead to computer simulation. "We had these wonderful breakthroughs in computer technology and simulation and everything became computerized," Schwarzkopf told us. "An entire war was fought on the computers. We had our intelligence personnel playing the enemy because they were the ones who knew the enemy's tactics. I commanded 350,000 to 500,000 troops in Corps exercises against the enemy—against scenarios we actually expected to fight. Plus there were a bunch of type-A people who did not plan to lose. We were able to exercise the entire spectrum of the organization."

General Schwarzkopf said that the professionalism in the military was greatly enhanced by simulation training. "The great deal of success we enjoyed in the Gulf War, as compared to the lack of success we had in Vietnam, was a direct result of this entire change in the mentality of the armed forces.

"In World War I there were dogfights," recalled Schwarzkopf. "Everybody flew around on everybody's tail shooting each other down with machine guns." By the time of the Gulf War, most pilots sat in an airplane with a display screen. Schwarzkopf's description indicates how American military actions resemble high-tech electronic games:

"You can't see the enemy from where you are, but the display screen tells you he is there. You pop off a missile. That missile goes out there and knocks out the enemy. There is a total disassociation from what used to be air combat. Today pilots have what they call a pickle. With one hand they are manipulating this pickle and shooting off missiles. It's pure manual dexterity. If you watch my son play his computer games, he's got his joystick and he's fighting the damnedest war you ever saw. I personally can't do it! I didn't grow up in the computer age. I get on the computer and I look away, and I'm dead."

This disassociated warfare wouldn't have been possible without electronic game training, yet not everyone is as enthusiastic about simulation training as Schwarzkopf. In the colloquial language of a decorated Gulf War army lieutenant, J. T. Terranova, who spent months on the front lines, "Simulation don't mean dick. Put a guy in simulation—he's not suffering. Field training is the only thing that separates the men from the boys. Living in the dirt makes you aggressive. A soldier's got to be out in the cold, deprived of sleep and food. Technology has made a weaker soldier." When it comes to infantrymen, the general agrees. "The infantrymen's battle is eyeball to eyeball. Simulation only goes so far."

The two Littleton boys also trained "eyeball to eyeball" for the attack by playing paintball, a derivative of Laser Tag. At Wal-Mart, any kid sixteen or older can purchase paintball guns priced from $34 to $99. If accompanied by a parent, a child of any age can purchase paintball guns, which are in display cases next to real rifles, shotguns, and handguns and are hard to distinguish. It turns out that paintball, the next best thing to shooting real people with real bullets, is a growth industry. An Arkansas-based manufacturer of paintball equipment, Brass Eagle, is the second-fastest-growing company in the world, according to *Business Week*.

MARINE DOOM

Faced with budget cuts, the military is increasingly attracted to simulation and modeling technology. Military budgets have been reduced by 30 percent since 1988, and the number of soldiers enlisted in the U.S. military has decreased from more than 800,000 in 1973 to fewer than 500,000 in 1998.

In recent years the military has increasingly found that simulation training can be beneficial to the recruits as well the commanders, and the military looked into using cost-effective, commercial off-the-shelf (COTS) electronic games as training tools.

"Kids who join the marines today grew up with TV, video games, and computers," said Lieutenant Scott Barnett, one of the creators of Marine Doom (a modified version of Doom tailored for military training). "So we thought, how can we educate them, how can we engage them and how can we make them want to learn? [Marine Doom] is perfect."

With only about 4 percent of the Department of Defense's (DOD) budget, it is hardly surprising that marines have turned to commercially produced simulation games. Warren Katz, cofounder of MÄK Technologies, a privately owned electronic game company, says, "The DOD views modeling and simulation as a cost-saving mechanism. If they are using modeling and simulation for training, they're burning less gasoline and firing fewer real bullets. It costs about $15,000 an hour to fly a helicopter. It costs about $5,000 an hour to drive a tank around. Large-scale tactical team training is very, very expensive."

When Marine Corps Commandant General C. C. Krulak took office in June 1995, he reaffirmed the marines' commitment to the use of simulations and games for training. "The use of simulation, virtual reality, models, and various war-fighting games can make subsequent field training more effective," the Commandant wrote in the Marine Corps planning guide.

By the time the Commandant's directive was released, one marine was already looking to commercial electronic games as a training tool for infantrymen. Sergeant Daniel Snyder, a self-trained computer whiz working on his own time, was knee deep in the process of customizing Doom.

The manufacturer of Doom, id Software, had released the electronic game as a "shareware" program, which allows players to modify it to suit their tastes, skills, and preferences. Instead of battling aliens on Mars, for example, the game could be altered to fight cops in the New York City subway. Simply by downloading a set of editing tools, players can tweak Doom to shape their own fighting environments and choose their own weapons and characters. Over the course of several months, Snyder replaced Mars monsters with marines, chainsaw weapons with authentic marine weapons, and dark cybermazes with jungle combat scenes. In the end, Snyder produced a realistic, combat-oriented game that allowed multiple players to participate simultaneously in the same war.

When he showed Marine Doom to Commandant Krulak in 1996, the Commandant's reaction was so positive that Snyder spent the rest of his military career traveling around exhibiting Marine Doom and demonstrating how effectively the military could import commercial games and upgrade them into prime training tools. Subsequently the Marine Corps Combat and Development Command in Quantico, Virginia, evaluated more than thirty commercially available electronic games for their potential use as training tools for marines.

"We were tasked with looking at commercial off-the-shelf computer games that might teach an appreciation for the art and science of war," recalled Lieutenant Colonel Rick Eisiminger. These days the Marine Corps is focusing on a electronic game called TacOps, a battle simulation game developed for the commercial market by a retired major in Texas. Commandant Krulak ordered a copy of the game for every computer in the Corps.

"For the marines to build a proprietary game, we are looking in excess of $200,000 to $300,000," said Major Saul Hernandez, director of Logistics for the Marine Corps University. "[TacOps] in particular has already gone through a life cycle of profitability, so we are getting it dirt cheap. Dollar for dollar, pound for pound, this is much more effective."

THE MILITARY-NINTENDO COMPLEX

Links between the military and the electronic game industry have been around since the early 1980s when the U.S. Army asked Atari to create a special version of the game Battle Zone as a training tool for drivers of the Bradley Fighting Vehicle (a relatively light, fast-moving tank). Since then talent and product have flowed between the two, creating a symbiotic relationship.

One of the best-known military migrants to the entertainment industry, J. W. "Wild Bill" Stealy, chairman of Interactive Magic, a North Carolina–based company, is dedicated to realism in gaming. "I don't play fantasy games," says Stealy. "I don't play adventure games. I went to the Air Force Academy and I'm a military officer. I've learned that we have to take reality and make something of it."

Stealy's most recent project highlights the increasingly blurred line between military technology and civilian games. His company recently released a flight simulation game called Carrier Strike Fighter starring an aircraft called the iF/A-18E *before* the actual aircraft was put into general operation. In an effort to make the game as real as possible, Stealy and his research team observed not only test flights of the iF/A-18E but spent time on the aircraft carrier USS *Abraham Lincoln*, taking photos and videos so that artists could render the game with precise accuracy.

"Now," said Jim Harler, a retired Marine Corps pilot and Interactive Magic's lead game designer, "we can truly simulate the thrill of flying one of the most lethal jets in the navy's arsenal."

Another defector, the talented creator of Marine Doom, Daniel Snyder, now works in the private sector, where he creates commercial games that will also be sold to the military for training. Game designers such as Snyder migrate from the military to the private sector for a more fluid and responsive environment, with shorter design cycles and higher pay. But they also leave because of people like Dante Anderson, former senior producer at GT Interactive, who lure skilled military personnel into the commercial gaming world. Anderson is no stranger to the increasing synergy between the military and gaming industry, and is a veteran of the annual Connections Conference, an impressive example of the Military-Nintendo Complex.

The conference, hosted by the U.S. Government, invites anyone "involved with modeling or development of military or popular wargaming packages." Attendees include personnel of the Defense Intelligence Agency and game companies like GT Interactive. Conference agendas have included such topics as "Wargaming Design Fundamentals" and "Department of Defense Wargaming 101." Cooperation between these two cultures is being actively encouraged by the National Research Council, which advises the government on matters of science and technology, to "better leverage each other's capabilities in modeling and simulation technology and to identify potential areas for greater collaboration."

Collaboration has taken a step beyond allowing game makers to observe the military or the flow of talent between the two sectors. In 1997 MÄK Technologies in Cambridge, Massachusetts, won the first-ever, dual-use contract from the Department of Defense to create Marine Exed Unit 2000, an amphibious electronic game for release in both the commercial and military markets. According to MÄK Technologies cofounder Warren Katz, "The dual-use business model that MÄK is pioneering between the DOD and the video game industry will yield professional-quality, low-cost training for our military customers in addition to the most realistic simulation games ever produced" for the civilian market.

MILITARY GAMES FOR KIDS

The Military-Nintendo Complex (much of it funded by our tax dollars) creates games that our children now have access to that advertise: "Total annihilation, the new landscape of war"; "Just like the real Army except for the syphilis"; "The smell of napalm"; "The joyous feeling of riding and guiding your missiles straight into enemy targets"; "The beautiful sound of your arsenal blowing away tanks and downing helicopters in head-to-head combat"; "You better fasten your military-issued seat belts, you're in for the adrenaline rush of your life."

Young children play the very same games that the U.S. military uses for training soldiers. Children "play" more often and log more hours than military personnel, but without the well-known discipline that accompanies a soldier's training. "Real" high-tech military operations fought from screens and disassociated from enemy soldiers and civilians, result in few American causalities. "Virtual" high-tech battles fought from screens desensitize our children to violence and train them to kill. "Doom will become a reality" becomes the fantasy.

Play is becoming more like war and war is becoming more like play.

These games worry General Schwarzkopf. "I think it's scary. I get very nervous about the disassociation from reality in a Nintendo game. Kids are out there chopping people to death and blowing people up."

If computer simulation has taken the U.S. military to a new level of professionalism, how does the same training affect a child? The American Academy of Pediatrics reports that nearly 1,000 studies confirm a correlation between aggressive behavior in children and media violence. The vast majority of these studies conclude that there is a cause-and-effect relationship between media violence and real-life violence.

A friend of the Littleton killers at Columbine High School said, "They trained on video games like it was a real war."

Lieutenant Colonel David Grossman told us he firmly believes that electronic games condition and train children to kill. He was hired as a consultant after the 1998 school shooting in Paducah, Kentucky, and tells a chilling story about the fourteen-year-old assailant who had never picked up a gun before that day:

The FBI says that the average law enforcement officer in the average engagement hits fewer than one bullet in five. Trained, seasoned, hardened law enforcement officers hit with less than one bullet in five at an average distance of seven yards, which is pretty darn close. Now he [the fourteen-year-old assailant in Paducah], among a bunch of kneeling, scrambling, screaming children, fires eight shots. How many hits does he get? Eight. Eight hits on eight different kids—five of them are head shots, the other three are upper torso.

All the witness statements say that he stood there and that he got this blank look on his face. He held the gun up in a two-armed stance, he planted his feet, and he never moved them. He never fired the gun far to the left, never far to the right. He just fired one shot at everything that popped up on his screen. And this business of firing one shot, this is not natural. The natural reaction is to fire at a target until it drops and then move on to the next target. But if you are playing games such as Lethal Enforcer and many of the early-generation point-and-shoot games, what do they train you to do? You fire one shot at every target. If you are really, really good, you'll fire one shot, don't even wait for the target to drop, go to the next, the next, the next, the next.

His family had arcade-quality games in the house. He also had all the quarters he needed down at the local video arcade, and he played and played and played. When you actually play the point-and-shoot video games, what happens is that you are getting practice. Now, if I take my kid out and I teach him how to hunt, there is a tradition that goes back 5,000 years of hunting. What do I teach him? I say: Never point a gun at another human being. That is the cardinal rule: Never, never, never point a gun at another human being. And that kid will carry that gun around, you know a hunter, a policeman, a cop, a soldier will carry a gun around for days and never fire a shot. And that is normal. But when a kid puts a quarter in that video game, what does he do? Number one: He breaks the cardinal rule and begins to point and shoot at other human beings. Number two: He never puts that quarter in that game and doesn't shoot; he has this immediate expectation [that] when he takes a gun in his hand, he will shoot.

THE CATHARSIS CONUNDRUM

The electronic game industry claims that children can distinguish between real and fake and are in no way affected by violent electronic games. They embrace the notion that such violent games provide a cathartic outlet for children with violent tendencies.

Violence "is in our 'wiring,' so to speak," says Doug Faust, publisher of *PlayStation Magazine*, "and singling out games to blame for this problem reeks of scapegoating. It is a fallacy to assume that just because video games contain violence, they are in some way the cause of the violence present in our culture. In fact, it is possible that video games may even allow some naturally aggressive boys to release aggression in the form of fantasy play as opposed to acting out violently upon other people."

Some companies are using this claim in their product advertising. Net Fighter, an interactive Internet game, recently advertised in a magazine: "You can divert your anger off the streets and onto the Net against real live people all over the globe." The ad also quotes letters from fans: "I used to take out my bullets, and on each one I would write the name of each person on my [school] bus. Then a friend showed me I could purge my violent urges in Net Fighter on Heat. Net against other people. Thanks to Heat, the people on my bus will never know how close they came." Another letter in the ad reads: "The doctor said I had a bi-polar personality and I needed to practice anger management techniques, so I hurt him. Now that I beat up my friends in Net Fighter, I don't have to do that anymore."

Few media scholars or psychologists regard as valid the notion of entertainment violence as cathartic, particularly for children and adolescents. In fact, numerous studies have shown that gratuitous violence stimulates aggressive thoughts rather than purges them. It also has been widely documented that aggression is a learned behavior, not a primal urge that seeks an outlet.

"If we really believe that watching violence has a cathartic effect, then we should require that all kids watch violence every day before school to make them more manageable and peaceful," said psychologist and professor Roger N. Johnson, author of *Aggression in Man and Animals*. "It's a logical conclusion, and it indicates how weak and grasping at straws their argument really is."

It is illogical for the gaming industry to claim simultaneously that games can't influence behavior while suggesting they offer a cathartic outlet for violent behavior. "Catharsis to me is a cover-up for the fact that they are admitting that video games are emotionally very volatile," Professor Stephen Kline believes. "I say that's an admission." A cathartic purge from playing violent games is highly improbable, he says. More likely is "a cognitive rearrangement, a change in the emotional life of the child, in response to the highly emotional activity of playing video games."

The use of electronic simulation in the military, hospitals, and universities across the country points to the fact that what is on our screens has "real" consequences. "Researchers in California and Atlanta have relieved patients' long-standing fear of heights by having them walk over 'virtual' bridges and ride in 'virtual' elevators," reports Janet Murray, a senior research scientist at MIT. "Patients initially respond to the 'virtual' environments with terror, just as they would to the real-world experience. The therapist then accompanies them through the experience, helping them practice self-calming behaviors. Essentially, the patients are practicing coping behaviors in the 'virtual' environment; they are like actors at a dress rehearsal."

In Georgia, virtual reality is being used to treat Vietnam veterans with posttraumatic stress disorder. Using programs created by a company called Virtually Better, therapists are helping veterans learn how to manage their fear by bringing them back to the source—a ride on a Huey helicopter or maneuvering through a field surrounded by a dense jungle—but this time their experience is simulated.

Electronic simulation creates an ideal environment for desensitizing phobic patients who transfer what they've learned in the "simulated" world to the "real" world. So while the electronic game industry vehemently counters claims that interactive electronic games have any real-life consequences, psychotherapists and doctors have begun employing "virtual" reality precisely because it is so powerful in effecting real changes in people's real lives. In other words, screens are real.

Electronic games and other violent images delivered in films and on television are not cathartic but rather a steady diet of experiences that become a part of our memories, our dreams, and our conversations. The films we watch, the television shows we ingest, the games we play are part of our life experience and help shape our worldview, particularly as we spend ever more hours sitting in front of screens.

A CULTURE OF VIOLENCE

We live in an electronic culture of violence that we deny is real and believe is entertainment. Electronic games are perceived to be benign playgrounds, when in fact they are training grounds for violence.

We are so steeped in a culture of violence that even while lamenting its consequences, we unconsciously use the language and imagery of violence:

- Four days after the massacre, at the Littleton memorial service attended by 70,000 mourners, Vice President Al Gore said "What say we [sic] into the open *muzzle* of this tragedy, *cocked* and *aimed* at our hearts?"

- During minute-by-minute coverage of Littleton, CNN used as a graphic backdrop the image of pulsating, splattering blood.

- In the five-hour live coverage of the Littleton massacre on April 20, 1999, and in the reporting in the days that followed, there were repeated graphic images of the bloodied victims, fleeing, fearful students, and heavily armed SWAT teams entering the building.

- In an article in *Time* magazine, one reporter wrote, "We struggle to come to terms with the slaughter in Colorado and the *vivid gash* it has left on our psyche."

- The lawyers representing the parents of the Paducah school shooting victims in a lawsuit against the entertainment industry said, "We intend to *hurt* Hollywood. We intend to *hurt* the video game industry. We intend to *hurt* the porn sites."

- Five days after the massacre, in a forty-minute report on the culture of violence and the Littleton tragedy, CBS's prime-time *60 Minutes* aired clips from two ultra-violent films responsible for numerous copycat murders. They also aired clips from Doom and other violent electronic games. *60 Minutes* showed teen idol Leonardo DiCaprio, in *Basketball Diaries*, wearing a flowing black trench coat entering the classroom of an all-boys private high school and in graceful slow motion killing his classmates with a shotgun while a friend cheered him on. *60 Minutes* also showed a young couple terrorizing people in a small-town coffee shop in the movie *Natural Born Killers*. The teenage girl determined who would be killed first by using a children's rhyme, "Eeny, Meeny, Miny, Mo."

Like deer in headlights, we watch the screens while the entertainment industry and news services perpetuate the culture of violence, and our leaders invoke its imagery.

TELEVISION AND TOBACCO

Why is it so many of us turn a blind eye, a deaf ear, and are mute to media violence? Why do we continue to deny the effects?

Lieutenant Colonel Grossman finds that some Americans are willing to accept that violent content in the media contributes to aggressive behavior but deny that it fosters crime. That's "like claiming that tobacco causes cancer but not death," he says. During the years since the Surgeon General's 1964 report linking cigarette smoking with cancer, our view of smoking has been changed radically. As a society we no longer tolerate television commercials or billboards for cigarettes, smoking has been outlawed in most public places, and now, thirty-five years later, the tobacco industry has been forced to become fiscally and socially accountable. Smoking is now generally unacceptable—a sharp contrast to the 1940s and 1950s, when it was considered glamorous.

For decades, American's have turned a deaf ear to studies correlating media violence to violence in our culture. We like to watch violence, just like we enjoyed smoking—and the entertainment industry has added more and more violence to its products, just as the tobacco industry reportedly added more and more nicotine to cigarettes.

"If *Natural Born Killers* or *Pulp Fiction* had been released in 1939, the year that *Casablanca* was released, you can imagine how our society would have reacted," says Grossman. "But what has happened is generation by generation, we have been horrendously desensitized to human death and suffering and have learned to associate human death and suffering with our pleasure. And we have been taught to do that. The television industry learned very early on that the addictive ingredient was violence. The problem is, like the tobacco industry, the additive ingredient is also the deadly ingredient."

"Children's exposure to violence in mass media, particularly at young ages, can have harmful, lifelong consequences," said Leonard Eron, chairman of the American Psychological Association's Commission on Violence and Youth. "There can no longer be any doubt that heavy exposure to televised violence is one of the causes of aggressive behavior, crime, and violence among young people in our society."

The concern regarding media violence has existed for decades, though it's had little effect on the accelerating violence both on and off the screen. Since the first congressional hearing on television and violence in 1952, it has been the subject of many studies. In 1961 Newton Minow, chair of the Federal Communications Commission (FCC), warned that TV was becoming "a vast wasteland," in a time now considered the golden age of television by many. The President's National Commission on the Causes and Prevention of Violence in society cited TV violence as a "contributor" to violence in society. In 1972 Surgeon General Jesse L. Steinfeld issued a report citing a link between television and movie violence and aggressive behavior. In 1984 the attorney general's task force on family violence found "overwhelming evidence that TV violence contributes to real violence." The National Parent-Teachers Association (PTA) in 1989 "demanded," to no avail, that the television industry reduce the amount of violence in their programming. A study published by the American Medical Association in 1992 found that almost anywhere in the world that television appears, fifteen years later the homicide rate doubles. In 1998 the National Television Violence Study released the findings of its three-year-study and concluded that 60 percent of all TV programs had violent content and "there are substantial risks of harmful effects when viewing violence through the television environment." The study was funded initially by the cable television industry, which backed out as the unfavorable findings piled on. Another study found that children committed seven times as many acts of aggression in play after viewing one episode of *Mighty Morphin Power Rangers* (a children's show that averages 200 acts of violence per hour) than children who hadn't seen the show. Jumping spinning kicks and rapid-fire punches performed by the *Power Rangers* are too irresistible not to mimic.

Why do we deny the effects of media violence when copy-cat murders are regular news? Why do we turn a blind eye when teenage homicide is twice as common today as it was in the mid-1980s? Why do we turn a deaf ear when fully three-quarters of all homicide deaths in the entire industrial world among children fifteen and younger take place in the United States?

The massacre in Littleton, Colorado, is proving to be a powerful watershed event, as Americans search for answers to questions of why kids are committing acts of violence. Our tolerance for media violence will change forever once we accept that screens have real consequences. For decades, studies have been reporting a link between media violence and violent behavior in society. Is it possible that, in time, purveying and consuming media violence will become as socially unacceptable as lighting up in an airplane.

THE MAGICAL KIDDY WORLD

Until then, we are dishing up electronic violence to our children like it's candy.

Some electronic games package violent content in deceptively childlike boxes. Sony PlayStation's Croc (rated Kids to Adults) stars a gun-toting cartoon crocodile yet advertises, "Don't be fooled . . . this is no kiddy game." And advertisements for cartoonish Worms 2 (rated Everyone) urge children to "leave slimy trails on the corpses of your enemies" and "wreak havoc on rivals in an addictive game of revenge and mean-minded cruelty."

Cartoon packaging signals to small children that products are made for them, but kids don't understand that the content may be inappropriate, and often neither do their parents. Ann Breed, elementary school principal at Francis W. Parker, a private school in

Chicago, says, "Children are attracted to the games and the shows like *South Park,* because they look cute and innocent. That kind of marketing is disturbing."

While the age of game designers continues to drop (most are between nineteen and twenty-five years old) and as they pursue their "art" through new violent games that they claim are meant for adult consumption, the kids still think the games are for them.

ELECTRONIC PARENTING

Parental response to media violence varies: giving children limitless viewing rights, banishing television from the home, teaching children critical media literacy skills, or monitoring a child's media involvement with hypervigilance.

Victor Strasburger, pediatrician and author of the American Association of Pediatrics' study on media violence, alerts parents to "a third electronic parent [the television set] in the household," which he argues "can teach children good things or bad things." How much control the "real" parents exert over what comes into the home determines what the child will learn electronically. Strasburger reminds parents that they would not invite strangers into their home and give them free access to talk to their children. The television, he believes, can be just that: an intrusive stranger.

If the television is the third parent, then the computer may be the fourth. Psychologist Jane Healy, who has authored three books on children and computers, warns against relying on the computer to parent your child. "We are all busy," she says. "I have been a working mom forever. It is wonderful to believe that there is a parental substitute when you are tired and really don't have the patience after a long day to sit down with a three-year-old, or a ten-year-old, or a fifteen-year-old. It is so tempting to believe that the computer is doing more than you can do (which parents actually believe) and that belief has been encouraged in the computer ads. It is really annoying to find out that the thing that is best for your children is still your time and attention. And the computer may actually be doing your child harm."

Although advertisements have created a belief that computers are educational, and therefore desirable, Healy advocates keeping children away from computers until they are seven; other experts push that number up as far as ten or eleven.

"In this country, we as a culture—and I put myself in this category too—we are desperately eager to believe that something we have purchased can make things better," said Healy. "As a clinician, I truly believe that I am already seeing children who would have been well within the range of normal, whose responses are already distorted by having computers pushed on them since they were about eighteen months old."

CONDITIONS OF A CULTURE OF VIOLENCE
Desensitization

For a class assignment, the two Littleton shooters made a videotape of themselves pretending to blow up cars and kill jocks in the school hallway—a foreshadowing of the massacre to come. In another prelude, one of the boys described in an essay for psychology class a dream he had of killing his classmates in school. For a yearbook photograph, one of the two killers wore a T-shirt emblazoned with the words "Serial Killer," and no one seemed to care. One of the boys brought a pipe bomb to the pizza parlor where he worked, which went unreported. Also, his blatantly violent, obsessive, hate-filled website was called to the attention of local police officers, who failed to notify his parole officer. In a culture accustomed to a steady diet of violent images and language, it is not surprising that the killing video was interpreted as a spoof, the essay dismissed as harmless, and the T-shirt ignored as teenage shock-wear. America's culture of violence, delivered daily through high-tech media, is causing mass cultural desensitization to the consequences of violence and the warning signs given by our children. It is severing the soul of our humanness.

Lieutenant Colonel Grossman suggests we are creating a generation of children with a new, lethal disease: acquired violence immune deficiency. "We're letting our children watch vivid pictures of human suffering and death. And they learn to associate it with what?" he asks. "Their favorite soft drink and candy bar, or their girlfriend's perfume [from the advertisements]. We have raised a generation which has learned to associate violence with pleasure."

The average American child plays electronic games for an hour and a half a day, and Professor Kline points out that all it takes is an hour to begin to feel the effects of desensitization. "I played some of those violent games just to get the feel," he says. "And after an hour, I honestly felt completely numbed and pushed to the limit emotionally. I was playing alongside a twelve-year-old lad who had recommended that we get this game because it was fun. It becomes an emotionally grueling experience to shoot one more person, even if it is an imaginary person. But he could do it. And he could experience that as excitement and fun. And that really disturbs me."

Desensitization to violence and a cultural acceptance of violent imagery is making it difficult for people to recognize real danger. One student, who was outside when the Littleton boys crept toward the school before the massacre began, didn't respond when he saw the trench coats and guns because he thought it was a "senior prank." He was shot at. Kids in line at the cafeteria, waiting to buy their school lunches, were told by other kids that some boys had guns. They laughed and didn't respond because they thought it was a joke. Then bombs exploded. During the massacre, one neighbor heard the bombs blast, the guns pop, and the police car and fire engine sirens. She blankly described it as "a scene from a police movie."

Compassion Fatigue

In a culture of electronic violence, images that once caused us to empathize with the pain and trauma of another human being excite a momentary adrenaline rush. To be numb to another's pain—to be acculturated to violence—is arguably one of the worst consequences our technological advances have wrought. That indifference transfers from the screen, TV, film, Internet, and electronic games to our everyday lives through seemingly innocuous consumer technologies.

Sissela Bok, in her important 1998 book *Mayhem,* calls it "compassion fatigue." "Empathy and fellow feeling," Bok points out, "form the very basis of morality. The capacities for empathy, for feeling responsibility toward others, and for reaching out to help them can be stunted or undermined early on, depending on a child's experiences in the home and neighborhood."

It becomes too easy to turn our backs on fellow human beings. Technology, we are learning, is not neutral.

Mean World Syndrome

According to Bok, "mean world syndrome" is another consequence of media violence. American children live in media war zones.

Tragically, for many poor families, whose neighborhoods are infested with guns, gang violence, and regular echoes of *pop, pop, pop* that sound harmless compared to the gunshots enhanced for film and TV, it is safer to keep children at home behind locked doors watching television than allow them to go out and play. A Roper poll reported that 46 percent of adult Americans believe their neighborhoods to be unsafe, and the number-one concern of our children is a fear of kidnapping. A growing number of American children are afraid to go to school.

Everybody's 15 Minutes

Today everybody wants to be a star, especially our children, whose lives have been steeped in advertising and media images conveyed through information technologies: magazines, billboards, films, television, and now the Internet. In a poll of high school students, two-thirds of respondents answered "celebrity" when asked what they wanted to be when they grew up. Children who spend so much time ingesting images from screens want to be on those screens.

In America, the way to be noticed above the rising din of a modern world is to be increasingly outrageous: Madonna, Dennis Rodman, Marilyn Manson, Howard Stern, and Jesse "The Mind" Ventura have propelled their careers by shocking contemporary standards in the same way the networks have attempted to raise their ratings with "shockumentaries." To gain one's 15 minutes of fame only requires one to be extreme. If a child shoots another child in an city alley, it will go unmentioned on the evening's news and in the newspapers. But if a kid flushes out his classmates with a false fire alarm and lets fly rounds from a semiautomatic weapon, killing four kids, a teacher, and wounding dozens of others, that merits the cover of *Time*, international TV news, newspapers around the world, and possibly a book and movie deal.

Some nations have drawn the line already, refusing to publicize outrageous acts on television or in print. The journalistic custom of Norway and Sweden is to withhold names and photos of violent offenders and refrain from "identification unless it is necessary to meet just and fair demands for information." The result of this custom is that these countries don't have criminal celebrities or the ensuing copycat crimes.

Here in the United States, it took the media just under eight hours from the beginning of the five-hour Littleton siege to air the school yearbook photographs and names of the two student terrorists.

Lieutenant Colonel Grossman advocates the Scandinavian policy for the United States, noting that several of the 1998 school shootings were inspired by the celebrity status of other child killers whose pictures were printed in the media and shown on television. "The media has every right and responsibility to tell the story, but they have no right to glorify the killers by presenting their visual images on television."

But the Littleton boys' faces and names were plastered on television screens, newspapers, and magazines. The result: students across the country copied aspects of their actions:

- In Colorado Springs, Colorado, four high school students were arrested for trespassing after arriving at school in black masks and trench coats.

- In Prosser, Washington, a high school student was arrested for threatening to blow up his school.

- In Palmdale, California, two high school students were arrested for making references to the reputed Trench Coat Mafia of Columbine High School, threatening a fellow student, and talking of making bombs.

- In Cherry Hill, New Jersey, three teenagers were suspended for standing in the high school hallways in black trench coats and acting as if they were shooting weapons.

- Two sixteen-year-old males who claimed they were members of the Trench Coat Mafia were arrested for making bomb threats to Castle Rock High School in Colorado.

- Northwest of Dallas, more than 200 students were taken out of school by parents after a rumor spread that a fourteen-year-old had threatened to shoot a classmate.

- A seventh grader in Mesquite, Texas, was suspended after showing classmates a list of thirty-five students she wished were dead.

- In Tuscarawas, Ohio, a thirteen-year-old was arrested for threatening to bring a gun to school to "kill all the people that he didn't like." Three other students in Ohio were taken into custody for making similar threats.

- Schools in Florence, Colorado, were closed after a local TV station received e-mail from a "Satanist" who said he planned to continue the Columbine massacre at the local high school. The message was traced back to a school computer.

- In a Berks County, Pennsylvania, high school, authorities found and detonated a package containing a pipe bomb that was stashed on the school's roof.

- In Taber, Alberta, Canada, a fourteen-year-old opened fire on classmates, killing one student.

All these incidents, plus dozens of others, were reported in the first week alone after the Littleton massacre. Within a month, hundreds of copycat incidents had been reported, including a shooting at a suburban Atlanta high school, by a fifteen-year-old fellow student, where four students were shot exactly one month after Littleton.

All of the adolescent assailants in the spate of school killings between 1997 and 1999 were deeply engrossed in media violence. The fourteen-year-old student killer in Moses Lake, Washington, who was reportedly addicted to violent electronic games, imitated a particular killing pose of Mickey, the star of his favorite movie, *Natural Born Killers* (the most imitated murder film in history). The student killer in Pearl, Mississippi, was obsessed with Marilyn Manson (the "gothic" rock star) and violent electronic games. The boy from Springfield who opened fire on his classmates delved regularly into violent Internet sites and violent films. And as was widely reported, the two Littleton boys were absorbed in the nihilistic music of a German rock band, violent Internet sites, violent electronic games, and watched *Natural Born Killers* repeatedly.

When children are all but invisible to their parents, the consequences are devastating and dehumanizing. A mother of one of the many boys who killed his classmates in 1998 said that she never even "thought" about her child. Her child felt invisible, and he figured out a way to be seen. This deadly combination of desensitization to violence, a loss of compassion for human life, a paranoia that the world is a bad place, and the desire to be a celebrity, creates the need to be seen as important, good-hero or bad-hero. And technology is only too willingly used as the conduit for incendiary information.

American children are shooting each other, but they are also sending out signals of their ensuing crimes. And the hundreds of children who mimicked the Littleton boys in the days following the massacre (without the massive carnage), were signaling that they are stuck in an adult sanctioned electronic war zone, and they want out.

If we think of this copycat violence by children as a cry for help rather than another opportunity to lay blame, we might begin to reverse America's culture of violence. If we begin to understand that what is on our screens is real, we will no longer send our children into an electronic war zone daily and expect them to remain unaffected and unscathed.

Bewilderment and the Blame Game

At the Sunday memorial in Littleton, Vice President Gore offered little hope when he said, "Nothing that I can say today to you can bring comfort. Nothing that anyone else can say can bring comfort."

Andy Rooney's commentary on Littleton, which aired on *60 Minutes* days after the killings, was just as bleak. "I have this feeling that there is not always an answer," he said.

Most Americans were bewildered by the killings in Littleton. The May 3, 1999, cover of *Newsweek* and the cover of *U.S. News & World Report* on the same day, both read "WHY?" We seem to have few answers. It seems so incomprehensible.

Others Americans were quick to place blame on the two handiest targets (besides the boys themselves): easy access to guns (technology) and bad parenting (human beings). In his first address to the country about Littleton, President Clinton blamed American parents for not shielding their children properly from media violence. At that time he did not condemn the creators and promoters of that violence. He said, "Parents should take this moment to ask themselves what else they can do to shield our children from violent images and experiences that warp young perceptions and obscure the consequences of violence."

A little more than twenty-four hours after the massacre, at a nationally televised memorial service at the Denver Civic Center carried by CNN, a local minister said flat out, "I blame the parents."

In the gun blame game, Denver's mayor Wellington Webb publicly asked the National Rifle Association (NRA) to cancel its annual convention scheduled to take place in the city a week after the mayhem. (The convention was held, though shortened.)

Republican congressman and NRA member Bob Barr of Georgia said on CNN, "It's not a gun control problem, it's a cultural problem."

The blame game can get dizzying. And besides focusing on guns and parents, a growing number of Americans are beginning to suggest that media violence is the third cause; others have added a fourth, "bullying."

MTV sporadically runs a video called "Warning Signs," a show about young people and violence. The young MTV commentators, by and large, blame increasingly deadly violence among teens on easy access to guns.

Disagreeing with charges of a connection between his music and teen violence as rumors spread that the Littleton killers were devout fans, Marilyn Manson lashed out at the media for "irresponsible finger pointing." Manson then blamed "ignorance, hatred, and an access to guns." Nonetheless, he canceled both his Denver appearances, scheduled for the week following Littleton, and the rest of his 1999 concert tour.

Mike DeLuca, the president of the production film company that made *Basketball Diaries*, said after the Littleton killings: "I've thought about our own films and what we've put out. I think you'd have to be without a conscience not to think about it." But he believes that singling out the media "skirts the issue and the real problems: bad home life, bad parenting, having guns in the home, parents fighting and drinking."

Also commenting on Littleton, Senator Dianne Feinstein (D.-Calif.) said the most effective lobbyists in Congress are gun lobbyists. She believes that gun access "is adding to the violence that we see permeating our culture. Now guns aren't the only thing. There's certainly violence in the media. It becomes so easy to kill, everybody sees how easy it is to kill. And when you have low-maturity people under some kind of stress, they can easily go out and replicate what they have learned on television. They can make bombs [from information gathered] on the Internet. I think as a society, we have to begin to say, enough is enough."

When will we stop spinning in the circle of blame and try to find solutions? Littleton, by all signs, will be seen as the tragedy that marked a cultural turning point. For the first time, flashes of a new conscience are appearing across the American landscape.

A New Conscience or Token Response?

The Chicago *Sun-Times* did not run the Littleton story on its front page because it feared copy-cat acts and traumatizing children. "I belicve," said the editor Nigel Wade, "as a newspaper man that people are influenced by what they read in the paper. We hope they are—that's why we carry advertising and express editorial opinions." The decision to run the story inside the newspaper came as the result of a resolve to "balance our duty to report the news with our duty to society as a whole."

Two days after Littleton, MGM asked video stores to return copies of *Basketball Diaries*. "We are going to attempt to get as many of these off the shelf as possible. We think it's the responsible thing to do under the circumstances," said an MGM spokesperson. Days after announcing this plan, MGM discovered that as the new owners of the movie rights, it didn't have the legal permission to pull the movie until June of 1999. Seagram Co., which still owned the distribution rights at the time, declined to recall the film.

A number of television shows and movies whose plot lines were uncomfortably close to the events in Littleton were pulled (some just in the Denver area) following the massacre. Included were CBS's *Promiseland,* in which a gang shootout occurred in front of a Denver school; an episode of CBS's show *Buffy the Vampire Slayer,* because the story line included a fantasy about a mass murder at a school; NBC's miniseries *Atomic Train,* which features sawed-off shotguns and bad men in long black raincoats; and the film *Idle Hands,* which includes a scene of a psycho hand attacking students at their high school Halloween party.

Fox Network Newsmagazine "considered" pulling the story of a neo-Nazi leader who distributes his hateful message on the Internet and the story about young people making homemade bombs from information gathered on the Internet.

In the first few days following the events at Littleton, executives at CBS, NBC, ABC, and Fox all said they had no plans to air any movies about the massacre.

A continuing debate in the Colorado state legislature to liberalize gun control laws, including the right to carry a concealed weapon in a school, ended abruptly after the slayings.

Four days after his initial response to Littleton, President Clinton turned his words to the entertainment industry during his regular Saturday radio address: "To the media and entertainment industries, I say just this: You know you have enormous power to educate and entertain our children. Yes, there should be a label on the outside of every video, but what counts is what's inside and what it will do to the insides of our young people. I ask you to make every video game and movie as if your own children were watching it." Clinton even quoted Lieutenant Colonel Grossman's warnings about the dangers of electronic games.

The events in Littleton highlighted violent programming that is regularly served up through our information technologies, causing a ripple of self-consciousness in the entertainment industry. When MGM thinks of pulling a violent film off video shelves, when television stations cancel violent programming, when the publisher of Sony *PlayStation Magazine* suddenly won't answer our questions "in light of recent tragic events in Colorado," perhaps the creators and distributors of media violence are beginning to recognize their culpability.

Finally, politicians, educators, lawyers, doctors, students, and parents are asking for accountability from the entertainment industry for the creation of the electronic war zone, but no one is questioning the military's role in the creation of the Military-Nintendo Complex.

EDUCATION, LITIGATION, LEGISLATION
Lion and Lamb

Some parents want to unplug, but they don't know how.

Daphne White, founder of The Lion and Lamb Project, a nonprofit organization dedicated to removing violence from children's play, represents a growing number of adults who are concerned about violence in our society and the way it is marketed to children:

I decided to do this because my son wanted Ninja Turtle stuff. He was two or three and we watched almost no television. He had never seen Ninja Turtles, didn't know what one was. He saw it on a soup cup in a store and wanted one. It was kind of an awakening and a bell went off. I noticed that even though I was doing everything in my power to say no and protect my son from these things, they were in his face all the time. I called the American Psychological Association and other groups because I wanted to learn more about this and figure out how I could deal with it. When I called around to see what group could provide a workshop on merchandising to children, there was not one. There was no group that was helping parents deal with this issue.

In 1996 White, who has a background in journalism, created Lion and Lamb to serve an important unmet need. The organization covers a broad range of topics, from violent toys to violent electronic games. Lion and Lamb's basic premise is founded on a broad-based perspective:

Everything is interrelated. That's a Buddhist point of view. You can't talk about toys without talking about how they are marketed for television. If you talk about network television, you get into cable and into movies. What I found out watching this industry for a while is that if you attack one portion of it, like television, they will say cable is worse. If you talk about the cable industry, they'll say, well, look what is happening in the movies. Movies will say, well, video games are worse. I decided it was important to talk about the entertainment and marketing industry as a whole and how they relate to children.

Doug Faust, publisher of *PlayStation Magazine,* echoed White's experience when asked about violence in electronic games. He said, "It's no secret that some video games depict violent content. However, you need go no further than any prime-time TV cop show or latest action/adventure or horror flick—or TV news for that matter—to find confirmation of the ubiquitous presence of violence in our society."

Lion and Lamb "is an initiative *by* parents, *for* parents, helping families find alternatives to violent toys, games and entertainment," and offers monthly newsletters, a website (www.lionlamb.org), workshops for parents, and information on how to organize trade-ins of violent toys. Lion and Lamb's centerpiece is the Parent's Action Kit, an appealing, easy-to-read, step-by-step set that recently won a Parents' Choice Award. The kit helps parents understand how to protect children from media violence, teach peaceful resolution to conflict, and promote peaceful play and peaceful toys. In 1999 White began holding training sessions so others could run workshops across the country. Ideally, she would like to see her kit incorporated into schools and distributed to parents though pediatrician's offices.

White's organization is already having an impact on the toy and entertainment industry. Hasbro gets worried when White shows up at a toy convention, and she was called to testify before a Senate committee hearing on media violence in May of 1999.

White is no longer alone in trying to bring her message to public attention about violence merchandised to children. Other national organizations have begun to take up the cause, recognizing the detrimental effects media technologies and media violence have on the health of children and families. The National Parent Teacher Association, American Medical Association, American Academy of Pediatrics, and American Psychological Association all have programs to educate parents about media violence and teach children critical viewing habits. The American Medical Association, for example, offers tips to reduce family exposure to media violence:

- Don't use TV, radio, electronic games, computer games, and videos as baby-sitters.

- Keep TV and electronic games out of children's bedrooms and turn them off at mealtimes.

- Teach children about advertising and the influence the media has.

- Set guidelines on what is appropriate to watch and what isn't.

- Set a good example by limiting your own use of media and by speaking out for more wholesome programming for children.

Media Literacy

Schools have begun recognizing the need for media education.

"Today there is less reading, less direct parenting, less opportunity to engage the imagination," says Tom Rosenblooth, admissions director of Chicago's Francis W. Parker School. "Kids have less time with parents and spend more time passively unengaged [with screens]. There is also less of an appreciation for what we should expose kids to. Among other things, kids need to learn some filters. We educate people to read. But in the future as people spend less and less time reading, we will have to educate them to 'read' the media."

Media literacy belongs in the curriculum of schools, believes pediatrician Victor Strasburger of the American Academy of Pediatrics, alongside drug education and sex education. Media literacy can teach children to be savvy media consumers and to think critically, to question the motives behind the programmers and the advertisers—recognizing what is being sold, how, and to whom. Quick-fix solutions such as V-chips are the wrong approach, according to Strasburger. The only universal solution is media education, he believes. "It starts at home and belongs in K though 12."

A pilot project called Creating Critical Viewers, introduced in 1997 in the Seattle public school system, offers a good example of a media literacy program. In the project, seventh and eighth graders discovered how sitcoms unrealistically portray romantic breakups; in response, they created a "public service announcement" video on how to break up compassionately. The Seattle program aspires to teach children to watch TV with a discriminating mind rather than a passive one.

Creating Critical Viewers could be reproduced anywhere, but as yet there is not a broad-based, organized effort to include such media awareness programs in schools. Nevertheless, there are indications of a rising concern among educators about the influence media has on student behavior. Some schools are sending home a steady stream of letters urging parents to turn off the *Jerry Springer Show*, *South Park*, *Dawson's Creek*, and *Wrestlemania*, to name a few.

The question of media literacy recently was raised at Francis W. Parker School, when a particular pattern of behavior crept into the schoolyard. The teachers identified the source of the new problem as the TV show *South Park*. "Racially hurtful and sexist remarks were cropping up on the playground more and more frequently among first, second, and third graders," said Rosenblooth. "Characters in *South Park* have personalities and the kids find them attractive. Maybe it began with such irreverent media as *Mad Magazine* or *Saturday Night Live*, but today shows are more outrageous in their desire to get a laugh. Some are willing to cross the line to ethnic putdowns and racial slurs, competing to provide the most radical, offensive, Howard Stern kind of stuff. Anything that gets a reaction to boost the ratings."

Parker School sent letters home, suggesting parents turn off *South Park*. But the elementary school head, Ann Breed, realized that perhaps a letter to parents wasn't enough. "We probably should have created a dialogue with the children," she said. "We missed an opportunity." To be effective, Breed believes that a dialogue must begin at a very young age, especially as television and computer software increasingly target younger and younger children with television programs such as *Teletubbies* (age one and up) and computer programs such as *Jump Start Baby* (ages 1.5 to 5 years).

When asked about *Teletubbies*, Strasburger responded: "I think it is unconscionable to market to kids under two. PBS has temporarily lost its sanity. *Teletubbies* is not a bad show for four-year-olds. It's nonviolent, nonsexual. But not two-year-olds, not one-year-olds."

Professor Stephen Kline believes media literacy is most effective if offered to parents as well as children. "What I think you can achieve through media education is limited. But I certainly believe that a media education program out of the hands of the industry and one which supports the creation of a vigilant parental consumer wouldn't be a bad thing."

Arthur Pober, executive director of the electronic game industry's Entertainment Software Rating Board (ESRB), promotes the idea of media literacy. "We are a technological generation, and part of media literacy is understanding the visual message," he says.

Daphne White finds a mixed message in the promotion of media literacy. "Media literacy is better than nothing and it is important, but I think the secret underside is that you can't get toothpaste back in the tube." Once the violence is out, it is part of the culture. "Media literacy says we'll watch TV, but be an critical viewer," White continues. "The premise of media literacy is to teach some critical viewing skills, but the message is not 'watch less of it' or, 'don't watch it at all.'"

The Ratings Game

In 1994 the leading trade association for the electronic game industry, the Interactive Digital Software Association (IDSA) set up the ESRB in response to congressional inquiries and threats of government regulation. ESRB has rated more than 5,000 games, and the ratings appear on the front and back of most electronic game boxes. The incentive for game makers to submit their games is clearly an issue not of moral responsibility but of fiscal practicality. "The retail community, including Wal-Mart and Blockbuster, has said [they] won't stock games unless they carry a rating," explained Pober. "And that really has been a big impetus, in addition to which they want to be responsible. I mean they would rather be self-regulated than possibly face government intervention."

The ESRB rates electronic games according to their intended audience: Early Childhood, Everyone, Kids to Adults, Teen 13+, Mature 17+, Adult. "We did a lot of research at the very beginning," explains Pober. "We talked to parents, we talked to consumer groups, we looked at various clips [from electronic games], we spoke with parents, adults, consumers, and kids, and that's how we basically were able to define what seems to be appropriate."

In a desensitized culture, how easy is it for the average consumer to know what is "appropriate violence"? In a culture of violence, isn't it interesting that we consider *any* level of violence to be acceptable?

Perhaps more revealing than the ratings are the tiny content descriptors on the back of game boxes. A game like Vigilance, for example, may be rated Teen 13+, but its content descriptors read "animated blood, animated violence, suggestive themes." Violent content of electronic games are classified into eight categories: comic mischief, mild animated violence, mild realistic violence, animated violence, realistic violence, animated blood and gore, realistic blood and gore, animated blood, realistic blood. Sexual content, in contrast, is divided into only three categories and language into only two. Clearly, the overwhelming emphasis of electronic games is on violence.

"A very interesting exercise is to look up the ESRB rating and then look at the National Institute on Media and the Family's website [www.mediaandthefamily.com]," says Daphne White. "You will see quite a contrast between how parents rate things and how the ESRB rates things, and I would highly recommend that parents look to the other side—and not rely too heavily on the ESRB."

The ESRB maintains that it is a completely autonomous entity from the electronic game industry, yet it receives its nonprofit funding in part from the electronic game trade organization, the IDSA, and in part from the game makers, who pay between $100 and $500 to have their games rated. ESRB raters don't even *play* the games they rate; they merely watch a video clip provided by the gaming company.

"The rater's job is not to actually play the game; it is to look at the content," explained Pober. "This is sexual content, this is language, and so on and so forth. You don't have to necessarily play the game in order to be able to identify the kind of content that's there.

What we are looking to do is just label what the content is. We don't make judgements."

This self-regulation, as the electronic game industry calls the ESRB, is not regulation at all but rather an excuse to lay responsibility and blame at the feet of parents. As Doug Faust notes, "The ESRB standards specifically rely on consumers to make informed choices as to what type of interactive entertainment is appropriate. In other words, the standards rely on parents to be aware of and directly involved in game buying decisions in one way or another."

Game prices, once high enough to be considered natural barriers for children, have fallen so low that now violent games such as Duke Nukem ($14.99), Wild 9 ($24.99), and Doom II ($9.99) are well within piggy-bank budgets.

On the whole, ratings systems have had the opposite effect of what was intended. The self-imposed industry ratings of electronic games gives the industry a free rein to generate ever more violent games. "I approve of the rating system. As an artist, I like to have freedom to do the work I want to explore," says Roberta Williams, a renowned doyen of adventure gaming and creator of Phantasmagoria (rated Mature 17+). She concedes that mature ratings may attract kids to inappropriate games but likes to think "most people are good parents and watch what their kids are doing. We said our game was not for kids and we were applauded for doing that."

Game designer Dave Perry of Shiny Entertainment, the game company that produced Wild 9, the first interactive torture game, says:

You have to decide whether or not you want to be socially responsible or even whether that enters into the art. Social responsibility doesn't really enter into the equation. In making the games we want to play, the games are becoming more twisted and weird than they used to be. I don't think it's a bad thing, but I think certainly those young seven- and eight-year-olds who are strolling into the marketplace have a lot less choice than they used to have. There's not much in the way of Mario clones, but there's a lot of death and mayhem. The magical kiddy world is all very well, but what the public actually wants is violence.

John Romero, co-creator of Doom and Quake, the two games that changed the course of electronic gaming, has no qualms about what he makes. "I'm the one who made this stuff—why would I care about that?" he answered when asked about Littleton. "I make games I want to play. If I want to see more gibs [chunks of flesh] I make it. If people don't like it, they don't need to play the game."

"We're not going to start making games where you hand flowers to other people," said John Carmack, considered the "God" of gaming programming and the other creator of Doom and Quake. "That wouldn't sell. We make games that sell." (Quake II made $28 million its first year; 80 percent of that was profit for his company with only fifteen employees.)

Critics point out that while voluntary ratings allow society to skirt thorny First Amendment issues, the system has a crippling flaw: No law exists to punish businesses that sell mature-rated products to children. *PlayStation Magazine*'s Faust admits, "It's true that the ratings system has little or no 'teeth' when it comes to prohibiting the sale of mature rated games to youngsters, but ultimately it is the responsibility of parents to make informed decisions."

The ratings system continues to be controversial, and many believe that voluntary rating systems do little to keep violent games out of the hands of children. "Ratings," said Dan Gerstein, an aide to Senator Joseph Lieberman (D.-Conn.), who is heading the congressional effort to curb media violence, "are a stop-gap measure. The real task is to cut the problem at the stem: Stop manufacturers from producing violence and make them stop marketing to children."

Limiting children's access to violent images goes beyond rating systems, believes General Schwarzkopf. "It's not just the parents' responsibility. There is responsibility in the community. There is responsibility in the church. There is responsibility in the schools." There is responsibility in the entertainment industry.

Children Activists

Virginie Lariviére, a thirteen-year-old Canadian girl whose sister was raped and murdered, was "convinced that the influence of violent programming had been a factor" in her sister's death. She gathered and presented more than 1.5 million signatures to the prime minister in 1992 in the hopes of banning all media violence. This young girl was the catalyst for the Canadian Radio-Television and Telecommunications Commission, the cable industry, Canadian Advertising Foundation, and Canadian Home & School & Parents-Teacher Federation to study media violence and furnish solutions. The commission's summary included media literacy in public education, financial support of quality programming, industry self-restraint, ban of excessive violence, and enforcing a no-violence period on television before 9:00 P.M.

Some children as young as seven are becoming activists. A class of second graders in Oregon conducted its own study of media violence. Each child watched a half-hour of television at home and recorded every act of violence. Stunned by the fact that they witnessed nearly one incident of violence per minute, the children developed a "Declaration of Independence from Violence" for the rest of their school.

In Chicago an interracial demonstration of about fifty children and adults protested the *Jerry Springer Show* by passing out flyers titled "Broken Promises" and urging people to speak out against violence on television. Springer had vowed to remove the fighting from his talk show but reneged.

Following the Littleton tragedy, one Columbine student sent an e-mail chain letter through the Internet to collect prayers for the victims. It was circulated globally.

While some children are using violence as a cry for help, others are becoming activists in an effort to call attention to the electronic war zone.

Suing the Entertainment Industry

A friend of author John Grisham was murdered by two teenagers reenacting the movie *Natural Born Killers*. The victim's family sued Oliver Stone, the writer and director of the film. Grisham urges others to follow:

The second and last hope of imposing some sense of responsibility on Hollywood will come through another great American tradition, the lawsuit. Think of a movie as a product [real], something created and brought to market, not too dissimilar from breast implants, Honda three-wheelers, and Ford Pintos. Though the law has yet to declare movies to be products, it is only one small step away. If something goes wrong with this product, whether by design or defect, and injury ensues, then its makers are held responsible. . . . One large verdict against the likes of Oliver Stone and his production company and perhaps the screenwriter and the studio itself and then the party will be over. . . . Once a precedent is set, the litigation will become contagious, and the money will be enormous. Hollywood will suddenly discover a desire to rein itself in. The landscape of American jurisprudence is littered with the remains of large, powerful corporations which once thought themselves bulletproof and immune from responsibility for their actions. Sadly, Hollywood will have to be forced to shed some of its own blood before it learns to police itself.

The United States Supreme Court agreed to hear such a case against Oliver Stone in 1999.

The parents of the victims of the Paducah school killings are suing the entertainment industry for $130 million. The suit claims that the student who did the shooting was influenced by *Basketball Diaries* and electronic games like Doom and Quake; it charges that the games trained the assailant "to point and shoot a gun in a fashion making him an effective killer without teaching him any of the constraints or responsibilities needed to inhibit such a killing capacity." Among the twenty-five defendants are Time Warner, Nintendo, Sega, Sony, Polygram Film Entertainment Distribution, and id Software.

What moved the tobacco industry to greater accountability will soon move the entertainment industry.

Top-Down Washington Pressure

As educators, parents, and children are beginning to speak out against media violence from the bottom up, elected officials are taking on the entertainment industry from the top down. The aim of both is to create public pressure on the media and shame the industry into changing its habits. Speaking about the epidemic of youth violence in the spring of 1998, for example, President Clinton blamed the glorification of violence in Hollywood movies and the rise of violent, fantasy-based electronic games as factors contributing to the culture of violence.

One of the most vocal political critics of media violence is Senator Lieberman, who in March of 1998, joined a bipartisan group gathered to present the first Silver Sewer Award to Edgar Bronfman, president and CEO of Seagram, the owners of Universal Studios. Bronfman, who was not present at the ceremonies, was chosen by Lieberman and conservative cultural critic William Bennett for his "outrageous contributions to the degradation and coarsening of our culture and unswerving dedication to the pursuit of profit above principle." Bronfman owns the companies that own and/or promote the *Jerry Springer Show*, the "shock rocker" Marilyn Manson, and the electronic game Carmaggedon.

"At a time when it appears that the traditional conveyors of values in our society—like parents, religion and education—have diminished, the entertainment culture has filled a void," said Lieberman. "Television, music, video games now become the conveyors of values and I am convinced they are pushing this country downward."

Lieberman, who held Senate hearings that resulted in the creation of the ESRB, also has focused attention on the Internet by publicly appealing to ten of the leading Internet companies "to limit children's access to clearly inappropriate content." Lieberman favors government incentives as a means of curbing violent, sexual, and vulgar content in the media over direct government involvement or censorship. He believes that there is a "definite possibility" that the American people will become much more tolerant of censorship "unless the entertainment industry sets some limits on its own behavior. People are generally agitated about the electronic culture, especially as they consider the effects it is having on their children. So there is a danger of [a growing tolerance of censorship], and it ought to be heeded by the industry."

Violence and the First Amendment

In his book *Slouching Toward Gomorrah*, Judge Robert Bork describes the First Amendment issue starkly: "Sooner or later censorship is going to have to be considered, as popular culture continues plunging to ever more sickening lows. The alternative to censorship, legal and moral, will be a brutalized and chaotic culture, with all that entails for our society, economy, politics, and physical safety."

Censorship is complicated because Americans want both protection and freedom of speech. "I hate to tell you this, but the First Amendment is so abused that anybody can say anything or do anything, and they are subject to no recourse," said General Schwarzkopf.

American courts today view with strict scrutiny any legislation that appears to infringe on the First Amendment. Court rulings point out the difficulties governments face when attempting to regulate media violence. In 1989 a federal court ruled unconstitutional the Missouri law preventing minors from renting or buying videocassettes containing violent content. In a June 1997 ruling on its first Internet-related case, the U.S. Supreme Court struck down provisions of the Communications Decency Act as unconstitutional under the First Amendment. Addressing First Amendment concerns, the Court ruled that "in order to deny minors access to potentially harmful speech, the [law] effectively suppresses a large amount of speech that adults have a constitutional right to receive and to address to one another."

Media industry leaders argue that the censorship dilemma can be solved by technologies like the V-chip and Internet filtering software, which place the power of censorship in the hands of parents instead of the government. Filtering software supposedly allows parents to restrict access to sites with explicit content, but in all likelihood these technological blocks will not work because it will be the parents who have to do the programming. Many parents turn to their children to program their VCRs, fix the fax machine, or decode the new camera. Kids are infinitely more sophisticated than their parents; many even are capable of blocking their parents from knowing that they've tampered with the block.

Eliminating media violence does not necessarily mean abolishing or abusing the First Amendment. We already have a standard for exceptions to the right of free speech. Chief Justice Oliver Wendell Holmes in his famous 1919 *Schenck v. U.S.* decision set forth his clear-and-present danger test, which is "whether the words are used in such circumstances and are of such a nature as to create a clear and present danger that they will bring about substantive evils that Congress has the right to prevent." Holmes offered as an example falsely crying "fire" in a crowed theater.

Professor Kline explained how the issue was handled in Canada, where

it was found by the Supreme Court that the government has the right to protect children as a special class of consumers because of their vulnerability to commercial manipulation. You cannot constitute children twelve and under as being rational subjects and capable of evaluating a complex risk/benefit situation. An important point that seems to have been lost in considering U.S. legislation [against media violence] is that we have a long tradition of regarding children as a special category of consumer. We don't sell them tobacco because we don't believe that they can make the judgments about their health and the long-term consequences effectively. We don't allow them to buy alcohol. We have whole areas of protection. With products like video games, children should also be protected.

Token or piecemeal solutions will not work in a culture of violence. Janet Parshall, of the Family Research Council, said, "You can't say that you're going to fill the cultural stream of life with sludge and grime and slippery, cultural ooze and then say to parents, now I hope Johnny can swim through that without getting caught."

Electronic games, in particular, and media violence, in general, constitute "a clear and present danger." These games and other media violence are visiting "substantive evils" on our young children, which, under the Holmes doctrine, "Congress has a right to prevent." The danger to our children presented by the electronic war zone should be equated with crying "fire" in a crowded theater—absolutely unacceptable and punishable by law.

Are we really aware of how acceptable violence has become in American culture? Violence is humorous, pleasurable, and entertaining. Until we recognize that Americans have become acculturated to violence and that it is poisoning our spirit and the souls of our children, we will readily turn it on, pick it up, download it, go to it, watch it, play it, and, of course, pay for it.

PART TWO

TOMORROW: UNDERSTANDING GENETIC TECHNOLOGY THROUGH RELIGION AND ART

Galileo → Darwin → DNA

Our nascent understanding of genetics is beginning to rattle our world in much the same way as Galileo did 500 years ago when he argued that the earth revolved around the sun and as Darwin did 150 years ago when he challenged the theory of creation. Forever our thinking changed. Forever our sense of man's place in the universe changed and our understanding of man's place in nature changed. The mapping and sequencing of DNA and the technologies that this knowledge spawns will permanently alter our understanding of man himself. These monumental paradigm shifts have narrowed in scope from the universe, to nature, to the human being, and each has had profound implications for religion.

Genetic technologies are presenting perhaps the greatest challenge ever to traditional religious faiths. Decoding the human genome and the philosophical underpinnings of that quest are forcing a deep reexamination of what it means to be human. Theories of genetic determinism—that our genes determine not only our physical makeup but also our sexual preferences, our levels of aggression, and possibly even our propensity to be religious—are causing theologians to examine their ideas of free will, the human need for religion, and the very existence of God.

"Frankly, if it turns out that genes control 100 percent, I think religion is in trouble," said orthodox Rabbi Irving Greenberg, president of the Jewish Life Network in New York City. "I think the whole world's in trouble because ultimately religion is predicated on the belief of free will."

Science has steadily narrowed the divide between what science explains and what religion explains. Princeton microbiologist Lee Silver believes that "all of these questions that people thought were unanswerable, like when does life begin, we can answer. We can do experiments which basically invalidate old points of view. Galileo challenged people's view of the universe and their place in it, and the church imprisoned him for that until he recanted. And I think what's happening here is that all of these genetic technologies are frightening to people because they are challenging traditional points of view. It's worse than challenging it. It is basically demonstrating the inadequacy of traditional points of view."

Because of this profound challenge to religious orthodoxy and the powerful consequences of the new genetic technologies, it is critically important to listen to the views and thoughts of theologians and philosophers from different faiths. We interviewed leading thinkers from both Eastern and Western denominations, from fringe groups and the mainstream. Their thoughtful, decent, humanitarian perspectives offer rich hope in what otherwise would be a frightening new landscape. Their insights provide a human context, one that scientists alone simply cannot give us. They provide the human lens through which to understand the technologies that will forevermore change the human species.

This chapter will make accessible the science of the emerging genetic technologies (germline engineering, cloning, transgenic engineering, and bioengineering), the promise they hold, and the social, medical, and ethical concerns they raise. Bioethicists are already anticipating ethical and practical issues that may be raised by genetic technology, but a far broader public debate is necessary.

GENETICISTS: THE NEW EXPLORERS

Genetic technologies will overwhelm all other technology, including information technologies, in the next century. Not since splitting the atom have we developed such consequential technologies. Nuclear power gave us the power to destroy mankind. New genetic technologies give us the power to create life from death; to create new hybrids between genuses, not simply between species; to rejuvenate an adult cell to a primordial cell; and soon to direct human evolution itself.

These new technologies have the potential to change who we will become. "We're unraveling our own blueprint and beginning to tinker with it, which is extraordinary," said biophysicist Gregory Stock, a director at the Center for the Study of Evolution and the Origin of Life at the University of California at Los Angeles.

But the state of genetic engineering is likened to the beginning of the space program or the days of exploration when humans thought the earth was flat. "Christopher Columbus. That's where we're at with genetics," said preeminent bioethicist Arthur Caplan, a pioneer in his field at the University of Pennsylvania. "We're just starting to sail into these new lands, and we have no idea who's there, how they work, what their resources are, what we might bring back. We know that there are new places to go, that's what the genome mapping is. But how it really works, what it says, what's interesting, what's the best place to go, what's a dead end, we don't know. In the next twenty, thirty, forty years, starting in the next century, it's going to take a lot of stumbling around. It's in its infancy." Nacent but inevitable.

Scientific inquiry insatiably seeks greater knowledge. "Germline gene therapy is going to be done. The issue is: When is it safe? When is it ethical to have it?" asks W. French Anderson, director of the gene therapy laboratory at the University of Southern California, who some have called the father of gene therapy. Microbiologist

Silver suggests that "anyone who thinks that things will move slowly is being very naive."

"The genie is out of the bottle," believes Ronald Munson, a medical ethicist at the University of Missouri in St. Louis. "This technology is not, in principle, policeable."

We are faced with technology that appears to be inevitable, as powerful as nuclear energy, possibly unpoliceable, still in its infancy, and changing the way we think. The good news is that we seem to be accepting a moral imperative to anticipate the consequences because we are cognizant of the potential power of these new genetic technologies now, *before* they are scientifically possible or practical. Given our history with technology, human beings today have the unique opportunity to anticipate the social, economic, and ethical consequences of these awe-inspiring technologies—to anticipate rather than react. It is an incredible opportunity.

In the past, there has been a lag in understanding the ethical and social consequences of technological innovation. "You know, our recent history demonstrates over and over again that we've been confronted with the technological realities long before we've thought out the ethical and moral consequences of them," says popular New Age health guru Dr. Andrew Weil. "History is not very reassuring here." The Industrial Revolution damaged the environment in unforeseen ways. The astoundingly destructive power of the nuclear bomb led some of the scientists who developed it to regret their contribution. The problem of waste disposal at nuclear power plants was not fully understood at the outset. Until now technology always was considered neutral. Technology, the argument goes, is itself neither good nor bad. It depends on people's use of it. (There is an echo here of the National Rifle Association's mantra "Guns don't kill people; people kill people.") Only now are we realizing that technology is not a valueless synonym for machines or tools of science but a term that embodies its consequences—good and bad. Fortunately, there are signs that the consequences-gap is closing, particularly in the life sciences. Bioethics was the first field to signal an understanding that there are human consequences to technological innovation. (We do not have physics-ethics or engineering-ethics, which indicates the transcending importance of the life sciences technologies.)

Bioethics began as a specialized field in the 1960s, in response to the unprecedented challenges created by advances in life-supporting technologies and reproductive technologies. In 1992 hospitals across the nation made it protocol to have a bioethicist on staff or specific ethical by-laws. The root of medical ethics can be traced back to the ancient Greek Hippocratic Oath and the professional code of ethics written in the nineteenth century by Thomas Percival, which became the foundation for the code of ethics established by the American Medical Association in 1847. At the end of World War II, the Nuremberg Code for research ethics was developed in response to the detestable human experimentation performed in Nazi Germany.

"Twenty years ago, bioethics started as a fringe, a fairly peripheral thing," says bioethicist Caplan describing the field. "Today it would be hard to find a medical school that didn't teach bioethics in some form. They may not have a whole center or program, but something will be there." Today twenty-three universities in the United States offer degrees in bioethics, and thirteen offer Ph.D.'s in philosophy or religion with an emphasis on bioethics.

These days bioethicists are not only responding to changes in the medical profession but are anticipating new technologies. They are debating topics such as eugenics, genetic privacy, genetic patenting, and the extent to which technologies are impinging on the laws of nature and on religion—developments that promise to make medical ethics an even more central part of social decision making.

The rapid growth of bioethics in universities and in hospitals is a good predictor of the type of anticipatory thinking we will give new genetic technologies in the future. Another predictor is the concern of scientists, as indicated by the unprecedented public dialogue fostered at a March 1998 UCLA symposium entitled "Engineering the Human Germline."

Invigorate and Deepen Public Debate

"Powerful techniques have powerful downsides," said biologist W. French Anderson, a panel member at this first significant forum (anywhere in the world) to focus exclusively on human germline engineering. At the UCLA symposium, a group of scientists called a public forum to describe the new genetic technologies and their potential benefits to humankind and the possible devastating consequences. Because this technology could change humanity's path, it deserves serious public discussion, they declared. The aim of the UCLA conference was "to invigorate and deepen public debate about human germline engineering" while at the same time providing a solid scientific foundation for future discussions. As a society we are beginning to learn that powerful technologies do have powerful consequences. And we have the responsibility to anticipate them thoughtfully.

Donald Shriver, president emeritus at the Union Theological Seminary in New York and an ethics professor emeritus at Columbia University, believes that "since we don't have absolute wisdom about consequences, we have every reason to be on the alert when those consequences begin to appear." He further emphasizes that "we're going to make mistakes as human beings. Societies are going to make mistakes. But the saving grace is both the forgiveness of our mistakes and the chance to try again to correct them. Religion has a great deal to say about the second chance that God seems to be able to give us humans."

The Wisdom Is in the Dialogue

Debate and public awareness increase our chances of acting prudently with these emerging genetic technologies. What is required is open dialogue among not only politicians, scientists, and economists but also theologians. Even bioethicists see theologians as key participants in the process because they grapple with more fundamental questions of our humanity and less with the procedural or legal aspects of new technologies. "I spend time in my line of work talking to people of varying religious traditions and theological perspectives," bioethicist Caplan told us, "because a lot of these concerns about personal identity, about the limits of human wisdom to engineer ourselves, about whether it is ever unnatural to change fauna or cross species lines really do raise fundamental questions."

Nicholas Wade, the *New York Times* science writer, agrees. "Religions tend to incorporate our values." The voices of theologians are critically important in creating an ethical framework for understanding and implementing these new technologies, yet as Wade points out, journalists rarely seek out the opinions of theologians. They report the science but not the religious or spiritual responses of clergy or scholars.

Theologians create a heightened sense of awareness about the assumptions of science, just as science challenges the assumptions of religion. Together, scientists, ethicists, and religious leaders are saying it's time to sit down at the table, get down to basics, and find common ground—because these issues are too big for any one sector to solve independently.

Jesuit Father James Keenan, who is one of an international committee of six Catholic ethicists established in 1997 to contemplate and write about the consequences of genetic technologies, describes the context in which theologians can contribute to the discussion on genetic engineering: "My work is in the field of virtue. We ask three basic questions: 'Who are we? Who do we want to become? And how ought we to get there?' Christian and Jewish and Muslim leaders could offer to the scientific community a context for reflecting. That context would be 'What type of human beings do you see us becoming, not simply what *will* we do, but *who* will we become?' " Theologian Donald Shriver concurs. "The power of scientific curiosity, technological ambition, and economic profit are together a very formidable power. My solution is not that the clergy or theologians should become the single agent on this, or become experts in this area, but what the clergy, engineers, and researchers need to do is to collaborate with each other. There is wisdom to be gained, which is not going to get constructed by any one profession alone."

Richard Doerflinger, of the National Conference of Catholic

Bishops, is the spokesperson on bioethical issues for the Catholic Church. He has appeared before the U.S. Senate to express the church's views about the use of embryos in research and argues for the inclusion of clergy in policy decisions regarding genetic engineering: "Religious leaders have the role, as others do, of participating in the debate, in bringing their values to the table. The concerns go so deep into understanding human nature that religion plays an even more significant role [than philosophy]."

New technologies can be "checked by upholding the full dignity of all human beings, by teaching reverence and respect for all kinds of people," believes Rabbi Greenberg. This is a way religion can deal with these technologies "rather than simply saying they're automatically dangerous."

Bioethicist Caplan argues for a world in which mankind consciously chooses which technologies it adopts. In other words, he does not believe that whatever can be done will be done. He notes that popular films portray a world in which science and technology must inevitably be our masters. As a man who has played a central role in a field that has changed from being concerned with improving physicians' bedside manners to one concerned with the ethics of complex reproductive technologies (including genetic engineering), Caplan firmly believes that "human beings can control the technologies that they invent. But to do so, they have to use their heads, not their genes."

Rabbi Greenberg advocates drawing from as many points of reference as possible. "There is no magic bullet here and there is no one religion that has all the right answers," Greenberg says. "I think we have to invite the broadest possible range of religions to speak up." The best protection is a pluralistic, democratic environment where people can challenge and criticize. Religion can play a role in creating that kind of environment. "Arousing awareness, I think, is the first step toward correcting [the classic moral lag]," he continued. "The religious establishment and the religious infrastructure should pay attention to these questions. I don't see any other way. Technology is obviously self-sustaining now. We have to recognize that we need every possible partner in this challenge. You'll not have the wise man or the great religious prophet who has all the answers."

GERMLINE GENE THERAPY

We Are Created in the Image of God → We Are Created in the Image of Man

Appearing as a panel before a packed auditorium on the campus of UCLA in the spring of 1998, eight prestigious scientists and two bioethicists announced to the world that in two or three decades, humankind would have the power to direct its own evolution. "We are talking about intervening in the flow of genetic information from one generation to the next. We are talking about the relationship of human beings to their genetic heritage," announced Gregory Stock, one of the forum organizers.

Darwin took evolution out of the hands of God, but he didn't put it in the hands of humans. The prospect of controlling our own evolution is turning solid religious doctrine upside down. Germline gene therapy, which potentially puts the power to alter the human gene pool in the hands of man, throws into question the age-old Judeo-Christian tenet "We are created in the image of God." Man in control of his own evolutionary destiny is evoking a sense that humans are moving into God's dominion and raising such questions as: Are we playing God? And even more profoundly, volitional evolution is bringing into question the very existence of God.

"I guess I'm just longing for the old days when you had a very clear line. It's either God's or human's work and never the twain shall meet," said Rabbi Greenberg, who continued with a story. "It's funny, when I was growing up in the 1950s, there was this drought in New York City and cloud seeding was one of the early uses of a technology [that caused theologians to question whether humans were playing God]. I remember a cartoon in *The New Yorker* where this group of very worried looking ministers were sitting around the table and saw through the window that it was raining. One minister says to the group, 'Is this our rain or theirs?' "

THE SCIENCE

Germline gene engineering involves making genetic alterations to the germinal, or sex cells, of a mammal. The procedure, which has been performed on animals, typically is conducted on a fertilized egg to ensure that genetic changes are copied into every cell of the body. Because sex cells are affected, successive generations are likely to inherit the changes. This ability to manipulate and transfer genetic traits from one generation to the next raises the possibility that one day parents could prevent hereditary diseases such as Down syndrome, sickle cell anemia, or Parkinson's disease from being passed on to their offspring and future generations. Currently somatic gene therapy (which does not affect the sex cells and therefore is not inheritable by the next generation) is being used as treatment for some human diseases, but with little efficacy. Germline gene therapy promises to be much more effective in treating diseases, but also more consequential.

These powerful new genetic technologies are *"life* sciences, not research on moon rocks," cautions theologian Shriver. "This research can effect the destiny of earth's *human beings.* This is a very big issue."

The potential for such medical breakthroughs for humans comes from our greater understanding of the human genome. Research is being conducted under the auspices of the government-funded Human Genome Project (HGP) in the United States, Généthon in France, University of Tokyo Human Genome Center in Japan, and fifteen other nations worldwide. But companies such as Celera, Incyte, Geron, Human Genome Sciences Inc., and Millennium are making swift inroads and major discoveries in the private sector. The Human Genome Project, begun in 1990, is big science—the U.S. government will spend a total of $3 billion over a fifteen-year period in the hope that scientists will identify and sequence the human genome (some 80,000 to 100,000 genes in human cells). They hope to determine the complete sequence of human DNA subunits by the year 2002, providing scientists in the twenty-first century with DNA sequence maps to explore human biology more completely than ever before thought possible.

The Human Genome Project website attempts to make the science of this massive endeavor accessible to the average American, thereby making a broad-based dialogue possible:

A genome is all the DNA in an organism, including its genes. Genes carry information for making all the proteins required by all organisms. These proteins determine, among other things, how the organism looks, how well its body metabolizes food or fights infection, and sometimes how it behaves. The order [of DNA] underlies all of life's diversity, even dictating whether an organism is human or another species such as yeast, rice, or a fruit fly, all of which have their own genomes and are themselves the focus of genome projects. Because all organisms are related through similarities in DNA sequences, insights gained from nonhuman genomes [such as the bacterium E. coli] often lead to new knowledge about human biology.

At the UCLA symposium (which was free and open to the public), the chair of the Department of Molecular Biotechnology at the University of Washington School of Medicine, Leroy Hood, also attempted to put the science of genetics into layman's terms. The symposium attendees were a diverse lot, as planned, and included middle and high school students, journalists, writers, and physicians who flew in from around the United States and from overseas.

"The human genome is about deciphering the twenty-four human chromosomes," Hood said. "And by deciphering, we mean a number of different things. The size of the task is gargantuan. There are 3 billion letters in the DNA language. And, of course, the human genome is probably the most incredible software program that's ever been written. So here's a program that dictates and directs the development of the most fascinating of all processes [human development], starting with a single cell, the fertilized egg. . . . [This program is] able to carry out the chromosomal choreography that specifies for each of the different cell types the right subset of those hundred thousand genes that have to be uniquely expressed."

In bringing science out of the laboratory and into public forums, both electronically and in town hall–style meetings, scientists make the language of science less intimidating, enabling us to understand the consequences—both intended and unintended—of these new technologies.

THE PROMISE

The promise of germline gene therapy is a world free of hereditary diseases, a medical field that cures rather than treats, healthier and longer lives, and, according to some scientists, an assurance that if geneticists make a mistake when tampering with the human genome, the technology is reversible. Most scientists, theologians, and bioethicists accept that these technologies will make a positive contribution to mankind in the treatment of major diseases. "I honestly feel that there's an incredible upside here," says Rabbi Greenberg. "The upgrading of human dignity, the extension of human life, the improvement of health, the extension of basic decent living conditions to many more people, not nearly enough, but many more than in the past. I think the new trends in science are entitled to respect."

Kevin Fitzgerald, a Jesuit priest and geneticist at Loyola University in Chicago, says, "We will use some of it brilliantly, with tremendously marvelous results and save lives and add to lives that would have been severely debilitated. We'll do wonderful things."

Even the Catholic Church, which only recently (in 1992) apologized for condemning Galileo and even more recently (in 1996) recanted on the evolution-creation debate, officially supports germline gene therapy. The church is optimistic about the benefits of genetic technologies. "In an age of limited medical resources," said the church's medical ethics spokesman Doerflinger, "better understanding of people's genetic makeup will allow us to target health care resources where they're most needed, to those who are most in need of help."

Scientists, bioethicists, and theologians cannot help but be awestruck by the potential of germline gene therapy to lessen human suffering and cure previously incurable diseases. Anyone who has had a child born with a degenerative disease, or a parent with Alzheimer's, or a loved one with cancer or AIDS has hoped for a miracle cure. "Human germline engineering may enable us to obtain the benefits of a century of genetic science," which up until now has been largely theoretical, said organizer Gregory Stock at the UCLA symposium.

The Human Genome Project states its promise on the World Wide Web: "The project will reap fantastic benefits for humankind, some that we can anticipate and others that will surprise us. . . . Information generated and technologies developed will revolution-ize future biological explorations. . . . Medical practices will be rad-ically altered. Emphasis will shift from treatment of the sick to a prevention-based approach. . . . The potential for commercial devel-opment presents the U.S. industry with a wealth of opportunity, and sales of biotechnology products are projected to exceed $20 billion by 2000."

Dr. Francis S. Collins, director of the National Human Genome Research Institute at the National Institute of Health, believes that "Most historians will look back on this project as the most important thing we did in science at the turn of the century. This is far more important than putting a man on the moon or split-ting the atom."

Humans will live longer, suffer less, and America will get rich in the process. Why the need for debate?

THE CONCERNS

Germline gene therapy raises scientific concerns about the efficacy of the technology, a loss of biodiversity, irrevocable alteration of the human gene pool, and the unforeseen consequences of genetic manipulation. It raises ethical concerns about eugenics, disparity of access, genetic patenting, and genetic privacy. It raises theological considerations about removing the act of sex from procreation, the uniqueness of each human life, genetic determinism, playing God, and idolatry of the individual.

Detractors believe the claims of science are overstated. "I think in some ways there is an extreme optimism about gene therapy that may not actually be true," says Archbishop Randolph W. Sly, of the Eastern Province of the International Communion of the Charismatic Episcopal Church. "There are many people who are optimistic about what we can do with genes—that cancer can be completely eliminated from the body, or AIDS, or of any number of diseases. Very optimistic viewpoint, but very practically we're not anywhere near that." Robert Thurman, leading American Buddhist scholar and professor at Columbia University, shares the skepticism and believes that in thirty years the claims of genetic scientists will be seen as vastly exaggerated.

SCIENTIFIC CONCERNS

Scientists themselves admit that the pace of technological innovation is somewhat unpredictable. At the UCLA symposium, Mario Capecchi, distinguished professor of biology and human genetics at the University of Utah, said, "We all have a tendency to overestimate what we can do in five years and underestimate what we can do in twenty-five years."

While the scientific community shares an enthusiasm about the revolution these technologies could bring to modern medicine, they admit they're hardly off the starting block. Biologist W. French Anderson, the first scientist in the world to attempt (noninheritable) somatic gene therapy in 1990, is optimistic about the future efficacy of germline gene therapy: "So the answer to your straightforward question, 'Does gene therapy work?' is, at this point, It does not work. Now, does that mean it's never going to work? Well, no. It will."

Scientists also differ in their opinions about the real potentials of the techniques. Biologist Wivel is less confident than Anderson: "We are having a lot of difficulty treating single-gene diseases," he noted. "There is not one scintilla of efficacy of any protocol to this point."

Loss of biodiversity is another scientific concern. "[We] have the problem of possible homogenization, which is like all of us driving a Toyota Camry," Michael Rose mused at the UCLA symposium. Rose, a professor at the University of California at Irvine's School of Biological Sciences, continued: "If we all have the exactly the same antiaging chromosome and as it turns out that [it] gives us a weakness to a virus which none of us has yet experienced—which we've not yet seen epidemiologically—and that virus comes in and kills all of us? Well, bummer."

Other unintended consequences might include the loss of unknown positive contributions of genes perceived as diseased or less than perfect. For example, scientists know that the genetic trait that causes sickle cell anemia also protects many people against malaria. The genetic trait that causes cystic fibrosis also may protect against cholera. Richard Land, longtime president and CEO of the Southern Baptist Ethics and Religious Liberty Commission, very vividly describes the potential downside of unintended consequences: "If we really succeeded in getting rid of hyperactive attention deficit disorder in children because they are difficult to control, how many artists and musicians and astronauts have we just taken out of the gene pool? And explorers and discoverers? We might make a whole human gene pool of accountants." No scientist fully understands how genes that cause pathologies also serve humankind.

Irrevocably altering the human gene pool is one of the most serious concerns for scientists. Many adamantly advise that germline gene therapy (which appears to be the most promising of the genetic therapies) be used only if a corresponding technology can be developed that will prevent the trait from being inherited by the next generation. In other words, create a therapy that is wonderfully effective but will not alter human evolution. Some have suggested microscopic "scissors" that snip the new genetic material from the sex cells of the embryo so its offspring will not inherit the manipulated trait.

Biologist Anderson issues a stern warning. "As opposed to every other decision made in medicine, this involves more than the patient, the family, and the doctor. The gene pool is not owned by anyone. It is the joint property of society. And when you manipulate the gene pool—before one attempts to do that—one needs the agreement of society."

ETHICAL CONCERNS

The heart of the gene therapy ethics debate (which includes issues of genetic privacy, disparity of access, and genetic patenting) is cure versus enhancements. Do we use germline therapy strictly to cure major diseases, or should we extend the technologies to enhance human traits?

There is deep concern that these technologies may slip from therapy to fashion, much as reconstructive technologies developed for soldiers wounded on the battlefield moved to cosmetic surgery. Among theologians, scientists, and bioethicists there is widespread repugnance to the idea of genetically altering human beings for superficial "enhancements," such as breast augmentation, but there is no consensus on whether a clear demarcation between cure and enhancement can be drawn. Scientists themselves cannot even agree on what defines a disease. Are dyslexia and attention deficit disorder diseases, or are they better understood as traits that clash with a sedentary, text-based society? Is obesity a disease, or the result of an overstuffed lifestyle?

"We know so little about the human body. We know so little about life itself that we should not try to dedicate engineering to try to improve anything," warns biologist W. French Anderson. "It is our duty to go into the era of genetic engineering in as responsible a way as possible. And that means to use this powerful technology only for the treatment of disease and not for any other purpose."

It is easy to imagine the outcome of germline therapy used to enhance rather than cure: designer babies as the ultimate shopping experience or a generation of kids who all look the same. Imagine generations marked not by the most popular names of an era, such as Henry and Ruth (1910), or Patricia and Charles (1950), or Austin and Kaitlyn (1998), or distinguished by styles such as tattooing and piercings, but by genetically determined traits such as height, facial structure, and waist and hip proportions. Parents could choose as a model of ideal beauty Mona Lisa, or Barbie, or Tom Cruise. Teenage daughters may find new disgust with their parents because they chose the wrong face rather than the wrong name. Sons may be disappointed in their parents' purchase of soccer talent rather than baseball talent.

The power of this technology to ever be able to manipulate and control complex traits is doubted by many. The skepticism of New York University art historian and artist Kirby Gookin is typical: "Lee Silver and some other people have suggested that we can actually shop for a child, select a type, select intelligence. This is hypothetical, but this is what they believe in—genetics as being essentialist— like a genetic strand identifies something very specifically and coherently and discreetly. Which I don't even agree with. Nonetheless, assuming that you can shop for height, and basketball talent and a certain kind of intelligence, mathematical intelligence or creative intelligence, why not an extra arm, right? Getting more things done, being more efficient. It *is* customization. But can you really create a six-foot-eight basketball player who is a rocket scientist? That's my question."

Eugenics

The idea of perfecting the human race has historic roots fraught with emotional land mines. "I think that the eugenic dreams and biological perfectionist aspirations of the Nazis and others were hindered, in part, by their not having the science," bioethicist Caplan says. "Well, look out world: The science is coming!"

The notion of eugenics came out of Darwin's theory of evolution and Mendel's laws of inheritance (which identified the mechanism for transferring biological traits), by the Victorian scientist Sir Francis Galton. According to Gookin, "The moral and aesthetic obligation of the artist to perfect the image of the human body in art has now been transferred to the field of genetic science. With genetics, the scientist was given the means with which to apply the aesthetic and moral concept of 'improvement' to the human organism itself."

Sir Francis Galton defined his idea of eugenics as "the science of improvement of the human race through better breeding." Gookin, who is writing a book on eugenics, explains:

Thus Galton, believing that everything was inherited, including moral character, pursued the study of human fingerprints, profiles, family histories, and the like in hopes of discovering a method for evaluating a single individual's physical, mental and moral stature. Using the breeding of animals as a model, Galton had hoped that once the machinations of heredity were understood, and once the methods for distinguishing "desirable" from "undesirable" members of society were perfected, eugenic science could be implemented. He believed that a superior human race could be developed through breeding. Ideally one could breed a desirable "temperament, character, and ability" into a species (as one does with dogs), and weed out of the species less desirable qualities such as "drunkenness," "criminality," "shiftlessness," "idleness," and "poverty."

The specter of Galton's eugenics and the Nazi pursuit of an ideal race fester in the objections to germline technologies used for human enhancements. "I'm really interested in how the sale of genetic information and the sale of genetic perfectionism is going to shape us," bioethicist Caplan muses. "The early signs are not good. I think that there will be an attempt to generate markets for people to feel bad if they don't get genetic report cards for their embryos and reproductive mates. Soon it will be 'How dare you create a child with a known mental disorder?' In a market society, notions of perfection will be sold. You can almost see the shops in the mall: Genes 'R' Us."

But not everyone is fearful. James Watson, who discovered the double helix structure of DNA with his colleague Francis Crick, is unequivocally in favor of full implementation of the technologies: "No one really has the guts to say it . . . I mean, if we could make better human beings by knowing how to add genes, why shouldn't we do it?"

Geneticist John Campbell, also speaking at the UCLA symposium, goes so far as to question who would rely on evolutionary chromosomes if there was an option. "At every generation, a parent will presumably want to endow his or her child with the newest and the best modifications and improvements that are possible, instead of relying on the chromosomes that were given to that person, to the parent, a whole generation."

Also at the symposium Daniel Koshland, professor of molecular and cell biology at the University of California at Berkeley, argued that genetically altered children would be superior: "If the criterion is that children should turn out to be at least as good as their parents, my guess is that germline engineering will compete very well with those conceived in the natural way. And if we make this criterion that the children should be up to their parents' expectations, then I think the engineered child may have a good edge over the child conceived in the normal way."

This enthusiasm is echoed by some theologians as well, particularly from the Eastern traditions. Hindu scholar K. L. Seshagiri Rao, religious studies professor emeritus at the University of Virginia and chief editor of the eighteen-volume *Encyclopedia of Hinduism,* sees no reason to limit the technology: "The knowledge that we get should be used in such a way that is for the benefit of all people. If looking good, being strong, and having sharp intelligence are the things being designed, more and more people should have it. What's wrong with it?" Buddhist scholar Thurman told us: "In fact, you would want to design the most admirable, most delightful, most helpful, most happy type of being you could think of. I mean, that's normal."

The possibility of genetically treating obesity, depression, short stature, hair loss, and of enhancing beauty, intelligence, strength, and athleticism is perceived as eugenics by some, fruitful by others, and highly unlikely by still others. In any case, undoubtedly there will be a market for it. Public opinion polls suggest that the demand for genetic enhancements may be substantial. Surveys in 1986 and 1992 showed that 40 to 45 percent of the American public approved of the concept of genetic technologies to bolster physical and intellectual traits. And that does not surprise bioethicist Caplan. "Americans, being entrepreneurial, believe that they can do better than nature, or for that matter, God."

Drawing the Line

The response from Western theologians runs the gamut from outright rejection of all application of the technologies (fearful of the slippery slope) to embracing full usage. But the general consensus is that healing is a natural response to human affliction, and new genetic therapies and medical technologies that relieve suffering should be encouraged and celebrated. But they generally agree that the uniqueness of each individual life and the value of each human being, imperfect as we all are, should preclude genetic enhancements, particularly cosmetic ones.

Theologian Shriver draws from Genesis to gain understanding. "That genetic engineering is attacking natural evils like disease, I think is justified. It's when we shift it over into planning the whole human gene pool according to our likes and revamping the human self according to some value system that is popular at the time, that, I find, is arrogant and an assault on the gift of the creation. The Genesis vocation of human beings involves both working the earth and preserving it."

Catholic ethicist Doerflinger recognizes that it will be very difficult to draw a line. "The Catholic Church's position is that it is valid in principle to use genetic therapy to cure disease, to correct particular defects. For example, to do germline genetic engineering to correct the defect that causes Down syndrome would be something to be praised. What the church has said is very dangerous and would generally oppose is the idea of using genetic therapies or germline engineering to do what is called positive eugenics. To make a better human being. But where you draw the line between negative and positive eugenics is very controverted. There are going to be gray areas. There's a tendency to male pattern baldness. Is that a defect? Or is it just part of the human condition—that I happen to have myself. People debate whether that's really a defect or it's just one end of the spectrum of natural human variation."

Rabbi Greenberg, while not opposed to enhancements on the theological grounds, says that man has a covenant with God to perfect himself and the earth, but he is emphatically opposed to aesthetic cosmetic applications of the technologies: "If it comes into pure cosmetics, it will be an abuse and a breakdown."

From Cure to Enhancements

However, many bioethicists and scientists believe that enhancements are inevitable. "I think it would be a big mistake to think we can say 'yes' to germline gene therapy and 'no' to cosmetic enhancements," said Erik Parens, an ethicist at the Hastings Center in Garrison, New York. Biologist Anderson is just as fatalistic: "Genetic enhancement is going to happen. Congress is not going to pass a law keeping you from curing baldness."

But the real driving force, scientists and ethicists believe, is love of an unborn child. Most parents will make whatever choices are necessary to provide what is best for their children. "Germline gene therapy will be done because of human nature," Anderson says. "None of us wants to pass on to our children lethal genes if we can prevent it. And that's what's going to drive germline gene therapy. In the last analysis, when you really sit down and think about the things really important in your life—your loved ones, your family, what you're going to do for your family, those things which really touch our core as human beings—you're not going to pass on a lethal gene to your child if you can have a simple safe treatment that prevents it."

The first applications of these technologies will be treatments to cure severely debilitating diseases, but as the prenatal germline technologies get more sophisticated, parents will feel pressure not to handicap their children in any way. The very definition of what constitutes a handicap will change. As a society increasingly comfortable with surgical enhancements—nose jobs, liposuction, laser eye surgery, lip augmentation, face peels, cheek and chin implants, breast enlargements—it is not difficult to imagine a day when homeliness or short stature or big ears or cellulite is considered a handicap. In fact, they already are. Technology critic Jeremy Rifkin illustrates the pressure he says may build on parents to conform: "What happens if a child is not programmed and deviates from culturally accepted norms, or has a 'disability' as we define it? Are we going to be tolerant of that child or see that child as an error that could have been corrected? What's wrong with that kid's parents?"

What constitutes ideal versus average is another central issue. "But how are they going to choose what is a beautiful being? Is it going to be because of commercial interests? So what would be the criteria of the design?" wonders Buddhist Thurman.

"In the case of genetic engineering, I feel that the motivation behind it actually evolved out of the history of art and that is what I call ideal beauty, the aesthetic ideal of perfection," historian Gookin has come to believe. "Genetics and eugenics—it's very difficulty to separate them. This is a very Platonic notion that eventually gets adapted by Christianity—the imperfection of your morality—the idea of working toward improvement. There are two main principles that come from art into genetics: One is the idea that nature is imperfect and that humans actually have an ability and moral obligation to perfect nature, perfect our species. The problem is, what are the criteria? The second premise is that there is an ideal human figure and the criteria are based on symmetry, primarily. The criteria come from classical notions of ideal beauty—which, simply put, are the proportions in the history of art."

These days America's standard of ideal beauty comes from mass media, from television, billboards, film, and magazines: Kate Moss, Uma Thurman, Naomi Campbell, Leonardo DiCaprio, Denzel Washington, Brad Pitt—none of whom is overweight, among other things. Obesity is a disease, many physicians currently believe. It also poses serious health risks. Being thin is the number-one criteria for being fashionable. Being overweight is most often a product of sedentary habits and overeating, and one-third of all Americans are overweight. One-third of that one-third are obese. Imagine how much easier it would be to stay thin if we could program a high metabolism. Correcting obesity may be the first application of genetic therapy that falls in that gray zone between cure and enhancement. Nineteen obesity genes have already been identified. Is wanting to be thin a health concern or a fashion statement?

What Makes Us Human?

What it means to be human is a central theme underlying the discussion of cure versus enhancement. The message of many scientists, bioethicists, and theologians is: Before we tamper with our humanness, we might want to think about what is it that makes us who we are. "I don't know that we have any agreement on what it is about human beings that's most human, or most valuable," says Catholic bioethicist Doerflinger. "I don't think we mere mortals are equipped to determine what kind of humans we need for a better society." Bioethicist Parens also questions the wisdom of manipulating the human genome: "There are real concerns about whether we are wise enough to mold ourselves to the extent these technologies may allow us to mold ourselves. It certainly makes me nervous."

Smaller nose, longer legs, broader shoulders, and narrower waists are all cosmetic enhancements that could be calculated in numbers. The very notion of genetic enhancements assumes that traits can be measured, weighed (so to speak), and then programmed. Historian Gookin wonders about the assumption that we can somehow measure even things like intelligence. "That kind of idea, of this mathematical or quantifiable form of the ideal translates into quantification of intelligence—the IQ test. All forms of certain numerical measurements—20–20 vision, for example—assume not only measurable perfection but measurable average. The idea [of germline therapy] is to raise the average. Why not raise the average of all people? The process of objectifying the human body through measurement lies at the core of the establishment of ideal standards of the human body for both art and science."

One extensive 1996 international study led by scientist Randy Thornhill at the University of New Mexico attempts to establish a

biological, scientific basis for human sexual attractiveness. The findings concluded that the perfect waist to hip ratio of a female is 0.7,
which the study correlated scientifically to fertility, and 0.9 for a
male. Firm symmetrical breasts, large eyes, small nose, delicate
chin, and smooth skin also attracted males to females, it said, regardless of nationality or race. The males most attractive to females were
slightly above average height, had prominent chins and cheekbones,
broad foreheads, symmetrical wrists and ankles, and were muscu-
lar—all indicators of "biological quality." Hearing of the possibility
of genetic enhancements, measurable standards of sex appeal,
backed by scientific research, the alarms of eugenics are ringing.

Beyond beauty or sex appeal, theologian Shriver cautions that
we also place too much emphasis on intelligence: "I don't think
intelligence is the one authentic mark of human beings. There's also
goodness. Plato talks about the good, the pure, and the beautiful.
The human capacity to love is at least as impressive as the human
capacity to know. And the overestimation of the virtue of knowing
things is something to be protected against." Ethics, morality, goodness, love defy quantifiable measurement.

Disparity of Access

Another ethical concern echoing among the theologians, scientists,
and bioethicists is the potential disparity of access to these new technologies between rich and poor families and rich and poor nations.
There is solid agreement that this is going to be a problem, but thus
far no one is formulating any solutions.

Microbiologist Silver is very pragmatic about what he sees in the
future. "Genetic engineering will allow parents who have the
money to give their children advantages before birth, in addition to
the ones they've always given to their children after birth. The real
problem with genetic engineering is that it's so good that those who
are unable to afford it will be severely disadvantaged, though I am
not against use of the technology."

Bioethicist Caplan is not optimistic about the disparity. "There
will be people who can afford genetic testing, there will be people

who can afford gene therapy, but that will produce what we already see in the United States, a very two-tiered healthcare system. I don't applaud it. I just think it's likely to happen."

Jesuit Father James Keenan has global concerns about access. "We're very concerned that the real thing will be runaway prices for wonderful gene therapy that will be only accessible in the First World and to those with healthcare coverage in the First World. We thought, as Christian ethicists, our responsibility is to think about the question of justice and accessibility in gene therapy treatment. I think sometimes we get caught up in the questions of playing God instead of really looking at the brutal, hard economic, justice questions."

Microbiologist Silver predicts a world straight out of science fiction: When genetic reproduction technologies are made commercially available and distributed unequally, the technologies will over time (in 300 years or so) create a subspecies of humans (he refers to them as the Naturals) incapable of mating with the genetically enhanced (GenHaves).

BENEATH THE SKIN:
GENETIC PRIVACY/GENETIC DISCRIMINATION

Artist Iñigo Manglano-Ovalle, whose work addresses genetic technologies, suggests that the old classification of race will be replaced with new ones based on genetics: "With genetics there is a possibility that the categories at stake in the future are not going to be the old categories. Let's say black and white. Or let's say brown and yellow. Let's say kinky hair or straight. If the categories are going to be different, they are going to be beneath the skin."

Discrimination based on genetic information already exists today in the insurance industry and the job market. We don't need to wait centuries or even decades to get a taste of a new dimension of prejudice, a new category upon which some people can judge themselves superior to others or be judged as inferior or simply viewed as a business risk not worth investing in.

At the same time that this new form of genetic discrimination is emerging, the Federal Bureau of Investigation (FBI) and other law enforcement agencies are championing DNA identification as an essential new tool for justice. With the cooperation of law enforcement agencies in thirty-two states, the FBI has formed a new national database of genetic information. The name of this computer database, The National DNA Identification Index, rings of the nomenclature in Terry Gilliam's classic film *Brazil*, in which information was used systematically to control the citizenry.

A legal battle between civil liberties groups, like the American Civil Liberties Union (ACLU), and law enforcement agencies, like the FBI, is inevitable. The inherent conflict is that the more genetic information that is generated, the more likely that information will be misused to discriminate and control.

The ACLU invokes the constitutional right to privacy and the right to protection against unreasonable search and seizure. Along with other advocacy groups, it opposes the creation of genetic data banks. But genetic information is proliferating and is being stored in a variety of ways. Genetic databanks contain genetic profiles, genetic test results, or preserved biological specimens. The FBI index currently contains the DNA profiles of 250,000 convicted felons. Additional plans include testing and recording the DNA profiles of an estimated 1 million felons on probation or parole for serious crimes and possibly recording the DNA profiles of everyone arrested (not just those convicted) in the United States—about 15 million people per year. In the not-too-distant future, run a red light without your license and your DNA profile becomes part of your permanent record. Even today, make the mistake of loitering near a public toilet in California and police officers have the right to take a DNA sample.

DNA specimens are being gathered from convicted or suspected criminals, newborns, fertility patients, school children, employees, and military recruits. (Eventually 2 million members of the U.S. armed forces will have DNA on file, and soldiers have been court marshaled for refusing the test.)

With the proliferation of genetic information arises the need for legal protection against genetic discrimination. Misuse of medical information is already prevalent today. Companies routinely access the medical records (often without consent) of potential employees, or insurees, or loan applicants, and make judgments—to hire or fire, insure or cancel, loan or refuse—based on that information. In this era of national databases, electronic records, and now genetic information, no comprehensive medical privacy act exists in the United States, although there are bills before Congress.

The ACLU is actively pushing for the creation of a comprehensive federal law protecting the medical privacy rights of Americans. It is acutely aware that DNA specimens are much more consequential than traditional fingerprints or traditional medical records. DNA, once collected and stored in databases, has the potential to identify 4,000 (and that number is growing as we continue to map the human genome) genetic markers, such as susceptibility to a specific disease or traits such as the propensity for alcoholism. Leaders of the National Breast Cancer Coalition (NBCC) also are championing privacy laws as a necessary precaution to protect from discrimination the millions of American women who have had breast cancer.

Barry Scheck, one of O. J. Simpon's defense attorneys (he handled the DNA aspects of the trial) believes the ACLU and the NBCC are overly concerned. The national DNA databank, he believes, is being used only for identification purposes and reveals nothing about the person's health, heredity, or psychology. Law enforcement officials maintain that widespread DNA testing can be used to catch the guilty while maintaining civil liberties of the rest of the population.

The ACLU has an interesting perspective on the expanding use of DNA testing called "function creep." Barry Steinhardt, associate director of the ACLU, points to the social security identification system enacted in the 1930s. At a time when fears of fascist dictatorships were very real, advocates of the numbering system expressly stated that it would be used only for purposes of this new retirement program. But over the past six decades it has become our country's universal identification system. Our social security number serves as our personal identifier, as our tax ID number, driver's license number, health insurance number, employee ID number, and student ID number. Applications for jobs, mortgages, bank accounts, car insurance routinely solicit the number, as do some retailers.

Similarly, Steinhardt notes, the national census was developed for general statistical purposes by the government, but during World War II, census data was accessed to intern Japanese Americans in concentration camps.

DNA testing has experienced rapid function creep. In less than ten years, tests originally administered only to sex offenders (on the assumption that they are most likely to be habitual criminals and to leave behind biological evidence) were then administered to criminals convicted of other violent crimes, then to criminals convicted of burglary (on the grounds that they are likely to progress to more violent crimes), then to juvenile offenders. Now our federal government is pondering whether to test everyone arrested.

DNA function creep is spreading to hospitals, schools, workplaces, and insurance companies. The state of Michigan has even proposed to create a permanent data bank of blood samples collected from all newborns for better detection of rare congenital diseases, other medical research purposes, and possibly for law enforcement needs down the road. A strand of hair or a drop of blood provides enough DNA for hundreds of genetic tests. Encoded in DNA is information we can't even access yet, because we simply haven't learned how. In another twenty to thirty years the DNA samples collected for identification purposes could be revisited to reveal amazingly detailed information about an individual—past diseases, future diseases, sexually transmitted diseases, likely time of death, nasty habits, family lineage—things that we may not even want to know about ourselves, or our families, but that we certainly don't want others to know. We can only speculate about what information our DNA will reveal once the human genome is completely mapped, sequenced, and marked.

While traditional medical records reveal only existing conditions, medical records that contain genetic information have the potential to reveal future conditions. The story of a Maryland banker provides an example of how discrimination based on medical records gets progressively worse with the advent of new genetic information. In 1993 an enterprising Maryland banker accessed the medical records of his bank's mortgage holders, then recalled the loans of those people who had been diagnosed with cancer. With genetic information the bank could recall even more loans—loans of mortgage holders, for example, whose genetic records reveal the presence of BRCA1 or BRCA2, genes believed to be indicators of future breast cancer. Even if a bank customer hadn't yet developed the disease, the banker could recall the loan or refuse to issue one on the grounds that she might. A new classification, that the ACLU calls "asymptomatic ill," may become part of the American business lexicon, despite the fact that genetic tests cannot accurately predict how disabling a certain condition, such as breast cancer, will be for a specific individual.

Ironically, as genetic sciences are learning to identify and treat certain hereditary diseases, insurance companies are using that very same information to deny coverage for that treatment. In documented cases, insurance companies have eliminated or refused healthcare coverage for children on the basis that hereditary diseases found through genetic tests were "preexisting conditions." According to geneticists, we are all born with preexisting conditions encoded in our DNA that expose us to all manner of inherited diseases and conditions. Previously, insurance companies couldn't label genetic predispositions as "preexisting" because the technology to do so didn't exist. The more sophisticated the technology, the greater the information, the more insurance companies are making questionable and prejudicial predications about the long-term health risks and future disabilities of its customers.

Insurance companies access genetic information from standard medical records, from special insurance medical data banks (like the Medical Information Bureau in Westwood, Massachusetts, which contains the medical records of up to 20 million Americans), and possibly, in the future, by requiring genetic testing of their customers. Insurance lobbyists from the American Council of Life Insurance argue their right to use genetic information to determine rates and rate structures and to refuse to insure certain individuals because of their genetic profiles, despite the fact that actuarially, inherited diseases have been factored into their rate structures for decades. In response, Congress has formed a committee to investigate genetic discrimination in health insurance. So far nine states have passed laws against genetic discrimination by insurance companies.

Genetic tests have become less expensive and more expedient. Where that information goes, who has access to it, how it's gathered, and in what ways the information is used are real social concerns. Use of this technology raises serious questions about Americans' right to privacy and our Fourth Amendment right to protection against unreasonable search and seizures.

Genetic privacy advocates argue that a judge's court order—a biological "search warrant"—should be required to obtain genetic identification. In certain criminal cases, however, law enforcement officers have used what's called a "DNA dragnet" to identify perpetrators of sexual assault and murder. DNA samples taken almost randomly from men in a certain vicinity were compared to DNA material left at the scene of the crime. More than 2,000 men in the United States were tested for one case, 4,000 men in the United Kingdom for another, and 16,400 men in Germany for yet another. No perpetrator was found directly through these tests. Some "suspects" are now refusing to summit to such testing, and some American prisoners are beginning to challenge DNA testing as coercive in court, but with little success.

Law enforcement officers and prosecuting attorneys laud DNA fingerprinting—an effective new tool perceived to be a huge improvement on the mug shot or traditional fingerprint. It solves crimes faster, more reliably and definitively, without need of witnesses. And in some cases, genetic evidence is freeing innocent men who have been imprisoned for decades. DNA samples currently are used to identify decomposed bodies, finger criminals, exonerate the innocent, settle paternity suits, and identify infants switched at birth. Famous DNA cases, of course, involve O. J. Simpson's glove, Monica Lewinsky's dress, and the now-known "unknown" soldier.

The Florida Law Enforcement Agency is so enamored of DNA identification that in 1999 it offered three school districts an opportunity to ID their schoolchildren for free. (The cost to the agency was only $1.50 per test.) Identifying bodies is a major problem for law enforcement officers, and if all the children in the state were identified genetically, solving certain crimes would be more expedient. But only one school district accepted the offer. The others, wary of "big brother" and the gruesome reality of why DNA identification of children was being sought, refused. Only 300 of the 500 children in the participating district took the test. Parents had to give permission and be present at the testing, and it was the parents who walked home with the specimen, not the state. If their child turned up missing in the future, the parents could present the police with the DNA identification to make a search and conviction easier, but their child's DNA would not become part of a permanent record otherwise.

Today it is becoming more common for corporations to gather genetic information. Genetic testing is the current upgrade to the urine analysis, a test many consider normal for employment application. A survey of 6,000 companies by the American Management Association in 1997 found that 10 percent already use genetic testing for employment purposes.

A central concern of the theologians we spoke with was that a profusion of genetic testing could lead to the creation of a genetic underclass systematically denied employment, insurance, or housing because they are a business risk not worth taking. "Unacceptable genetic profile," "preexisting genetic condition," "genetically at risk," "early morbidity factor" are potentially new stereotypes. Redlining could take place not by neighborhood but by DNA. Discrimination is rearing its ugly head. Most frighteningly, this discrimination uses the authority, the "objectivity," of science and technology as its basis.

The Council for Responsible Genetics, a national, nonprofit organization founded in 1983 in Massachusetts by scientists and public health advocates, has recently recorded more than 200 cases of genetic discrimination in which genetic "predictions" prevented currently healthy applicants from securing employment or health, life, or car insurance.

It is not hard to imagine the day our DNA profile replaces our social security number—a biological smart card of sorts—but not without a legal battle first, between those championing the need to protect our citizens from criminals and those championing the need to protect the privacy and equality of all our citizens. DNA has the power to stigmatize, and a hodgepodge of state laws is not enough to prevent genetic discrimination from growing. The Council for Responsible Genetics is one of the major advocates for stringent federal laws prohibiting genetic discrimination. This organization also argues for the elimination of all genetic databanks because they are far too costly: the financial costs versus information gained, especially in the areas of forensic and military databanks, and the cost of potential social abuse.

But elimination of databanks seems an unlikely possibility as long as we have war and crime. Parents of soldiers want to know what happens to their children, as "missing in action" is more devastating in the long run than a definitive pronouncement of death. Similarly, a missing child is torture to parents. No legislator, in the name of privacy, could stand up to the testimony of a parent whose dead child was identified by DNA testing or to the testimony of another grieving for a child still missing. No legislator wants to tell the parents of soldiers that the military's identification system is being dismantled in the name of privacy and cost/information ratios.

Comprehensive federal laws upholding constitutional rights, coupled with strong medical ethics and frequent review of these laws and medical practices by panels that include philosophers, theologians, and scientists will be critical to keeping insurance and employment discrimination in check.

GENETIC PATENTING AND MARKET-DRIVEN TECHNOLOGIES

Microscopic genetic material, including entire genomes of plants and animals, and certain human genes, is now being patented and owned and sold. Like the formula for Coca-Cola or the design of the Pentium chip, DNA has become a commodity.

Duke University owns patent number 5,508,167 for the

Alzheimer's gene. Johns Hopkins University has patented the colon cancer gene. Geron found and has exclusive license to the gene for cell immortality. Millennium Pharmaceuticals owns the patent for an obesity gene and has licensed the patent to Hoffman–La Roche. Companies and universities locate genes, patent them, and then license therapeutic development rights to pharmaceutical companies, usually retaining a royalty of future sales. By early 1999 the U.S. patent office had issued approximately 1,800 gene sequence patents for plant, animal, and humans genes with applications for another 7,000 pending.

Genes responsible for obesity, epilepsy, blindness, high blood pressure, asthma, osteoporosis, melanoma, human growth, arthritis, breast and ovarian cancer, cardiovascular disease, and Parkinson's disease have already been located and sequenced.

Bioethicist Caplan sees a strongly market-driven world of genetic technology in the near future. "The genome will be patented. Genetics is moving from the university to industry. Monsanto and places like Dow and Hex will own more and more animal and plant genes. Different biotech and pharmaceutical companies will own human genes and that will be that. We will have a lively industry registering trillions of dollars in sales of all manner of genetically engineered products built on the patenting and licensing of the genome."

"It's analogous to computer technology," says microbiologist Lee Silver. "It began through government funding of military operations and military applications, then computers went out to the private sector and they exploded. The same thing's happening to the biotechnology."

Locating and patenting genes promises better and more cost-effective medical therapies and diagnostic tools. Americans spend billions on prescription drugs, which are prescribed regardless of the patient's genotype. In the near future, the administering of prescription drugs promises to become precision engineering.

But patenting (something once limited to mechanisms) of life is morally opposed by some, most notably technology critic Jeremy Rifkin. In 1995 Rifkin organized public opposition to the patenting of transgenic animal and human genes, garnering the support of some 200 religious leaders. "If you start off from birth with a society where all of life is seen as simple chemicals that are patentable," Rifkin contended, "I really don't see where there's any room for theology or intrinsic value in the equation. What role would there be for theology in a world where all of life is considered human invention?"

"We've always allowed people to patent therapeutics and diagnostics," microbiologist Silver counters. "A gene patent is really worthless. What does that mean? I think it means nothing. It's what we do with that information in terms of development diagnostics and therapeutics. The only thing that's useful, that's going to make money for people, is if they can find the true uses of a gene: (1) develop a diagnostic test, or (2) use the genetic information to develop a cure for a disease."

The ever-pragmatic bioethicist Caplan agrees with Silver: "I'm not so interested in gene patenting because I think the issue has ended. I know people are wrangling about it but genetics will become commercialized, private. The patenting issue is moot; there is nothing left to argue about. I'm not applauding it, I'm just saying it's over."

The theologians we spoke with in 1999 were less concerned with the morality of patenting genes and more concerned about leaving the application and development of new technologies strictly to the marketplace, particularly in a society where most people would agree with Mary Lake Polan, chairman of the department of gynecology and obstetrics at Stanford University, who says, "If there is a market for it, and it is technically possible, then someone will do it."

Theologian Donald Shriver takes the long view. "We ought to be much more careful about what has impact on generations hence. One of the problems of our economy is that corporations have planned their activities according to quarterly or annual reports. Whereas they're doing things that impact on natural systems, that could have effects hundreds of years from now. It's very hard, especially in American society, to think long range. But I'd rather have caution as the spirit of this thing precisely for that reason."

A common opinion among the theologians we spoke with is the need for greater reflection than markets provide. "I would go back to those original questions as to what types of goals are these pharmaceutical firms setting," Jesuit Father Keenan suggested. "How much is the buck going to dictate where they are going—the fast buck? Cosmetics will always be the fast buck. They spend a lot more time on promoting than they do on reflecting, but I do think in some ways that the future of humanity is in the hands of the pharmaceutical companies."

Theologian Shriver warns, "And indeed, the whole idea of letting the course of this applied technology be determined by the market seems to me very risky."

Rabbi Greenberg, however, has faith in our democratic, capitalist society. "It's one of the paradoxes of the modern system: There's no question that free capitalism, that the free market is so strong, that sometimes it sweeps aside what should be moral considerations to worry about. But you know, one of the great things about democracies is that they also correct themselves. They make mistakes, but they correct themselves. I see no other way."

THEOLOGICAL CONCERNS

Playing God

On March 26, 1997, Greenpeace activists scaled the exterior towers of the Cologne Cathedral in Germany, protesting genetic manipulation of plants and animals with banners that read: "Man is not God—down with genetic manipulation." This new or imagined world of designer babies, strawberries with frost-resistant fish genes, and immortal cells has also prompted a New York Times headline to ask: "Are Scientists Playing God?" We asked theologians.

"Well, I think that it's one of those phrases that expresses deep-down concerns," said Catholic ethicist Doerflinger, describing a general fear that we may be stepping over a line.

The theological responses to our question fell into four categories: (1) Yes, we are playing God (a minority opinion); (2) playing God is overstated—we give technology too much credit and God too little (the general opinion); (3) it is as it should be—we have a covenant with God to become more Godlike (a Judeo-Christian perspective); and (4) it is not a religious problem but a political one (a practical approach, and particularly Eastern).

Falling in the first category, Southern Baptist Richard Land strongly believes that "if we manipulate the genetic code, we play God. Playing God," he continued, "is a very appealing temptation to fall on mankind—which is almost an irresistible temptation to people, unless checked by a relationship with God himself. And our technology has made that temptation uniquely powerful in the modern era."

Hindus, Buddhists, Muslims, and Jews generally expressed the opinion that the notion of genetic scientists playing God gives technology and the scientists too much credit. Hindu scholar Rao suggests that "critics are exaggerating the importance of inventions and underestimating the infinite knowledge of God. God is supreme intelligence. God is infinite intelligence." Similarly, Rabbi Greenberg puts it this way: "The notion of playing God is overplayed. Only God is absolute."

The Jewish faith stresses the covenant man has with God, and Rabbi Greenberg believes the development of powerful genetic technologies is a positive religious fulfillment. He speaks of man's partnership with God and suggests that genetic technologies are placing man in a more senior position with God, no longer such a junior partner. He says, "The positive principle remains. We are called to become even more human. Part of the Bible says, all humans are created in the image of God. Rabbi Joseph Soloveitchik, one of the great Orthodox thinkers of the twentieth century, suggested that 'we are created in the image of God' means we are godlike. And that it is a commandment to exercise and to develop that capacity. So our development of mind or science is a positive fulfillment of that command." Rabbi Greenberg believes that genetic technologies that enhance the human capacity for intelligence, health, and strength are as God intends.

Catholic ethicist Doerflinger, on the other hand, points to the political aspects of the question. "I think where the charge of playing God comes into play in a valid way is when one set of human beings begins to acquire the power to determine and limit and control the specifications for other human beings on some model of what a good or better human being should be. So I think charges of playing God has some truth to it."

The idea of scientists playing God has no meaning for Buddhists. Buddhist scholar Thurman frames the question historically and politically: "You see, the problem in the Western spirituality is that there's kind of an antitechnological view because they have the view that God is in control. And so, therefore, it's hard for them to develop ethical guidelines about dealing with this sort of intervention that technology makes possible. They basically feel we shouldn't be messing with it. But the main view in Buddhism would not be that there is some sort of religious controller of the world and therefore human beings cannot tamper with things. The Buddhist concern, rather, would be given that power, and the ability to tamper with things, who has the wisdom to define what to do?"

All in all, the whole notion of playing God seems to be more of a media obsession at the moment than a theological one.

The New Meaning of Virgin Birth

Contraception technologies introduced in the 1960s allowed us to have sex without having children. Today's reproductive technologies allow us to have children without having sex. There will be increasing social pressure on parents to procreate "responsibly" through technology.

Reproductive technologies in use today include embryonic prenatal testing, embryo selection, gender selection, surrogate mothers, donor sperm, donor eggs, postmenopausal pregnancies, and use of dead men's sperm. The promise of these technologies, besides treating infertility, is healthier babies—and ultimately the elimination of the "Russian roulette" style of natural birth.

Gender selection is already possible and may become commonplace. Geneticist Edward Fugger and his colleagues at the Genetics and In Vitro Fertilization Institute, a fertility center in

Fairfax, Virginia, assert that the clinic can offer couples an 85 percent chance of ensuring a girl. They've done it by staining sperm (which have a gender X or Y) with a fluorescent dye that latches on to the DNA. Measuring the glow of the sperm allows them to find the females. X chromosomes have 2.8 percent more DNA than Ys and therefore glow more brightly. Preliminary results say that they can pick boys 65 percent of the time. It costs $2,500 a try.

Soon sex will *not* be the way to make a baby, and we can go back to telling our kids about the stork. "The link between the sex act and reproduction will no longer be seen as sacred," wrote microbiologist Lee Silver. "Ultimately, this may prove to be the real significance of sex selection: By breaching a powerful psychological barrier, it will pave the way for true designer babies, who could really turn society upside down."

Silver vividly describes how today's assisted reproductive technologies will be transformed in the near future with our increasing knowledge of genetics: "What IVF [in vitro fertilization] does is to bring the embryo out of the darkness of the womb and into the light of the day. And in so doing, IVF provides access to the genetic material within. And it's through the ability to read, alter, and add genetic material to the embryo that the full force of IVF will be felt."

And while Silver takes a very practical approach and believes that these new genetic technologies will be used in much the same way as in vitro fertilization is used today—to increase life span, to increase health of yourself and your children, and to give your children advantages—theologians and spiritual leaders across the spectrum have a problem with removing sex from procreation. Loss of sex as a sacred act, dehumanization of procreation, elimination of defective embryos in favor of more "perfect" ones, gender genocide, and the introduction of unmanageable complexities in the human condition are among their concerns.

Dr. David Frawley, founder of the American Institute of Vedic Studies, wonders: "You are trying to have birth without prana [vital life energy]. What kind of creature is going to be created without direct participation in the pranic force?" Another Vedic Hindu questioned the nature of a birth resulting from a conception in which love was lacking. For Hindus, souls are formed from the "consciousness and energies of the parents before and during coitus."

Rabbi Greenberg draws a distinction between contraception and reproduction. "Birth control enhances dignity. But clearly these technologies run scary images—could you remove sex from reproduction? It's the total removal that's objectionable. We stop having babies—we set up a great new world in which they are raised in test tubes. That would be crossing the line to idolatry."

"Genetic technologies might create the possibility of putting an individual into society without any familial connections," which gravely concerns University of Virginia Islamic scholar and bioethicist Abdulaziz Sachedina, whose Muslim faith dictates that family forms the moral basis for human beings.

Religion is conceived of in terms of human relationships. If you remove human relationships, then we do not have religion as such. Christianity, Judaism, Islam—we are all concerned with nurturing a sense of interpersonal justice within the relational dimension of human existence. In a secular society, the autonomy of the individual becomes such an important issue that we forget that the individual is actually part of the family, is part of society, is part of the nation. We are interested in the spiritual and moral development of the individual within a community, within a society, within the family as the first unit. So, if that is threatened by technology, we are moving toward a society that becomes meaningless.

Assisted reproduction technologies do not square with the sense of God's creation for Christian Scientist John Selover either. "The Virgin birth—we are profoundly grateful for the principle it puts forth. There is a remarkable sense of *birth*. In the human experience, that which most closely approximates the divine sense of father-mother-God is the most fruitful way for us to reproduce and care for ourselves." He also believes that assisted reproductive technologies fly "in the face of the fact that man is a spiritual creation, and not a creation of matter."

Catholic ethicist Doerflinger describes reproductive technologies as dehumanizing. "The cloning technique is at the far extreme of a long line of technologies which have increasingly objectified and depersonalized the process of creating human beings, from artificial insemination to in vitro fertilization to genetic engineering to cloning. There's something about these processes that seems to invite researchers, especially, to see the product of these processes as uniquely subhuman."

Another common objection to many of the new technologies is that they are designed to reveal embryonic defects and eliminate the embryos with those defects rather than to identify problems with the intent to cure. The approach evokes concern that human embryos, and by extension humans, are dispensable and disposable. It runs in parallel with the abortion debate.

Theologian Shriver wonders about our society's ready acceptance of reproductive technologies: "We live in a society which honors a certain amount of free choice, including family choices. That we should never even consider any kind of a limitation or curb on the decisions of families is rather questionable in my mind."

Genetic Determinism Versus Free Will

The question of genetic determinism versus free will is an intensified form of the old nature versus nurture debate—that is, are humans the product of genetic predispositions or environmental conditioning?

Harvard sociobiologist Edward O. Wilson is the most visible genetic determinist. Although he would not call himself that, his message is that DNA governs everything human. Frequent media announcements that scientists have identified yet another human gene which causes a specific illness, or habit, such as smoking or extreme risk-taking reinforces the validity of genetic determinism. Scientist Francis Crick told a congressional committee in 1996, "We used to think that our fate was in the stars. Now we know that, in large measure, our fate is in our genes."

But if any one person is upsetting the religious apple cart, it's Wilson, who has spent a lifetime exploring the physical basis of behavior. His name was brought up again and again in our interviews, and every theologian vehemently resisted the idea that genes supersede free will; the very notion, they suggest, threatens our humanity. "E. O. Wilson says everything about human behavior is really encoded in that double helix," theologian Shriver told us. "Everything about us has a gene and that includes our decisions, our religion, whom we marry, what kind of education we get, what our vocation is, etc., etc. I find that a very difficult thought. Determinism ultimately cuts the nerve of ethics."

Shriver forcefully continued: "The concept of freedom may be illusive but it's something I have to hold on to. It's part of what it means to be a responsible human being, and that gets into the business of humanity. Are we going to say that we're genetically predisposed to go to war with each other? That's a serious possibility, I think, according to some psychologists and physiologists. But it is a theory I have to resist on grounds that I think I'm obligated to obey the higher law that we seek and pursue peace."

The three main points theologians make about the notion of genetic determinism are: (1) determinism is a flawed theory, ironically arising from religion; (2) determinism renders morality a pointless illusion; and (3) humans are both body and soul.

The idea of genetic determinism echoes an old theological doctrine of predestination, which taught that no matter how you behaved, your fate was preordained—your place in heaven or hell was already sealed at birth. Many theologians find it very interesting, if not a little amusing, to see this religious doctrine echoed in a scientific form of determinism.

It also conjures up the philosophy of Calvinism. Dr. John Eagen, of the Regional Grace Church in Minneapolis, explains, "Calvinism is the notion that all the world is a play, written by God in some detail. We are actors on a stage following a script and free will plays no role whatsoever. And Calvinism has no small number of adherents across the world. But I understand the Bible to teach that we are in a much more interesting relationship with God than that—a much more dynamic personal one."

Jesuit Dr. Kevin Fitzgerald points to what he sees as the inherent flaw in Wilson's theory of determinism. "If you go back and look at what E. O. Wilson has written over the past twenty years or so, he flip-flops a little on determinism because he realizes himself that the logical consequences of his arguments can often drive him into a cul-de-sac where he doesn't want to be. So, in his various books, including *Consilience*, he argues for this big important sociobiology and how we're going to be able to ultimately understand everything through scientific investigation. Some people then confront him with the logical extension of his argument which is to say, 'Well, you know, Edward, by your own argument, you are doing only what your genes are telling you to do.' "

David P. Barash, professor of psychology at the University of Washington in Seattle, describes free will as an awesome responsibility, implying that genetic determinism is an easy out: "People are genetically complete at birth, but as selves they are woefully unfinished. Our essence is ours to choose, depending on how we direct ourselves with all our baggage, DNA included. This is not to minimize our gene-based Darwinian heritage. It is rather a reminder that within the vast remaining range of human possibility left us by our genes and our evolutionary past, each of us is remarkably, terrifyingly free."

This debate is likely to become a central religious concern over the next many decades. It also could become a central legal defense. The knowledge we gain about our DNA, as we continue to map the human genome, could, in fact, give rise to a new branch of law and ethics—behavioral genetics—where lawyers could argue that their client exploded in rage because of his dominant aggressive genes or because he was genetically prone, say, to alcoholism. A code of ethics may no longer be the rule by which we judge a person's behavior, and "My genes made me do it" may become an acceptable excuse.

Some scientists even believe that our studies of genetics will lead to new understandings of consciousness, formerly the sacred realm of the soul or the mind of God. Microbiologist Silver suggests that "someday we'll be able to use these genetic differences as a way to discover exactly what are the genes that allow humans to have a higher level of consciousness than chimpanzees."

Moral or immoral behavior explained as the result of DNA programming offends ethicists and theologians. And Southern Baptist Land blends the language of genetics, religion, and humor to argue against determinism: "God has uniquely prepared everyone geneti-cally to be what He created them to be and to do what He created them to do. Now whether they in the end choose to do that, or whether they choose to abuse the gift, is up to them. I mean, there are a lot of men who I believe God called—that God created to be preachers—who are selling used cars."

Another common theme, which precludes the idea of genetic determinism, is that humans are both body and soul, genetic and psychic. DNA shapes the body but does not govern the soul.

Archbishop Sly argues that "from a Christian standpoint, both in terms of scripture and the traditions of the Church, when you ask the question what is a human being, you have to go beyond mere human technology. Scripture teaches that a human being is not merely human technology; it is also spiritual. That we are created in the image of God cannot be defined in physical terminology. It has to be defined in a moral, spiritual terminology. So we've got to see the definition of being human as more than just our DNA. In the miracle of conception, God created a soul in his image and, in some mystery, connected that soul to a physical being."

Jesuit Father Keenan is hopeful about what genetics can teach religion and does not see a conflict between theology and genetic determinism. "There is genetic determination in us and happily we're going to learn more and more because I think we've spent cen-turies judging people's actions as sinful when they may have been genetically compulsive. And now we're going to know more about the extent of human freedom. This really will be astonishing for us to reflect on. However, we will never see human freedom erased. We'll just see human freedom in its proper historical context."

Beyond genetic determinism, theologian Shriver beautifully describes the context of free will as ethics.

We need to talk more, especially in ethics and theology, about finite free-dom rather than infinite freedom. Infinite freedom is a quality that can only be ascribed to God. All the freedom that we human beings know and all that we have a right to, is a limited freedom. We must always ask where are the limits, what are they, what is the context in which we are to make our decisions—a context that also gives us some limits. Somebody has rooted the word ethics back to the Greek word for the pen, or the corral, in which farm animals were put. To carry on that analogy further, you can say that a farm animal who is always free to run away is thereby free to starve to death. Nobody thinks this is as simple a problem in human affairs. We're always nudging up against each other's freedoms. And we always have to decide when my freedom is rightly limited by yours.

CLONING HUMANS

No other genetic technology fires the imagination or emotions quite like cloning human beings, perhaps because the technology already exists or because animal cloning is becoming routine. Or perhaps because it is easier to imagine a living breathing baby replica of another human than it is to imagine the process of genetically engineering an embryo in a petri dish. And we've all seen pictures of Dolly the sheep, the cloned mice, and the eight Japanese calves created from a single cell scraped off the innards of a slaughtered cow from the floor of a butcher shop. (Cloned prize beef is now sold in common marketplaces in Japan.) Of course we imagine humans will be cloned next. Aldous Huxley's 1932 story, *Brave New World*, of manufactured people is often referenced in discussions on cloning. Others imagine warehouses stocked with brainless clones, whose organs are harvested as needed by their rich twins, or a world full of soulless zombies. (Headless tadpoles and headless mice have already been created.) Will we see back-alley cloning or attempts to clone King Tut, Queen Elizabeth, or Lenin? (Scientists are already attempting to clone an extinct fish from a preserved one mounted on a plaque.) Still other eccentrics claim their genetic twin has a right to be born.

A Bahama-based company called Valiant Venture, Ltd., is offering a service called Clonaid and charging $200,000 to have a child cloned. For $50,000 Clonaid will store cells from a living person so he or she can be replicated when dead—although there is no evidence that the company can deliver what it promises. But Dolly's mother was table meat years before Dolly was born. The Kyunghee University team in Seoul, Korea, claimed to have cloned a female embryo from the cell of a grown woman in 1998, although their methods have been questioned by other scientists. In January 1997 nineteen European nations signed a treaty that said cloning people violated human dignity and was a misuse of science. The signatories agreed to enact laws to ban human cloning. Britain and Germany did not sign. Cloning humans is not illegal in the United States, but federal funding of such research and practices is. A Massachusetts company, Advanced Cell Technology, reported in December 1998 that it had created cloned human blastocysts using cow egg cells whose DNA had been removed and replaced with the DNA of one of the scientists. The purpose of their experiments was for "therapeutic cloning," that is, the creation of cells for medical purposes, not to make an entire person.

Cloning could turn family lineage topsy turvy. For the last thirty years in America we've been struggling with the changing face of families—single mothers and fathers, mixed-race marriages, mixed-faith marriages, ex-stepchildren, adopted children of one race with parents of another, gay parenting, surrogate mothers, donor fathers. Now we're really going to strain. We have names for half sisters, stepmothers, adopted children, stepgrandparents, but cloning would certainly overturn our understanding of family. Catholic ethicist Doerflinger vividly describes the possible ensuing confusion: "It's actually a blurring of language to even talk about someone who is your clone as your son or daughter. Genetically this is your twin sister or brother who happens to have been born maybe thirty or sixty or two hundred years later than you were. But that person's genetic parents are your parents and not you yourself. And so the whole concept of lineage, of parenthood, and childhood, family relationships gets distorted to the breaking point." Will a clone be a child or a sibling? Some bioethicists suggest that cloning poses *less* of an ethical issue than donor parents, because cloned children are at least products of their family's DNA.

Even the very fellow who cloned Dolly is fundamentally

opposed to doing the same thing to humans. "I can't believe that people would think of using this technology to produce people," Dr. Ian Wilmut says. He can't think of a single good reason to clone humans, including infertility. "I can't for the life of me see how you could have a normal relationship between any of those people—for a six-year-old to look at his sixty-year-old clone and see much of what life had in store for him."

University of Virginia bioethicist John Fletcher agrees that the interpersonal relationships would be too weird. "It is going to cut directly across the traditions we have inherited concerning the relations between the sexes and for responsible parenthood. Just the thought of trying to bring up a child who is a biological self-image of another person is a portentous issue. My own prediction is that there will be a kind of moral apprehensiveness and even a deep moral shudder when people think about real cloning."

One American company actually may be preparing girls to accept cloning as natural. My Twinn Doll advertisements, displayed prominently throughout the nation's airports, show a young girl holding a large doll custom made to resemble her (for up to $159.95), wearing identical clothes, the same hair color and style, same color skin and eyes.

Even children are aware of how befuddled familial relations could become with cloning. A boy, eight-year-old Jake, recently asked his mother if she would choose to clone his older brother, Rory, should Rory die suddenly in an accident. Jake then realized that, should that happen, *he* would become the older brother. He could teach little Rory to skateboard, he could boss little Rory around, he could throw Rory to the ground in a wrestling game. And that would change everything. Rory wouldn't be Rory anymore.

What exactly is cloning? The answer is not as simple as Dolly. The Human Genome Project again makes the science accessible:

To Human Genome Project researchers, cloning refers to copying genes and other pieces of chromosomes to generate enough identical material for further study. Two other types of cloning produce complete, genetically identical animals. Blastomere separation (sometimes called "twinning" after the naturally occurring process that creates identical twins) involves splitting a developing embryo soon after fertilization of the egg by the sperm to give rise to two or more embryos. The resulting organisms are identical twins (clones) containing DNA from both the mother and the father. Dolly, on the other hand, is the result of another type of cloning that produces an animal carrying DNA from only one parent. Using somatic cell nuclear transfer, scientists transferred genetic material from the nucleus of an adult sheep's udder cell to an egg, whose nucleus, and thus its genetic material, had been removed.

The future promise of cloning really applies to producing prize livestock reliably, growing genetically compatible human organs from a single cell of the patient in need, and replicating cells as a source of consistent genetic material for research. The cloning of full human beings appears unlikely. "Individuals, and particularly egotists, are usually interested in establishing a life record that is not only considerable but also unique," microbiologist Koshland suggested. "People like to get an Olympic gold medal, be an upstanding leader of the community, be a devoted patriarch of a family, and so forth. Some people even like to be a famous bank robber or a charming swindler or a distinguished artist—different goals for different souls, but unique to each. Would they really want to clone themselves? My guess is that people's demands for self-cloning will be very low. So outlawing the cloning of oneself seems to me a little like outlawing ballooning around the world."

The Reverend Heber C. Jentzsch, president of the Church of Scientology, is equally unconcerned about the technology of cloning, "We believe that the human spirit is not cloneable, not replicable. It can't be copied. The material is only animated by the spiritual, so we are not concerned with people rushing off to Lenin's Tomb and somehow creating a new Lenin, literally the same being. There is only one of him around, whatever he might be doing today."

All in all, the theologians we talked to put cloning on the back burner. It is an issue that is secondary to genetic engineering, perhaps because it occurs in nature. We have all met identical twins.

Cloning is the media darling of the day, and a lot of hype. By and large, because theologians staunchly believe that humans are more than their genetic makeup, a cloned individual would have a unique soul. Many theologians are unopposed to research using cloned cells because of the promise of organ "manufacturing" in an age of organ shortages. Some, however, most notably the Catholic Church, view any embryonic research as morally reprehensible. The church believes that cloning embryos for research is creating human life for the purpose of experimentation, then disposal—a far too utilitarian view of human life.

The myths of Eastern faiths actually may predispose followers to cloning. In Hinduism, according to the text Markandeya Purana, during any battle in which the mythological Hindu demon known as Raktabija fought, from every drop of his blood shed, another one of him arose. And Lord Ganesha was formed from the skin of his mother and Lord Murugan from a spark that came from Shiva's third eye.

According to the Buddhist scholar Thurman, "Buddhists believe that every individual clones themselves in some sense. For example, when you die you choose your next embodiment by the way you lived, by the way your mind is. And enlightenment is really defined as the ability to choose where you live to be of most benefit to others and then to yourself."

ANIMAL, VEGETABLE, MINERAL → AS, TS, CS, AND GS

Our old grade-school science classifications of animal, vegetable, mineral, which seemed so inexorable and so apparent, may no longer adequately describe our world. What scientists are discovering is that we are all very nearly the same. The distinctions between species, between races, between flora and fauna are perhaps less clear in nature than in people's minds. New classifications based on DNA undoubtedly will arise.

While working toward mapping the human genome, the Human Genome Project, along with the other eighteen countries involved, and private companies have decoded and sequenced the entire genomes of single-cell organisms like yeast and bacteria and more complex multiorganisms. The results are startling. "In the last ten years we have come to realize humans are more like worms than we ever imagined," declared Dr. Bruce Alberts, president of the National Academy of Science.

All mammals, for example, contain virtually the same number of genes; it's the DNA sequencing that's critical. "Gene for gene, humans are very similar to mice," the Human Genome Project website reports. The difference is a 1 to 5 percent variation in the gene sequence. "What really matters is that around 100,000 very subtle changes add together to make quite different organisms."

DNA pioneer and chemist Ned Seeman, of New York University, believes: "Ultimately we will be able to see what all things look like on the atomic level and we will find that we can't tell much of a difference on that scale between us and a bacteria or a chicken. That's just the way it goes. We will have to seek other means ultimately to figure out what the things are about us that make us uniquely human."

So genetically we are no different (really) from a worm, a bug, or a dandelion. What good does this somewhat deflating news do for us? How about a pig liver or rat sperm? Ralph Brinster, professor of reproductive biology at the School of Veterinary Care at the University of Pennsylvania is working on a new procedure in which human sperm would be implanted in the testes of mice and rats. The procedure would enable a scientist to remove a genetic deficiency, say, a gene for sickle-cell anemia, from the sperm. The rodents then would generate an endless supply of healthy human sperm, which could be tapped for fertilizing the human female egg before being placed in the mother's womb by in vitro fertilization. In another project one American company, Nextran, has performed trials in which blood from human patients with unhealthy livers is passed through livers of genetically modified pigs and then back into the patients.

Scientists are splicing and dicing the DNA of plants, animals, and humans as well as placing the organs of one species into the body of another. They have added fish genes to beets, human genes to pigs and sheep, replaced the nucleus of a cow cell with human DNA, transplanted the heart of a pig into the chest of a baboon, grown a "human" ear on the back of a mouse, injected rat DNA into mice embryos, introduced spider genes into bacteria, and injected human DNA into a pig then transferred the transgenic pig brain cells into rodents and baboons. Fish-beet. Spider-germ. Rat-mouse. Human-pig. Why?

Understanding the similarities among all living things, scientists are now comparing biological data among human, plant, animal, and bacteria in an effort to develop organs suitable for transplants, cure previously untreatable diseases, and develop new pharmaceutical and agricultural products. Daniel Vasella, chief executive of Novartis, a life sciences company formed by a merger of two large established European companies in 1996, describes this new approach: "The common denominator of our business is biology. The research and technology is applied to discover, develop, and sell products that have an effect on biological systems, be they human beings, plants, or animals."

The driving force behind transgenic research is the desperate need for donor organs for transplant surgery. Transplants have proven to be successful in treating disease and extending life. For liver recipients, for example, the three-year survival rate is over 70 percent. Kidney, pancreas, and heart transplant patients have even better odds. In 1954 the first successful organ transplant, of a kidney, was performed, and today more than 18,000 transplant operations are performed each year in America. But for every 18,000 performed another 40,000 patients hope for an organ to become available, and 10 die each day waiting. Companies are vying to create a reliable, affordable bank of organs or the technology to grow them as needed.

Significant biomedical research is geared toward finding ways to provide those organs—by growing them in a lab or in another animal. While the idea of transgenic organ transplants is not new, the technologies are. Genetic engineering is making both techniques possible, but the science of simulated tissue growth conducted in vitro is estimated to be five to ten years in the future, so some researchers are turning to pigs as a quicker solution. While pigs may not seem a likely first choice, their size and organ arrangements are similar to humans, and pig heart valves have been used in humans since 1974. Our closest relatives, chimps, are not seen as a viable choice; their long gestation periods, small size, expense, and a fear of related viruses stand in the way. Pigs, on the other hand, have been domesticated for centuries, and they multiply quickly, ensuring a steady stream of spare organs. Until now organ rejection has been a big hurdle. Researchers have been injecting human DNA into fertilized pig eggs in the hopes of fooling the human body into not recognizing the pig organ as foreign and thereby accepting it.

Transgenic technologies raise old fears of mythological monsters (centaurs, griffins, werewolves) and the objections of animal rights activists, but few theological questions are raised. Ethical questions of disparity of access will apply to transgenic organs as it does to all the genetic therapies, yet the possibility of an "endless" organ supply will temper far more ethical issues than it creates. Currently hospital bioethicists have an overwhelmingly difficult task distributing scarce organs to so many needy patients.

Questions of playing God could clearly come into consideration. But again, transgenic engineering is not a huge theological issue. Healing human suffering is one of the fundamental purposes of religion. And in 1998 religious leaders from different denominations created a weekend dedicated as the National Donor Sabbath to let their congregations know that they support organ donations.

"I think healing is highly moral," Christian Scientist Selover told us. "We join wholeheartedly in that sense of the alleviation, the recovery from suffering, pain, disease, and we would certainly stand for the rights of anyone to choose the means they wish to turn to bring about that solution. A student of Christian Science might choose a rather different path than genetic therapy, but we would not deprive ourselves of these technical advances for the sake of continued human suffering."

Beyond the relief of human suffering, the new transgenic technologies raise the possibility that all life is one. The technologies suggest a shift away from "man is the keeper of the earth" and "man has dominion over the earth" toward the teachings of Eastern philosophy, in which all life is to be cherished and respected—all bugs, plants, trees, water, sky—because we are all one. The difference between a cockroach, a tulip, a dog, and a human are clearer in people's minds than in nature.

One of Selover's stories speaks of a spiritual wholeness: "A number of years ago a very experienced, seasoned Christian Scientist was looking at an absolutely, magnificently beautiful scene: the sky, mountains, lakes, water, trees. Looking around at this scene, he suddenly turned to the one standing next to him and said, 'My, what a beautiful body I have.' His consciousness, his recognition included a sense of the earth's beauty and grace and strength and depth and grandeur and awe and wonder as aspects of his identity and his body."

GENETIC ENGINEERING IN AGRICULTURE

Field after field of frost-resistant, pest-proof, supernutritious, sumptuous, extra-plump crops that feed the world with increased yields and fewer applied chemicals is the promise of life sciences companies like Monsanto and Novartis. Their scientists are working to genetically engineer potatoes without brown spots, soybeans with bolstered nutrition, vaccine-delivering fruits, sticky wheat for high-quality Asian noodles, or wheat high in amylase to help dieters in food-rich nations shed pounds.

Humans have been cultivating the land for close to 10,000 years. What place does genetic engineering have in this long history of agriculture? Evolutionary biologist David Dilcher of the University of Florida and the Florida Museum of Natural History, who has found evidence of the earth's first flower in China after a thirty-year search, takes the long view. He provides a unique context for understanding the place of genetic engineering in the coevolution of plants and animals. While others turn to hybrid seeds of the early twentieth century, or to Mendel's nineteenth-century laws of heredity, or to the first evidence of domestication of animals and cultivation practices to understand humans' historic manipulation of nature, Dilcher looks back millions of years to posit that people may not control as much as they think. He points to the long interconnected relationship between plants and animals.

Dilcher's theories of plants may sound a little sci-fi at times, he admits. "The spin that I put on this is that plants are in the business of controlling animal behavior. Plants, given that they are not thinking entities, developed a strategy to co-opt the behavior of animals. They first developed bright colors to attract animals to come and visit them. And then they offered rewards of pollen and nectar to keep them coming back." As Dilcher explains, flowers are "advertising their sexual organs" in order to lure animals to their vicinity and hence carry their genetic materials some distance away for fertilization and cross-pollination (an essential component of their survival).

"When social insects developed, flowers developed special other strategies," he continued. "Things like snapdragons, peas, orchids not only attracted insects with bright colors, but they presented a landing platform and showed them the front door. Then flowers developed fleshy fruits and nutritious seeds when there were other animals available, such as rodents and birds. Now humans come into the picture, and there are particular plants that are benefiting by humans growing lots of their seeds."

Today, thousands of years after agricultural cultivation began, people are worried about the consequences of genetically altering plants and animals. Fears include human control of evolution, loss of biodiversity, catastrophic crop failures due to homogenous weaknesses of an entire crop, widespread famine, superresistant weeds and insects, and the patenting and control of seeds that have been free for thousands of years. Protests, concentrated in Europe, against companies genetically altering seeds have even turned violent, with policemen opening fire on activists with automatic weapons. But Dilcher thinks human control of agriculture is not the issue.

"The plants have got us right where they want us," he says. "We are dependent upon them. We have to go get them and reproduce them, and grow them, in order to feed ourselves. So who is in control? Are the plants in control or are the humans in control? So my science fiction extension is that the plants have actually co-opted animal behavior to such an extent that they control human behavior. Because we are in need of them; they aren't in need of us. We have to manage them. We have to reproduce them. We have to maintain them. Or we would go extinct."

Dilcher's more scientific perspective is that plants and humans have co-evolved, co-opted each other in such a way as to support 6 billion people in the world today. "Why do you think there's nearly 6 billion people in the world today?" he asks. "It isn't because we are going around looking for some wild plants and wild animals to eat. And human population is projected to go up to 10, 11, or 12 billion in the next 50 years," he adds. Thus genetically engineered food with higher yields may be part of the evolution of this plant-animal relationship.

If Dilcher is right, it's amusing to think that perhaps plants just want to be more beautiful, more voluptuous, and more perfect, at a time when genetically altering humans may result in the same thing for our species.

European Resistance

The American Soybean Association's Joseph Zak, who is trying to get Europeans to be more open to genetically altered soybeans, says, "It is just another step in the history of agricultural technology. What is this 'mad' science business? It falls in the same line as when tractors replaced the horse. It's like when fertilizers came into the picture or when we moved to breeding to make a better product." Similarly, Michel Cazale, head of the French corn producers association, says he can remember the same arguments lobbed against the introduction of hybrids years ago.

European nations are much more cautious about introducing genetically engineered foods than the United States. Over the past few years activists have staged repeated protests against early applications of genetically altered seeds, not dissimilar to the Luddite protests 300 years ago against early signs of the emerging Industrial Revolution. Demonstrations have been staged in London, Paris, Prague, Barcelona, Helsinki, Milan, and elsewhere. The European Union has approved only twelve genetically modified organisms compared to forty approved in the United States.

In the spring of 1999 the United Kingdom passed a law requiring restaurants to list all genetically altered ingredients used in the preparation of their dishes; fines for noncompliance are as high as $8,750. Until the law also applies to farmers bringing produce to market, however, it will be impossible for restaurants to comply. Farmers may soon be required to do just that, however. In May of 1999 the British Medical Association, which represents 80 percent of all Britain's doctors, called for mandatory labeling and segregated processing of all genetically modified foods so consumers could choose to avoid them. They advise a cautious approach because there is no proof of genetically modified food's safety. Britain's Prince Charles is even more emphatic. Genetically engineered food, he believes, "takes mankind into realms that belong to God, and to God alone."

Bioethicist Caplan puts into perspective the difference between European resistance and tacit American acceptance. "History shapes the response. Germans don't trust science not to go off the rails," he said. "The massive abuse of genetics is still in the memory of some people in that country. It isn't true for Americans. Literally, the Nazi dabbling with eugenics seared the memory of France, Germany, England. It will be tougher to do things there. At the same time, I think the Europeans have a more pristine view of the wisdom of nature." The disastrous problems associated with mad cow disease — something Americans only read about — also have produced a widespread skepticism among Europeans.

"There is some sickness spreading across Europe right now," says Swiss farmer Kaspar Gunthardt. "A bunch of people are trying to get rich by telling us that nature isn't good enough and that we will have to take genes out of a fish and put them in a strawberry if we want to survive. They are changing the basic rules of life and they want to try it all out on us."

In contrast, of the nearly 14 million acres of cotton planted in the United States in 1998, more than 5 million were planted with Monsanto's genetically modified Roundup Ready Cotton or Bollgard's Insect Protected Cotton, just three years after the products were introduced to the market. In Europe, similar crops have not gotten out of the trial stages. Between 25 and 45 percent of major crops in this country are genetically modified.

American Resistance Is in the Marketplace

What began as a movement to avoid ingesting any of the almost 1 billion pounds of pesticides, including herbicides, fungicides, and insecticides doused on crops by American farmers each year, has now extended to genetically modified foods as well. In a country built on freedom, Americans figure they have a choice of eating genetically altered foods or not. But that's tricky. Thus far food growers and manufacturers are not required by law to label genetically altered products as such, so an increasing number of Americans are choosing to go organic.

Organic food sales in America increased from $178 million in 1980 to about $1 billion in 1990, and it is estimated that sales will surpass $6.5 billion in the year 2000. Organic food sales as a percentage of all food sales are expected to reach 20 percent by the year 2010, and organic food sales have been increasing 20 to 25 percent a year since 1990, compared to 3 to 5 percent for the food industry as a whole. By the year 2000 organic food is expected to account for 10 percent of all crops in the United States, up from around 2 percent 1998.

The already confusing label of organic could get even more confusing, thanks to a brilliant move by life sciences companies. "We believe biotech ought to be equally included [as organic foods]," says Alan Goldhammer of the Biotechnology Industry Association. In 1998 Monsanto asked the U.S. Department of Agriculture (U.S.D.A.) to expand the review process an additional three years before certifying genetically modified foods as organic or not. Much of what is engineered into the seeds is the pesticide or herbicide itself. So while companies like Monsanto are moving away from an agricultural system based on chemicals sprayed repeatedly on crops throughout the growing season, they are not moving away from the use of herbicides, pesticides, and fertilizers. The vehicle for administering the chemical is just different. One is crop dusting, the other is genetics. The federal jury is still out. Whole Foods is working to collect 1 million signatures to present to the president, Congress, and the U.S.D.A. asking for mandatory labeling of genetically altered foods and the preservation of the organic label.

As a reaction to the lack of labeling regulation, many manufacturers of organic products now advertise on their product boxes or produce stickers the ingredients *not* found in their food—"no pesticides," "no growth hormones or antibiotics," "no dangerous chemicals." But if the big life science companies succeed in gaining government approval of labeling their genetically altered seeds as organic, the protests that have been restricted primarily to Europe may begin in the States. Americans want clear choices, and a growing portion of Americans don't want to eat genetically altered foods.

"The whole concept of organic is that you feed the soil, not the plant," says Jim Riddle, an organic farm inspector who recognizes the growing need for organic farmers to organize politically and to rethink cultivation techniques. Farmers are barely getting by, says Warren Weber of the organic Star Route Farm in Marin County, California's largest vegetable farm. But "this new movement must be organized by the growers. The coalition hasn't emerged yet, that's all. . . . We have to work more closely with ecologists and set goals that are both practical and achievable to improve habitats. It means taking into account watershed issues, endangered species, and habitats, among other things." Weber sees the need for a new set of rules and thinks California farmers can be in the forefront on this.

Agriculture in America seems to be splitting into two camps: genetically altered crops on one side and organic on the other. The U.S.D.A. would be wise to keep the division clear, because Americans like to make informed choices.

ANTICIPATING THE CONSEQUENCES
The Human Context

"Guidelines, not prohibitions, are needed. Knowledge has to be expanded," Hindu scholar Rao recommends. "The more you know, the more you know that you know so little. The mysteries of the universe are being opened up, as it were. As the mysteries open, we will have to work out some way of dealing with those things in society in that time."

Genetics is a technology as pervasive in life sciences as the computer chip is in information sciences. Genetic technologies will transform life on this planet, literally. But the public is not yet aware of the potential power of these technologies. "I would say that most people that I've encountered still see genetic engineering as a *Star Trek* episode," Archbishop Sly observed.

The power of this technology is portentous, and Jesuit Dr. Fitzgerald reminds us of the potential dangers, if we are not reflective: "As we move rapidly, as we move quickly, as we move now with greater potency than we've ever done before, we can move in the wrong direction. We can move poorly. We can make bad decisions, and we have a possibility of disastrous consequences much more rapidly, much more expensively."

To many thoughtful people, genetic technologies are as frightening as the development of nuclear energy, and in our interviews the comparison was commonly drawn. But signs that our relationship with technology is maturing, that we are learning to anticipate the consequences of future technology through pluralistic discourse, has many theologians cautiously optimistic. They point to the fact that despite the destructive power of nuclear energy (developed before we understood the need for anticipatory dialogue), we have not blown ourselves to smithereens. Pastor John Eagen of the Grace Church in Minnesota draws a hopeful comparison between genetic engineering and nuclear power. "The greatest threat to humanity on the planet today is still nuclear weapons," he believes. "And when they were developed the question was not should it be done? It was *could* it be done? Well, then we faced the prospect of annihilating ourselves. So, we've done pretty well in the last fifty years in keeping that beast in the cage." Perhaps with a little reflection, a little anticipatory preparation, we won't develop a genetic beast we'll have to struggle to keep caged. Rabbi Greenberg also draws an optimistic comparison. "It is scary to be so powerful and so potentially destructive. But look at the Cold War. There were moments when we were literally hanging by a thread and could have blown up the whole world. Science in retrospect opened a Pandora's box that was destructive but somehow people and the cultures managed to assert themselves and pull back and exercise that control. It turned out democracy won out, so I remain optimistic."

By anticipating the consequences of nascent technologies, we will arrive better prepared to apply the new technologies—judiciously and intelligently—when they are fully realized. By anticipating the consequences, we behave not impulsively but maturely as a society. And the most fruitful context for reflecting on these new technologies is a human one: Who are we? Who do we want to become? And how are we going to get there? as Jesuit Father James Keenan advises.

By examining genetic technology through a human or spiritual lens, we gain the ability to make thoughtful, compassionate, reflective decisions, decisions not blinded by fear or prejudices. By reflecting on technology, new and old, in the context of what is good for humanity, we can glimpse a kind of wisdom that encompasses more than rational intelligence. We must look through a lens that includes empathy, respect, and a sense of awe. And we should always examine technology with theologian Donald Shriver's counsel in mind: The human capacity to love is at least as impressive, if not more so, than the human capacity to know.

THE DOGMA OF SCIENCE AND RELIGION

Science can be stifled by its own biases, as can religion. In the West today, the purpose of science is to explain the physical universe; the purpose of religion is to shed light on the spiritual universe. It is unlikely that either will succeed in altering the fundamental worldview of the other any time soon. Nor is that the purpose of a dialogue.

Avoiding narrow thinking, dogmatic stances, and blind hubris is the basis of an open, sustained dialogue among theologians, scientists, and others.

But there are hurdles to be overcome if a truly open dialogue is to be fostered. Scientists must recognize the hidden assumptions of Western scientific thinking and theologians must stop viewing science and technology as an affront.

Buddhist scholar Robert Thurman, who considers discussions between scientists and theologians to be one of his major academic interests, explains the traditional barriers erected by both science and religion.

Science thinks that it has no philosophy and it's just empirically examining things and measuring things. But actually it does have a philosophy: It is going to consider *only* material things to be important. And it's not going to train its people to think philosophically. They're just going to learn all kinds of formulas and technologies. They just have rats that they give neurotransmitters to. And that is a bad miseducation of the scientific people and that has to be changed.

And on the other side, religious people have to be trained in a different way to think or they are left dogmatically theistic. We have to think of religion as something other than faith. They should go back to some of their own monastic thinkers like the Quinoas and Bonaventures and those people who were ready to be a little more flexible than the simplistic Inquisition way of thinking.

Thurman describes Eastern philosophy, particularly Buddhism, as a kind of middle way between Western scientific and religious thinking. "India had a notion of what they called inner science, which meant psychology and philosophy—the king and queen of sciences. They had very elaborate systems of botany, biology, medicine—much better than the Western ones of contemporary times." All their scientists had to be well trained in the inner sciences "because that was the *key* science." That's why India developed Yoga and "evolved a much more sophisticated way of dealing with the mind than the West did. And this is something the West has to learn about. But the West, and our whole educational system, is still brainwashed in the Greco-Roman, Euro-American thing. As if that is *it*, and there is nothing else. It's really mistaken."

Hubris of Science

Scientific thinking is prone to a kind of hubris, an arrogance that can blind scientists and shut them off from a broader discussion. Nobel Laureate James Watson provides a case in point. He discounts any theological discussions of the inviolability of the human genome: "Evolution can be just so damn cruel, and to say that we've got a perfect genome and there's some sanctity to it [is wrong]. I'd just like to know where that idea comes from. It's utter silliness." The idea, of course, comes from religion, but it is not verifiable in a scientific kind of way.

Biologist Daniel Koshland mimics Watson's hubris: "We should start, perhaps, with the question raised by some who say we shouldn't tamper with the germline. I frankly don't understand these people. Where are they living? We are already altering the gene line right and left. When we give insulin to a diabetic who then goes on to have children, we are increasing the number of defective genes in the population. No one is seriously suggesting we refuse to give life-saving drugs to genetically disadvantaged people."

Watson also tends to discount discourse. "I think we can talk principles forever, but what the public wants is not to be sick. And if we help them not to be sick they'll be on our side."

Even some bioethicists can be shortsighted about the glories of scientific discoveries and close-minded regarding the role theologians might play in setting a context for a broader, more holistic dialogue. "On the whole, religion plays a very conservative role in response to genetics," bioethicist John Fletcher stated at the UCLA symposium. "And actually, in its worst features, [religion] makes people afraid and passive in the face of the terrible things that nature and genetic roulette does to children."

One central underlying assumption of Western science is a veneration for objectivity, which is not always apparent to scientists or bioethicists themselves but needs to become apparent for dialogue to be constructive. Historian Kirby Gookin says that it is not science "but rather the supposed 'objectivity' that science imposes upon our views about the world" that is dangerous. The threat is amplified when this objectivity is pointed in the direction of living organisms, in the direction of humans themselves. "Again, the enemy is not science," he says, "it is not technology. It is the insistence that a rational order and control permeate *every* facet of our lives."

In addition to a scientific reverence for objectivity, scientists themselves often separate their pursuit of knowledge from the application of that knowledge. Chemist Ned Seeman believes that while to some extent we're all responsible for the way our work is used, scientists basically produce knowledge. "And knowledge can be used for good purposes and bad purposes and it's very hard to control it once it's out there," he concedes. "The essence of scientific enterprise is that it is public. It could be used for all sorts of magnificent purposes, and also for many evil purposes. There's really no control there from the point of view of the scientist." Seeman goes on to muse, "If they gave us control, we'd all probably be kind of unhappy."

Dr. Michael West, chief executive of Advanced Cell Technology, concurs that "any technology can be abused" but believes we should focus on the positive applications. He asserts: "Once the public understands how these cells can be used to treat any disease caused by loss or malfunction of cells, from Parkinson's to diabetes to heart disease, the concerns will be overshadowed." This kind of dogmatic belief in the technologies and the separation of the pursuit of knowledge from its application has theologians skeptical of science's ability to regulate itself.

Theologian Shriver suggests the need for a broader perspective and some curbs. "To put it rather simply, everything that we can do is not necessarily something we should do," he believes. "Scientists have some problems with that because science sees itself on a course of more and more knowledge and if something can be known, try to know it. And that's all right so long as knowledge is sort of cooped up in a laboratory and so forth. But we're talking about a technology here which is very close to our everyday human living."

Shriver also raises the concern of corporate self-interest determining the outcome of genetic technologies. "A discovery in the laboratory (especially when it's already financed by some corporation) is itself a potential profit center. It is something to be developed because of the self-interests of the people who developed [and financed] it. On the other hand, I think we have to have a free-enough society so that people can indeed pursue some of their own interests. But we need to have a responsible-enough society so that some of those interests are curbed and given some limitation in the light of a larger human good."

Religion: The Willing Friend of Science

At a time when some scientists are displaying a kind of arrogance about their work, religious leaders are taking a rather humble stance vis-à-vis technology and science. Theologians are coming to the table more judiciously, due in part to a somewhat embarrassing past of resisting and denying the validity of science and from a history that has treated technology as an enemy. Jesuit Father Keenan illustrated the point: "You know what happened to the Jesuits? We had to side with either the Pope or Galileo. We sided with the Pope and we lost a lot of credibility."

Expressing the usual criticism, microbiologist Silver said: "Ultimately the church accepted Galileo. It's just that it took them a couple hundred years to realize that it didn't weaken them. The Vatican was very stubborn in the beginning. And it's sad if you look at the Pope's latest announcements. In fact, the Pope now accepts evolution and the Pope accepts genetic engineering, when it's used to cure disease." It took the Catholic Church almost 400 years to concede that Galileo was right, and almost 150 years to accept the theory of human evolution, but it took them less than ten years to accept controversial genetic therapies, including germline. Things are changing.

"I don't feel the religious record is so great," Rabbi Irving Greenberg acknowledges. "For religion to be involved constructively, the approach should not be one of constant suspicion." Rather, he says, religion should serve "as the participant observer and as the willing friend in this process. I think religion's first task would be to encourage and respect and honor science and technology. In other words, I think for too long, and for too many, religions have been defensive and frightened and seize upon every mistake made by science."

Some theologians, such as Pastor Eagen, are acutely aware of the pitfalls of an overly dogmatic approach. "The people of faith have got to figure out the difference between education and indoctrination. And I would say religious leaders need to become students. They're just going to have to accept the burden of reading journals and studying the questions and not feeling they have to have all the answers. The task of people of faith is to be able to address these issues not uniquely from a sectarian perspective but in the language of public discourse. And that is, I think, far more pervasive."

Archbishop Sly is a willing student of genetics. He says, "I think what really shook the church in this respect was the evolution-creation debate, and I think we're seeing that theologians are beginning to approach this not from a reactionary standpoint but from a very proper perspective of being well informed. I find myself not only having to study theology, I'm having to face the issue of reading papers on genetics."

Pastor Eagen, theologian Shriver, Rabbi Greenberg, Buddhist Thurman, Catholic Doerflinger, Jesuit Fitzgerald, Muslim Sachedina, and Archbishop Sly, among others, all take a proactive role in studying genetic engineering. Pastor Eagan emphasizes that theologians needn't approach genetics from a literal biblical perspective. "It's not an issue of taking the Bible and deriving commands out of it. The Bible doesn't have the words 'in-vitro fertilization' or 'genetic engineering' or 'surrogate motherhood' in it. So, what we do from our perspective is take principles of how to think and how to apply them to new dimensions, not how to answer questions [literally]. I'm exhilarated to be in that generation that has to face these brand-new issues."

Foster Dialogue

There have long been efforts to stimulate dialogue between scientists and religious leaders, but only now may the climate in the United States be ready to foster it. In March 1999 the Templeton Foundation awarded physicist Ian G. Barbour the Progress in Religion prize worth more than $1 million for his lifelong dedication to fostering dialogue between theologians and scientists. Barbour, who also has a graduate divinity degree from Yale, strongly advocates public discourse on genetic engineering and believes that theologians must be included in the debate to address such topics as human dignity and the value of the individual. "Science can tell you what's possible, but it certainly can't tell you what's desirable." Barbour suggests that scientists respect and honor the wisdom of theologians, much as Rabbi Greenberg argues that theologians must begin to honor and respect science and technology.

Ascribing scientific findings to the hand or the mind of God has come into vogue among the world's greatest scientists, including theoretical physicist Stephen Hawkings of Cambridge University and astrophysicist George Smoot of Lawrence Berkeley National Laboratory. Even Francis Collins, director of the Human Genome Project, admits to feeling a sense of religious awe about his genetic discoveries. "I am unaware of any irreconcilable conflict between scientific knowledge about evolution and the idea of a creator God," Collins said. "Why couldn't God have used the mechanism of evolution to create? In my field, biology, because of the creationists, the standard assumption is that anyone who has faith has gone soft in the head. When scientists like me admit they are believers, the reaction from colleagues is 'How did this guy get tenure?' "

But Buddhist scholar Thurman questions whether faith and science are simply coexisting today: scientists becoming comfortable with their own religious faith and religious leaders reconciling the big bang theory with Genesis. "There has been this split between religion and science in the West for some time, and it makes dialogue very difficult. But these issues of genetic technology are very, very worthy of discussion. We have to go into multireligious dialogue and be willing to take help from the Eastern brothers—Taoism, Hinduism, and Buddhism" to have a truly constructive dialogue.

A consilience between religion and science in the West must go beyond personal faith, or the acceptance of God among scientists, or the Pope's apology to Galileo, or a tacit coexistence. Public forums in diverse venues need to be held among Eastern and Western theologians, scientists, a variety of academics, artists, and policymakers.

"Theologians should be involved. Sociologists should be involved. Philosophers should be involved. Scientists should be involved," Jesuit Fitzgerald suggests. "Our understanding of ourselves does not come from one particular slice of academia. It doesn't come from one particular methodology. It comes from an integration of all of these things. We get an enriched idea not only of who we are but of where we want to go, what kind of society we want to have. In the past, that integration was often left to, or perhaps rested upon, people in particular areas of philosophy, let's say metaphysicians for instance, who tried to ask the big questions, create the overarching paradigms. Now, I think what's happened in this century is, with the advent of very, very powerful technologies, these big questions are forced to be asked, to be wrestled with, from different perspectives."

Human Suffering

One issue consistently raised in our interviews was a concern that today's intense focus on the human physical body, on prolonging human life here on earth, comes at the expense of moral, ethical, and spiritual pursuits. This myopic lens is viewed as problematic by most Eastern and Western theologians and by some bioethicists.

"I am struck by the fact that no matter how much our health is improved in this country, it is never enough," says bioethicist Daniel

Callahan of the Hastings Center. "As our life expectancy and over-all health have steadily improved, our sense of being healthy has grown much worse. It is as if we are unwilling to accept any suffering at all."

And suffering is not limited to physical suffering. Hindu scholar Rao suggests that suffering of the soul and psyche are equally important to the suffering of the physical body. While genetics may improve the overall physical health of the human race, we can never postpone old age and death, or mitigate the pain of living a human life. "People are going to become old and die, and that brings suffering. So we have to realize that there is a limit beyond which the life sciences cannot go. Improving health is not an end in itself. How do you use your health? That is more important. Do life sciences have something to say about that?"

Islamic scholar and bioethicist Abdulaziz Sachedina believes that suffering is a grim but important reminder that we are human and will remain human. "We have lost touch with suffering as being educational, as being purposeful, as being something that reminds us of our fragility, our humanity, our temporariness. The pain that we are trying to control through these sciences, the suffering that we are trying to control, the aging process that we are trying to control is beyond our control—and they are *not* evil. Secularist culture seems to be pushing us to conquer suffering as an evil. They are reminders; they are some kind of divine celestial intervention in human materialistic and consumeristic concerns which are dragging us to believe that we can really overcome pain and suffering."

He also worries that technology offers false hopes and is not always the appropriate solution. "I'm afraid we are not helping people overcome the fear of suffering." Technology, he believes, provides a steady dose of fresh optimism that the human race can conquer pain and suffering. He tells the story of a woman with cancer. "She goes to her doctor to complain, 'Look, you are my doctor. I want you to shorten my life because I can't handle it.' But what she's really complaining about is human relationships, because she feels lonely in her life. There's no one to say 'Here I am. I'll support you. I'll take care of you. I will be your moral support.' And the technology is saying 'We can correct the situation.' But technology can't correct what this woman is really looking for. Technology is not the sole answer to the human search for inner peace, for inner faith. I am very skeptical about whether technological advances can really lead us to any better way of living as human beings in this world."

Archbishop Sly talks about the limits of gene therapy. "So while we are inherently unified here on earth, soul and body as one, there comes a day of separation, and at that moment, whatever gene therapy has been applied to my body, has no application to my soul."

Hindu scholar Rao goes one step further. The *most* important thing, he believes, is the soul, not the body. Rao believes that "People will improve not through the manipulation of organs but because of the potentialities of the mind. So, our focus should not be so much the body, although it is important because it is the window through which we see, but we should focus on psychological, moral, and spiritual evolution."

Archbishop Sly worries about what he views as an increasingly narcissistic emphasis on the importance of human life. "Scripture does not bear out that human life is the highest prize. It is God's will that is. And so I think we're moving through an incredible shift in our worldview of how we view our own existence." His emphasis on a more traditional, Christian view of eternal life points to our cultural obsession with avoiding death through medical technologies. "We recognize the importance of human life, the need for the relieving of suffering and disease. But we also have a bias that what we encounter here in this world is merely our preparation, a time of building a relationship with God that will lead to a life in eternity. But still our body can be assaulted. We can become sick and so at that point, the church's response is one of healing. We want to pray for physical healing and we want to pray for emotional and mental healing, but at the same time, that isn't the end of it and the avoidance of death is not, of course, the issue."

For decades, Americans have turned over two of life's most spiritual experiences, birth and death, to clinicians. Avoidance of death is precisely the reason. We have trusted medical science in an effort to save or prolong the lives of our children, our parents, and our loved ones. But it's time to ask ourselves what we have lost in the process and what we need to regain.

Christian Scientist Selover, whose faith advocates prayer as an alternative form of healing and who considers that the loss of such an alternative would be a desolate black hole, says, "It's sort of a dichotomy, isn't it? In a sense, right now we see this raising of interest in things spiritual, in healing, in the mind-body relationship, and yet on the other hand we have what looks like a great locomotive coming down the track."

Leon Kass, another pioneer in the field of bioethics and a professor of social thought at the University of Chicago, explains the context more generally. "Does this mean I am in favor of ignorance, suffering, and death? Am I in favor of killing the goose of genetic technology even before she lays her golden eggs? Surely not," he says. "But I do insist on the importance of seeing the *full* human meaning of this new enterprise in biogenetic technology and engineering."

Rabbi Greenberg proposes that religion can play an active role in understanding the human context of genetics. "We've got to develop a greater sense of how religion can contribute to the fundamental values. I believe that religion will best contribute not by denying this scientific *process* but by truly teaching basic human respect for human uniqueness and the range of human talent, capacity, and work."

Religion gives us an awareness that we're spiritually part of a whole, that our own personal lives are set within a context of an everlasting universe, that birth and death are at least as spiritual as they are clinical, and that each individual life is unique and valuable no matter how imperfect. Science, with its greater understanding of DNA, is also teaching us that we are genetically part of a whole, that all living things are essentially the same. Artist Iñigo Manglano-Ovalle links science and religious teachings: "Genetics tells us that we all have a common origin. This mythic Eve may actually . . . be real."

Death, Sex, and the Body:
The New Specimen
Art Movement

Artists and scientists are society's antennas. They are the canaries in the mine. They pick up the first signals, map new territories, invite risk, and all the while are inspired by each other's work. They are the fringe voices and harbingers of things to come, and they offend our sensibilities.

The anticipated cultural upheavals associated with DNA technology are already apparent in the work of artists and scientists. The narrowing of focus from the universe, to nature, to the human has spawned a new art movement we are naming *Specimen Art*. Specimen artists, both scientists and artists, respond viscerally to the power of the new life sciences, much as theologians respond philosophically. And as theologians communicate through dialogue, specimen artists in America and overseas are expressing their concerns or approbation about these new technologies visually on the Internet and in art museums, galleries, public spaces, and science museums.

Specimen Art is art that borrows from, or critiques, scientific theories, technologies, and imagery. It is art that reminds us of our humanness through the human form or aspects of the body: cells, tissue, organs, limbs, and the whole body. It is art that exalts our humanness by visualizing the human body as sexual, as imperfect, as spiritual, and as corporeal.

This movement is distinct from figurative art of the past because Specimen Art is based on *real* human specimens, not their representation. Specimen artists rely heavily on photography, presenting "real" images of "real" stuff. These images may be simple photographs, holograms, videos, CD-ROMs, or Internet based. Sometimes they display the elements of the body as sculpture: body fluids, organs, or cadavers. Specimen artists frequently use themselves or their own body matter as the specimen, and the work goes beyond traditional self portraiture to MRI self portraits, DNA self-portraits, forensic self-examinations.

Artist Vito Acconci, the "grandfather" of performance art, laid the groundwork for Specimen Art and specifically artist as specimen. Acconci is best known for *Seedbed,* his 1972 performance piece at the Sonnabend Gallery in New York City, in which he spent two weeks lying naked under a wooden ramp, masturbating. Expressing the culture of his times, Acconci said he and other "body artists" of the 1960s and 1970s used their bodies as a medium for the discovery of "self." "My notion was to go within by going through the body. It's a kind of escapism—a way to avoid the world. The world was too hard to handle, so I went inside. This was a way of ignoring the flaws in the social system, the political system, the cultural system." Reflecting the culture of our times, many of today's artists are not concerned with exploration of "self," but explorations of the body as a biological specimen.

"I believe that the art of this time will emanate from the lab," said Harriet Casdin-Silver, a seventy-two-year-old artist who had a show called *Corpses* in 1992 and one called *Specimens* in 1994. "Art is supposedly about its time, and it is now a very technological time," she says. Technologies, theories, and the imagery of science will continue to flow from laboratories to the galleries as genetic sciences rapidly expand into daily life.

The context and the history of Specimen Art is museum science, the type of science we are all familiar with—butterflies pinned to trays, collections of shells, jars of pickled frogs—natural forms that have been collected, sorted, classified, labeled, and displayed. But the human being is the ultimate specimen. Photographed, plasticized, sculpted, dissected, dead and alive, the human body is being labeled and displayed like butterflies, in galleries and museums worldwide.

"Systematic taxonomy and the keeping of the specimen is really what you might call museum science," explains Terry Erwin, a research entomologist with the Smithsonian Institution who has specialized in beetles for thirty years. "And factually, we consider it to be art and science. The science part is gathering the observations, erecting hypotheses and testing them. But in order to get the observations, we go out, collect the stuff. We pin it; we put little precise labels on it. We line them up in little boxes. We put the little boxes in drawers. We have a very elaborate system that we call collection profiling, which ranges from Level One where the specimens are falling off the pins, to Level Seven, at the opposite end, where there are magnificently arranged drawers of specimens. When you pull it out, it's a work of art. Just beautiful." Many artists are making Level Seven Specimen Art and putting it not in natural history museums but in art museums and art galleries. Retail cool-hunters have borrowed from these specimen artists and now sell watered-down Specimen Art at Pottery Barn, Urban Outfitters, and even your local florist. Martha Stewart is no stranger to Specimen Art either, and she regularly gives her readers step-by-step instructions on how to make their own amateur Specimen Art projects.

ULTIMATE SPECIMEN

Within this context of the human as the ultimate specimen, there are two main schools of the new movement: Specimen Art that is raw, coarse, shocking, and disgusting (to some), and Specimen Art that visualizes the inner body as a translucent whole (or microscopically), aesthetically, abstractly, and beautifully.

Few artists epitomize the school of Specimen Art more than Gunther von Hagens, an anatomy professor at the University of Heidelberg in Germany. He is both a scientist and a sculptor. Sixty percent of the population of Mannheim, Germany, went to see his 1998 show. More than three-quarters of a million people lined up, waiting at times for as long as three hours, to enter the State Museum for Technology and Labour to see von Hagens's specimens — 200 glossy, lifelike, plasticized human cadavers, manipulated, cut and carved, stretched and pulled apart, skinned and sculpted.

The exhibition which was moved to Vienna the summer of 1999 begins with smaller sculptures — thin slices of human organs. Then whole organs appear. Then full bodies come into sight, perpetually frozen in everyday poses: sitting at a table playing chess, standing, leaping, thinking. Some are sliced in cross-sections, others split down the middle, all created with an eerie sense of humor and a spark about the eyes. One plasticized body is in the act of giving birth. A hole, cut in the forehead of another, provides a view of the brain. A six-month-old fetus dangles at the end of an umbilical cord. Sexual organs float unnaturally disconnected from the body. "My purpose is to push away the disgust associated with decomposition after dying," von Hagens said of his work. "I want to show the beauty of the inner body." These specimens (he calls it Anatomy Art) are beautiful, and the exhibition (which is on world tour) is spectacular. More than 2,000 people have donated their (as yet not dead) bodies to von Hagens for future work.

In a world where we increasingly view the human being as encoded information, what do we gain or understand about ourselves, about our humanness, from an exhibit such as this? "That we're meat," answers Melissa Alexander, public program manager for the San Francisco Exploratorium, expressing the most primal, visceral response. Unmistakably, von Hagens's work speaks to the fact that humans are basically flesh and bones and organs — corporeal. But the show evokes another response precisely because of its in-your-face rawness: Humans are more than material, more than information. We are spirit, soul, thought, love—intangible as well as tangible.

What's the appeal of such graphic rawness? "Authenticity," said Mark Dion, one of the most prominent specimen artists of our times. "One of the reasons why museums are incredibly important now, and people seem to be flocking to them like never before, is that, despite popularity of new technologies, people are still incredibly hung up on the actual thing, the object, the specimen—as a means of communication. A specimen, like one of von Hagens's anatomical sculptures, is a kind of representation, but not a two-dimensional representation, not an electronic representation. When you look at these prepared and displayed cadavers, you aren't looking at a film of the body. You aren't looking at a map of the body, or a chart of the body, or a photograph of the body. You are looking at a body."

Art is intensely personal and admittedly subjective, but there are recurring themes in this movement:

1. Sex: Sex is a spiritual act as well as a carnal one.

2. The Inner Body: Microscopically and translucently the human is beautiful, and encoded with information.

3. The Outer Body: The diversity of the outer body is to be celebrated.

4. Bodily Fluids: The corporeal body is universally the same.

5. Death: Reclaiming death from technology is a noble human pursuit.

This art serves as a cautionary tale as we march into a world increasingly defined by genetic technologies and its promises. Specimen Art reminds us that we are flesh and fragile and mortal and diverse and spiritual. It is, in its purest essence, a rejection of a scientific paradigm that reduces humanity to a set of classifiable, quantifiable, malleable chemicals.

And the work does not hold back.

SEX

In a time when reproduction is possible without sex, artists are creating stark reminders that sex cannot be removed from the human condition. And as the possibility of "perfect" designer babies and eugenics is discussed in the press, specimen artists celebrate the less-than-perfect human form, often documenting nature's "mistakes" as sexual beings. What is normal sex? is a recurring in-your-face theme raised by these artists.

Specimen artists sometimes directly and consciously call attention to the new genetic reproductive technologies. In 1997, when artist Iñigo Manglano-Ovalle was commissioned by the University of Washington's Henry Art Gallery in Seattle to create art using any new technology he wanted, he chose genetics. In a show called *Future Forward: Projects in New Media,* he will exhibit a fully functioning sperm bank as sculpture in an effort to break down boundaries around the discussion of genetics. The gallery offered him access to any of the university's facilities, which includes the Human Genome Project and its leading scientist, Lee Hood. Working closely with one of the university's geneticists, a director of the in vitro fertilization clinic at the university, on the science and with the university's legal department on ownership and insurance matters, Manglano-Ovalle's art will function as a real gender-selection sperm bank. The gallery and Manglano-Ovalle hope that by putting genetic technologies in the context of an art gallery, they will provide the average person an entree into the discussion of genetics. They also hope to "provoke further thinking and a little seeking," according to Sheryl Conkelton, a gallery curator. By placing gender- selection technology in the context of art, Manglano-Ovalle is pointing to the aesthetic choices implicit in genetic enhancements. The gallery's mission is to create cross-disciplinary public forums and cross-disciplinary art to discover conflicts and parallels that will open our thinking. Wisdom is in the dialogue, Conkelton said, "and that is the underlying theme of all our projects."

With the help of a tree specialist, Yale professor and engineer Natalie Jeremijenko recently cloned 100 hybrid walnut trees called

Paradox. The saplings were displayed as specimens in the Yerba Buena Center for the Arts in San Francisco. They will be planted in the year 2000 around the San Francisco Bay area near schools, off highways, and in parks, in a test of nature versus nurture. Jeremijenko hopes to counter the assertion made by biotech companies that they can produce industrial uniformity in living organisms.

Artists also bring into question the new reproductive and genetic technologies by displaying sex as primal, raw, sometimes dark, often humorous, and anything but normal. England's most famous contemporary artist Damien Hirst and Italian photographer Gianluca Cosci depict dead animals copulating. Hirst's proposed 1994 sculpture, *Couple Fucking Dead [Twice]*, was banned by New York authorities even before it was created, in part because they thought gallery visitors might vomit at the sight and smell of rotting cow and bull cadavers in hydraulic fornication. Cosci's photograph of two raw plucked chickens kissing passionately in a metal baking dish on a kitchen stove makes you feel as if you've walked in on your parents—very uncomfortable. But sex is the good old-fashioned way of making babies. It's how most of us were created, and it is often presented provocatively by artists.

Joel-Peter Witkin, one of the most collected and disturbing photographers of our time, takes the idea of a kiss to an extreme. Acting out of an old classic tradition in art whereby an artist re-creates for his own time a masterpiece of another, Witkin's photograph looks like a pencil sketch of Picasso's 1969 painting, *The Kiss*. But Witkin's *Kiss* is a cadaver's head split in half from the back and opened like a book lying flat on a table. The lips connect, the noses profile, and the eyes meet in a gaze. Witkin's talc-dusted head, against a black background, has the same stringy hair and balding hairline of Picasso's male lover, the same deeply creased face, and it simulates one of Picasso's signature cubist tricks, viewing the profile and the full face at the same time. And while Picasso's kiss is between a man and a woman, in this piece the cadaver autoerotically kisses himself, calling to mind Witkin's possible sexual feelings for his own identical twin.

Supermodel Cindy Crawford vomited at one of his openings in Los Angeles.

Witkin, who has seen hundreds of dead people "on tables," conceived of *The Kiss*, then hunted for the perfect specimen. "I waited several years for the opportunity," Witkin told us. "I asked a particular pathologist if he got a severed head to please get in touch with me. And that finally came about. I got the phone call and I was prepared. I got up early in the morning and had a good breakfast (which meant I might barf). I didn't know if I was getting a man's head or a woman's head. All I knew was that it was very much like a library book. It had to be back at a certain time. What was wonderful was the way its entrails were hanging, the shredded stuff of the throat and neck. It looked as though it were ripped out of the man's body."

Witkin treats photography as an elaborate painting, using staged tableaus with painted backgrounds, drapes, and copious props. The atmosphere of the photographs themselves is that of Civil War tintypes, scratched, posed, and old, with curved shadowed edges that draw you deep into the photo like a stage. His images compel, and the mind's eye revisits them, not hauntingly, but intelligently. But what is he saying by depicting cadavers, dwarves, bestiality, homosexuality, contortionists, pre-op transsexuals, sadomasochism, bondage, piercings, religious overtones, and sex toys?

Witkin's stunning images of sexual worlds most Americans know little about throws aside our sense of what is normal.

Andres Serrano, an infamous photographer, created a body of photographs called *A History of Sex* in 1977. His subjects, much like Witkin's, engage in taboo practices and are not Hollywood beautiful. He too photographs pre-op transsexuals and dwarves, bestiality and sadomasochism, extreme piercing and bondage. Shot outdoors in color, before strikingly blue skies or open seas, Serrano crops close in on naked bodies in a very matter-of-fact, crisp style. His portraits are huge, four feet by five feet, and are more suggestive than explicit. Nevertheless, they are very controversial.

In exhibitions of Serrano's work in Melbourne, Australia, which included *A History of Sex* as well as his immersion series and morgue series, the museum's director and curator received death threats and the gallery received bomb threats, after the Catholic Church failed in a legal attempt to stop the show from opening. One piece of art was attacked and damaged twice, and the show closed early after only a week, citing concern for the safety of employees. Serrano was dismayed that so much controversy surrounded his work. It is not as if sexuality had been invented in this century, he says. The new development, he believes, is the ability to display photographically these age-old practices. "Since the beginning of time people have been doing the same things. The only new thing is the way it can be documented."

The photographs by Serrano and Witkin show us the sexual human shadow and bring into question the scientific notion that sexual preferences can be genetically marked. Human sexuality is far too complex, this work makes clear, to be reduced to simple formulas. In the face of this art, the gay gene "discovered" in 1993 (yet questioned by many) seems an impossibility, as does a genetic marker for the diverse, sometimes dark world of heterosexual preferences. But what's next? Headlines announcing the discovery of the bestiality gene? The lesbian gene? The menopause gene?

Controversial British artist Damien Hirst could have been responding to Serrano's photos of sexual women in their eighties when he said, "We all want girlfriends like the ones in *Vogue* magazine. It's just not going to work. If you fall in love with somebody you'll be having sex with an old lady eventually. You can't really avoid it." On screen, on billboards, in magazines, sex seems reserved for the young and beautiful. In an aging society, these artists are asking the question: What is normal sex? Who should have sex?

Woody Gwyn's 1998 series of skeletal sculptures have not been shown yet. Using lifesize German medical models, he positioned realistic-looking human bones on eight-by-four-foot panels and embedded them in a mixture of dirt, bits of glass, gravel, tin scraps, and epoxy to create what looks like something an archaeologist might unearth in a field. A skeletal couple lay tenderly embraced in the unmistakable missionary position. Pompeii and sudden death come to mind, as do dry bones, fleeting flesh, and the blessing of sex as a spiritual act as well as a carnal one.

With stark, direct images, photographer Zoë Leonard created an unexpected "conversation" in a stuffy, damask-covered gallery of the Documenta Museum in Kassel, Germany. She removed half the Rococo paintings that are normally on view—landscapes, portraiture—leaving only paintings of women and an occasional still-life. Leonard replaced the others with much smaller black-and-white, close-up photographs of the genitalia of six female friends. "Once the genitalia went up, the whole gallery seemed to shift," said Leonard. "It was amazing to set up relationships between the photographs and the paintings. The facial expressions of the people in the paintings all seemed to respond to the photographs of vaginas. One older woman sits with her hands clasped in her lap, a befuddled look upon her face. Next to that is a still-life of a large fish. Two young girls, princesses, sit close together with knowing looks on their faces."

In a later exhibition at the Renaissance Society at the University of Chicago, Leonard hung the portraits horizontally, representing the vagina as a specimen. "In most art, the woman's genitals are invisible, a discreet curve or hairless mound. Or in most 'straight' porn, shaven into a tiny triangle, pink and neat. I wanted to photograph it in a way that looked real to me. Each one different."

Difference is normal.

THE INNER BODY

Within a two-year period, just before the millennium, the U.S. government funded three programs that are destined to radically alter the way we view—literally—our inner body and our outer universe. Two of the programs go deep into understanding the human body. The other goes deep into understanding outer space. And the more we investigate the human body visually, the more compelling its comparison to the universe. The new photographic images of inner space and outer space look remarkably alike, suggesting that infinity extends inward as well as outward.

In 1989 the Visible Human Project, commissioned by the National Library of Medicine, began to create the first complete digital record of the human anatomy. In 1990 the Human Genome

Project, commissioned by the National Institute of Health, embarked on a massive project to decode the DNA of the human body for the first time in history. In 1990 the Hubbell Space Telescope, built by NASA, was launched into orbit and began collecting images from the deep reaches of the universe.

Visualizing the Inner Body as a Whole

In 1989 University of Colorado scientists Dr. Victor Spitzer and Dr. David Whitlock were surprised to be awarded the prestigious Visible Human Project. They hadn't expected to win the $1.4-million contract because they were a small, relatively unknown team, and they faced stiff competition from big networked universities and other organizations vying for the project.

Spitzer, who possesses a quick wit, and Whitlock, whose enthusiasm for human anatomy is infectious, secured the contract not only because they were eminently qualified but because they inadvertently created a conceptual art piece that wowed the decision-making panel. A year before Spitzer and Whitlock received the contract, officials at the National Library of Medicine decided that the world needed a complete computer model of the human body, a digital catalog of the human anatomy, inside and out—its organs, muscles, bones, veins, skin, hair, teeth, visible as a transparent whole. Some virtual models existed, but none offered a comprehensive cataloging. The officials called for proposals and eventually narrowed the pool from one hundred applicants to three finalists, including the Colorado scientists. To aid the selection process, the officials asked the finalists to submit cross-sectional photographs of a guinea pig's body.

In the end, it was Spitzer and Whitlock's decision to submit other samples of their work, in addition to the images of the guinea pig, that got them the job. They had been developing techniques to image cross-sections of the human body long before the National Library of Medicine request, and they had twenty beautiful, large-format, color photographs of a small section of a human knee. The Library secretary who received the knee photographs assumed they were simply identical copies of the same image, so she separated and distributed them to the various members of the selection committee. However, someone at the meeting realized that the photos were a series. Once the photos were collected and stacked in the proper order, the committee fanned the stack like a flipbook and traveled three-dimensionally through the human knee. In a moment of excitement they knew their vision could indeed be realized and that they'd found their scientists. Spitzer and Whitlock had done something they hadn't anticipated or even orchestrated consciously— they had created a conceptual work of art—and in the process landed their biggest contract.

Spitzer and Whitlock set out to find a total of six appropriate cadavers, three females and three males. Ultimately one female and one male would be selected to digitally represent the human body for the National Library of Medicine. But their search wasn't easy. All bodies had to be under six feet tall to fit into the "scanner" the doctors had built specifically for the project. Also, the specimens had to be in good shape: no car accident victims (organs are usually damaged, or limbs severed), no drug addicts (they are usually malnourished), no gunshot victims, no obvious deformities, no deaths by disease. The search was slow, particularly because they were competing with 40,000 patients a year awaiting life-saving organ donations. In one frustrating incident, a mother donated her daughter's body to the Colorado scientists directly. The young woman had committed suicide but was otherwise intact and whole. A perfect specimen—until Spitzer and Whitlock discovered that she had a rare malady in which all of her organs were reversed. With her heart on the right side of her body and her gallbladder on the left, this young woman could not represent typical female anatomy.

Ultimately the female specimen chosen was a sixty-nine-year-old woman; the male a freshly executed convict. The Texas death-row inmate had donated his thirty-nine-year-old, 5-foot-11-inch, 190-pound body to science, but didn't realize he would be frozen, sectioned, sliced, and scanned into a digital textbook through which millions of cybersurfers would eventually take tours. He didn't realize he would become the most visible human specimen on the planet.

Spitzer and Whitlock were so thrilled to get their first, near-perfect (he was missing one testes) specimen that Spitzer flew to Texas to accompany the body back to Denver. Once in Colorado, the body was immediately frozen to −94F° for two days in a deep freeze chamber they had acquired from a local butcher shop that had gone out of business. Once frozen, the scientists glued (with glue purchased at the local hardware store, which would supply many of their materials) the specimen's arms to his sides, fingers and toes together, and penis to his thigh so that nothing would be lost or jarred loose in the cutting process. The body was then quartered with a contraption they jerry-rigged like something out of Frankenstein's laboratory. Each of the four sections was placed in blocks of blue gelatin and frozen again. Spitzer says they started with the foot block because it was the least important. He added, "No offense to podiatrists."

Spitzer and Whitlock spent months shaving off layers (the thickness of a credit card) from the frozen corpse and its encasing blue gelatin. Each buzz cut created brightly colored, frozen human "sawdust," which was carefully brushed into a garbage bag for later burial.

Looking down at a frozen block of glistening human flesh is a new perspective to the layperson. Spitzer's four-year-old daughter, Anna, had her own perspective of her father's work. Upon hearing an alarming description of her father's occupation in kindergarten class—"My daddy cuts up bodies and sticks them in the computer"—her concerned teacher phoned the Spitzer home.

Nine months after they received the prisoner specimen, the scientists had produced photographs of 1,878 cross-sections. The data amounted to 15 gigabytes. Over time their techniques improved, and the female was sectioned into 5,000 layers.

As part of the project, the scientists reassembled the digital images and pieced the prisoner back into a three-dimensional transparent whole. Digitally layered just right, the prisoner's body became whole again, and his tattoo reappeared on his chest. Today Whitlock and other anatomists are meticulously labeling each part of each layer of the thousands of cross-sections. And in a future application of the data, the scientists are looking to create a virtual patient to advance the field of simulated surgery, which they believe will revolutionize medical teaching. Using haptic feedback, the scientists have already created a virtual knee that can be "cut" with a special tool. Chronically underfunded, they wonder if the video gaming industry might want to co-produce a virtual surgery game.

The work of these two scientists has also directly inspired artists, most notably photographer Alexander Tsiaras and artist Justine Cooper.

From Science to Art

The work of Spitzer and Whitlock, whose considerations were scientific, not aesthetic, became animated art in the hands of Alexander Tsiaras. He bought the digital data of the male from Spitzer and Whitlock and created a stunning interactive CD-ROM that lets the viewer digitally fly though the layers of the body. Hit a few buttons on the computer and the skin disappears, then the muscles, then the organs. Cut away sections of the skull to reveal the brain. Twirl the figure in any direction. Examine the quartered sections one by one. In effect, Tsiaras beautified the data and made it commercially appealing. He made the human body dazzling and accessible to the average layman in Omnimax-style entertainment. His *Body Voyage* made the cover of *Life* magazine and is available in bookstores and on the Web.

With the help of new high-resolution imaging technologies (X rays, magnetic resonance imaging [MRI], computed tomography [CT], and positron emission tomography [PET] scans), a world once invisible has been made visible, and artists are latching onto the new technologies.

One artist, Justine Cooper, magnetically "sliced" the image of her own body like a salami and hung her 1998 self-portrait, *RAPT*, in the Julie Saul Gallery in New York. "I wanted to create a wandering footnote to the Visible Human Project and [then] something else again," said Justine Cooper. Using images from an MRI machine, the Australian artist transferred 78 life-size cross-sections of her body onto clear plastic sheets three by three feet, which she vertically suspended from the ceiling at eye level, in a long evenly spaced row. The piece hung in four sections (quartered to match the Visual Human) so the viewer could walk in and out of the body. Elongated by the distance between plates, her body stretched the length of the spacious gallery. Albeit a high-tech version, *RAPT* resembles a body on a table in a morgue.

In another piece that appeared in the 1998–99 Julie Saul Gallery show titled *SKIN/DEEP: A Survey of Interior Imaging from X-Ray to MRI,* Cooper used the same slicing technique to create a high-tech bust called *Self Portrait.* But unlike her *RAPT* piece, the glass plates of the *Self Portrait* are stacked. The horizontal plates form a transparent, three-dimensional, X ray–like image of the artist's head and shoulders. One edition of *Self Portrait* was quickly purchased by the Metropolitan Museum of New York, another by an eccentric wealthy art collector, a patron to many in the Specimen Art movement. The whole show was more beautiful than medical and included a CT scan portrait of performance artist Laurie Anderson by famous photographer Annie Liebowitz.

The Visible Human Project and other new imaging technologies give us a glimpse into the inner body, not on a molecular or cellular level but on the magnitude of tissue and organs—things we can see. Human anatomy has long been studied by dissecting cadavers, but the Visible Human Project and MRI imaging brings us a revolutionary advance in the history of human anatomy, enabling us to view the entire body, all its systems and structures, simultaneously.

"A real revolution is in how we image ourselves—a holistic view," says Harvard biologist Nancy Kedersha, who has shown her photographs of molecular structures in museums. "The most heartening thing I see is an increase in the emphasis on unifying everything. On trying to see the whole picture with technology, on trying to see how the little parts fit into the big parts, and trying to see the human body, not just as this piece or that piece, but how it works together—the systems, the flow."

But some artists and scientists prefer to focus on the little parts. Referring to the Visible Human Project, Ned Seeman says, "From the point of view of someone like myself, who's a molecular scientist, if you think about chopping up a body in that number of pieces [2,000 to 5,000], basically you're talking about pieces that are maybe a millimeter thick. I think of us as basically a bag of chemicals. The Visible Human Project is a very coarse display of the body—coarse in the sense that a fine one would entail billions of pieces." Artists and scientists can now photograph on that infinitesimal a scale.

Visualizing the Inner Body Microscopically

DNA IMAGING

Molecular photography captures a world invisible to the naked eye. Today high-tech imaging machines have opened the mysteries of the human body, allowing visual access to microscopic elements—DNA, molecules, and cells. Many specimen artists are delving into this new visual world, some with political motives and some because of the wonder it inspires.

As the double helix becomes a turn-of-the-century icon, one of the favorite new images of these artists is the DNA "fingerprint," which looks like supermarket bar code meets IBM punch card. According to artist Gary Schneider, whose recent work includes his *Genetic Self Portrait*, DNA fingerprints are not biology but rather information. Two works of his high-tech, self-portrait installation are black-and-white DNA fingerprints toned slightly to a muted red, called *The Mitochondria DNA* and *Gene SRY*.

Schneider, who has been "seduced" by the microscope since high school biology class, grew from painting, performance art, and film-making to scientific photography in the late 1980s. After conceiving the idea of this genetic portrait late in 1996, he sought out scientists who would work with him to create what would become fifty-five images that range in size from a tiny three- by four-inch image of a Y-chromosome to a huge nine- by seven-foot mitochondria gene. The tones of the photographs, which he carefully crafts in the darkroom, are subdued, earthy, and less adorned than the more common enhanced and manipulated scientific images. There is a straightforward honesty to his work. His "imperfect" specimens—a crimped gray facial hair, junk DNA—detailed and enlarged, are arrestingly human.

Also included in his portraits are those parts of the human body that are frequently used in forensic sciences. His show included photographs of his hands (the old-fashioned fingerprint), his teeth (dental record matches), retina (new laser identifying technologies), blood (murder scene), and sperm (sexual assault cases).

Schneider, who has an "anxious excitement" about the new technologies, wonders how this new information will be used in the future. He sees this work as "a kind of preparation" for the future as these technological discoveries become more integrated into our lives. "I'm not a political animal, particularly. But I feel like all aspects of this new world need to be discussed all the time," says Schneider.

Bill Ewing, director of the Lausanne, Switzerland, Musée de L'Elysée (which will devote the year 2000 to themes of the human body), understands the power of applying an artistic context to a highly politicized subject. In 1998 he asked Schneider to re-create the genetic self-portrait installation planned for the Santa Barbara Museum of Art. Ewing felt that the show would set a context for a referendum on agricultural genetic engineering that was up for vote in Switzerland. The show was widely covered in the Swiss media, and the pro-genetic engineering referendum passed with a cautious yes.

For Schneider, exposing his genetic material so dramatically and publicly addresses a recurrent political theme in his life. Raised in South Africa, the specter of an oppressive police state has always been with him. Much of his work addresses that anxiety. Genetic privacy is difficult to protect, so "why not just throw your DNA out there?" He continues, "It's a totally exposing portrait from the fingerprints of my hands all the way to my semen." And while average gallery visitors may see Schneider's portrait as one that could very easily be their own, to scientists nothing could be more private or more individual. "As a scientist," said Harvey Herschman of UCLA, "I'm familiar with each of these techniques—the retinal scans, DNA sequencing, chromosome swatches, micrographs of cells. Despite the fact that I'm familiar with all those techniques, the idea of representation of all of these things from one individual had never hit me. This is like standing naked but raised to the highest power. Not only are you naked at the surface, but you're naked all the way through from the level of macroscopic down to the level of atoms. Each observer sees Gary at every level of his body. To me it would feel like—if it were mine—I was being exposed. That's the sort of emotional response I got from this work."

His exposed DNA actually became a concern. While Schneider was in the process of creating the work, his backer worried Schneider might lose his health insurance if he pursued the idea of looking for a hereditary cancer susceptibility gene (due to his mother's death from the disease). Schneider felt it was all part of the process and went ahead, but the results of an abbreviated test were inconclusive. With respect to genetic discrimination, Schneider has almost literally become the canary in the mine.

Increasingly, portraiture is not about the face. In a 1998 show called *Garden of Delights* Manglano-Ovalle, with the aid of scientists, created a huge installation with forty-eight distinct DNA colorized "portraits," each five feet tall and two feet wide. Hung in triptychs, each set is a group of friends and titled by their names: *Lu, Jack, and Carrie* or *Luis, Chetas, and Pedro*. Like striped ink blots of color on a white background, the portraits make reference to the forty-eight Spanish "Casta" paintings made in Mexico in the eighteenth century as a system of classifying race. In the center of the vast room of DNA portraits were three sets of eighteen gray institutional lockers stocked with DNA testing kits.

Manglano-Ovalle's intention, he said, was to raise the question that whoever creates new categories based on genetics will be like the Spanish imperialists, in control of the social structure. His work asks: What sorts of new classifications will come from these DNA tests and what sorts of new discrimination will be based on that information? As DNA tests become as institutionalized and as accessible as a gym locker, how will we define a person? By genetic makeup? By a gay gene or an obesity gene or a cancer gene? Manglano-Ovalle was born in Madrid, Spain, in 1961 and grew up there as well as in Bogotá, Colombia, and Chicago, where he now lives. He has grappled with issues of identity and race in his life as well as his work, and he believes "that our contemporary circumstances present an ideal opportunity for reconsidering constructions of race and ethnicity."

Not all images of DNA are intended to tell a story or act as a portrait or jolt a political response or provide evidence, as in the case of paternity suits or forensic science. Some scientists are creating images of DNA as a way of communicating scientific information visually so it can be more clearly understood. Harvard chemistry professor George M. Whitesides teamed up with photographer and MIT artist in residence Felice Frankel to illustrate subjects of scientific investigations in their book, *On the Surface of Things*. DNA was one of their subjects. Unlike Schneider's clean, black-and-white images or Manglano-Ovalle's brightly colored, soft renderings, Frankel's rendition of a DNA fingerprint is orderly and looks dense with information. It is also beautiful, like five bamboo stalks glowing against a gray night sky.

To a chemist, this image of DNA becomes a teaching tool. "Each band shown here is a collection of DNA molecules of the same size," writes chemist Whitesides. "The separation of molecules of DNA by size is the basis for almost all procedures for genetic analysis, used for finding children of uncertain paternity, for ferreting out criminals. The molecules of DNA have a negative charge. When a voltage is applied to the electrodes placed at the ends of the pool [of water], they swim away from the negatively charged electrode and toward the positive . . ."

Frankel's aim is to popularize science through compelling images. She teaches scientists and students at MIT how to visualize their work and exhibits her own work in galleries around the country. As a popularizer, she says, "I want to be the Martha Stewart of science."

The purpose of documenting DNA images varies widely among specimen artists, as do their reasons for creating and displaying other microscopic worlds—from a celebration of the science to a profound questioning of it.

CELLULAR IMAGING

Harvard Medical School biologist Nancy Kedersha presents images of the body on a molecular level as an aid to her scientific research, but she is also seduced by their beauty. And although she says that the aesthetic part of her work is a "hobby," her work has been shown as art in the Santa Barbara Museum of Art, *DoubleTake* magazine (an arty photography publication), and *Wired* magazine. Her photographs of cells also have appeared as science in *Discover, Time, Newsweek,* and *The New Yorker.*

At times her work can be arduous. She says, "As a scientist, I do all kinds of things. I'm going to develop my own film in a little while. I'm going to go clean animal cages. I do tissue cultures. I grow little vats of cells in dishes and change their media every day. It's kind of the worst part of being a 'mother.' Your cells and your stuff take a huge amount of focus and nurture and attention at all times. It's not anything you choose to do in your right mind."

She is an expert in the techniques of "immunofluorescent molecular tags" with all kinds of cells. She dyes certain distinct things in cells and learns what other parts of the cells they associate with. "Essentially I worked out this method wherein colored molecules basically color code different things that preexist in cells," Kedersha explains. "The trick is to visualize these components in a moving cell, in a sitting cell, in a dividing cell. And it is beautiful because the dyes glow in the dark. They are fluorescent. At a purely aesthetic level, cells are beautiful."

Her photographs reveal information critical to the study of cancer, Alzheimer's, and other diseases. She collaborates with other scientists, trains people, and gives technical advice to scientists wishing to image their own work or use her techniques for research purposes. Her images become the covers of textbooks, slides at scientific conferences, and accompany articles.

Her friends joke that if she ever lost her job, she could set up shop taking commissions from rich patrons to create cellular portraits. Asked to describe how she might go about that, she said it would depend on the personality of the subject and noted she could get really creative if the subject were dead. Blood cells, she mused, would be readily accessible in the living subject. If the person were really centered, she might isolate certain parts of the nucleus. If outgoing and energetic, she would use the mitochondria of the cell because that's where the cell's energy comes from. Asked how she might make a portrait of President Clinton, she said, "I don't want to touch that," but added she's been working with prostate cells and foreskin lately.

The Santa Barbara Museum of Art group show *Out of Sight: Imaging/Imagining Science* that included Kedersha's work also displayed *The Natural Killer Cell* (1997) by scientist Oliver Menckes; *Drosophilia Chromosomes* (1998) by artist Pamela Davis Kivelson; *Nanoscape I: Encounter in the Blood Stream* (1998), a collaborative artwork produced by artists at (Art)[n] Laboratory and scientists at Monsanto; and a video *Blood Lines* (1998) by artist Dui Seid, in which his family portrait dissolves into his DNA. In another show, using simple chemical reactions, artist Hiro Yamagata created single-cell organisms in his studio, photographed them, blew them up to mural size, and exhibited them. Many artists are using the medium of molecular biology, with its striking resemblance to abstract painting, to create art.

Specimen Art and AIDS

In the late 1980s and early 1990s, the AIDS epidemic jolted some artists out of the self-referential, art-for-art's sake milieu into the larger context of life and death. While friends were dying left and right, pretty pictures and conceptual art that only referenced other art became irrelevant. Artists began turning to the medical sciences to protest the lack of research funding and public awareness. Their works of protest are part of the Specimen Art movement.

Photographer Zoë Leonard is aware of how the AIDS crisis affected her art, which shifted from nature photographs of water and clouds to Specimen Art. "The window frame of that airplane [from which she took her cloud landscapes] came into the picture at a time when I was dealing with a lot of very tangible horror in my own life because of AIDS," Leonard says. "I was beginning to become an activist and I realized I just could not keep doing these ambiguous, beautiful pictures anymore. I was frozen for about a year, and then one season I began shooting pictures of the wax anatomical models and all the medical history work. Those anatomical models are history. They are our inheritance. I wanted to see evidence. I wanted to find the roots of these problems, the proof of these problems, start untying the knot. I was like, okay, the plane is going down to land and I'm going to start looking at this shit around me."

Late one night in 1991, friends of New York photographer Nancy Burson papered two New York neighborhoods, Soho and Chelsea, with hundreds of her eighteen- by thirty-inch posters, which would become collectors' items in the gay and art communities. The posters consist of two big cells side by side, one infected with HIV and the other not, staring out with big bold words: VISUALIZE THIS. Today the piece has taken on almost mythic proportions. Stories have it that Burson appropriated city billboards, subway advertisements, and bus placards.

"They were plastered all over the place. They were all over the city, everywhere. Everywhere you went. It just said 'VISUALIZE THIS,'" remembers Anne Pasternak with slight exaggeration. Pasternak is executive director of Creative Time, a twenty-five-year-old nonprofit arts group that commissions artists to create experimental art in the public realm. Creative Time sponsored Burson's work. Their next project, which will be public art about genetics, is being sponsored by none other than the anonymous eccentric collector/patron of Specimen Art.

For VISUALIZE THIS, Burson collaborated with scientist Kunio Nagashima, who helped her image the cells on a S-4000 scanning electron microscope, a machine the size of a room, courtesy of Hitachi Scientific Instruments in Washington, D.C. Burson tinted the infected cell blue so it would visually pop but left the uninfected cell black and white. The poster explained the cells. "The image on the right is a normal T-cell which defends the immune system from infection. The image on the left is an HIV-infected T-cell." The healthy cell resembles a perky Koosh Ball, while the unhealthy cell looks like a dog got to it and chewed off most of the rubber strings. Burson's intent was to give HIV-infected people an image of a healthy cell. With a mental picture they might be able to begin healing themselves.

Anne Pasternak explains the impact of the work. "That was a very powerful thing for an artist to put out at the time. And it also was a very hopeful message at a time when there was an incredible sort of feeling, an incredible period of darkness. There was such a hot demand for these posters. It was something that was embraced." VISUALIZE THIS had a very personal connection for people with HIV and AIDS. The poster humanized the sick. The infected differ from noninfected only by cellular structure, not by spirit, not by soul, not by thought. "How do we get to healthy cells?" this work asked, says Pasternak. "And how do we help participate in making that happen?"

The Hubbell and the Helix

In the sixteenth century a collection of natural specimens was supposed to reflect the universe, a one-of-everything kind of idea. Today the ultimate specimen, the human, reflects the universe on a cellular level. "A mammalian cell up close and a cluster of stars far away are both too small to see; magnified but with no further indication of size, they may be difficult to tell apart," wrote Harvard chemist Whitesides in 1997.

Infinity extends inward as well as outward. When a child lies in the grass and looks upward and tries to imagine the universe he or she has heard about in school, it is just too incomprehensibly vast. The idea that each one of our billions of cells—cells of hair, toenails, a swab of the inside cheek—is life itself and contains the entire blueprint of our body and can be used to create a duplicate of ourselves is equally incomprehensible. As we have looked at an outer universe with awe, we now look at our inner universe with the same kind of awe.

"At a purely aesthetic level, cells are beautiful; they look like little galaxies," said biologist Kedersha. "You've got this big blue nucleus. You've got these swirls of little cytoskeletal proteins that are little dots that halo around from the middle. My closest friend works for NASA and we always exchange photographs of things that are taken through the Hubbell [which he works on] and things I take through my microscope. And it's sometimes amazing that a galaxy will look *exactly* like a cell."

Simultaneously, the latest imaging technologies are giving us insight into the interconnectedness of all matter, just as the latest genetic technologies are teaching us humans differ little from a worm or bacteria. At the cellular level, we now know that the human differs little from the universe. "Is there an organizational continuity" to all things? Kedersha wonders. "Are the principles of gravity and blood flow parallel? Can you mentally shift focus and learn something about one from the other?"

"For a long time we've known that there are universes that exist inside of us," said Donna Cox, a scientist who images outer space on supercomputers at the University of Illinois at Champaign Urbana and was one of the main creators of Omnimax's *Cosmic Voyage*. "The infinite depth in our cellular structure, the whole construction of the atom to the electron, is all very similar to the solar system and to very large intergalactic structures. The depth of the small, some scientists believe, goes much deeper than what goes on in galactic space. We hold galaxies, we hold the infinite within us."

As we slide into the new millennium, the cosmos and our own inner universe are the visual frontiers. The connectiveness of all galaxies, as well as the connectedness of all life, is somehow reassuring.

OUTER BODY

Specimen artists are documenting people with congenital deformities just as we are entering a time when such deformities are being erased through prenatal genetic testing. As geneticists strive to perfect the human body, some specimen artists are humanizing its imperfections. And just as genetic discrimination is rearing its ugly head, specimen artists are focused on human diversity, pushing the boundaries of tolerance and prejudice in a plea to embrace difference. In their world of the odd, the "freakish," "nature's mistakes," classifications of normal and defective, beautiful and ugly, real and ideal, come into question as appropriate categories for human beings. Compassion, acceptance, respect for each individual, and an awe-inspired celebration of the uniqueness of each human being suddenly become a transcendent context in which to behold another.

Artist Nancy Burson photographed children with craniofacial

conditions (disfigurations of the skull or facial bones), others scarred by burns, and youngsters with progeria, a rare accelerated aging disease. Using a mass-produced, low-quality plastic camera called a Diana, Burson photographed children at home with their families in the late 1980s and early 1990s. Beautiful black-and-white swirling images of young children with severe deformities playing peek-a-boo, being tickled, giggling, and swinging are difficult to look at—at first. They are simply children doing what children do. On second look, the love for these children of their parents, siblings, and friends, and the joy, intelligence, and humanity of the children themselves is overwhelming.

Burson's work, which has been shown since 1992 in museums and galleries in New York, New Orleans, Houston, Miami, and at the 1995 Venice Biennale, was inspired by an experience she had in the mid-1980s at a mall. She and her husband were experimenting with new computer graphic techniques they'd developed with two other artists, and one day the four of them headed for the Staten Island Mall to offer heart-shaped valentines to shoppers. "It was Valentine's weekend so people were getting pictures of their kids. It was great fun. I was happy because I was taking pictures of kids, and we were running this technology, these color printouts with various backgrounds," she said. It was lunchtime, and her three colleagues were away when "this man wheels up his severely palsied daughter. It was really much more like a bed than a wheelchair, and his kid was laid out in this thing." He asked Burson if she would make a valentine of his teenage daughter. Nancy attempted to make her look "normal" (something she never did in her subsequent photographs of children) by combing the girl's hair, adding a decorative barrette of her own, and trying to capture an image in which this child's condition was least noticeable.

"We had a very nice picture. But what I didn't realize until I looked around was that this crowd had gathered to watch us," Burson remembers. "It so moved me that the father was just so taken with his love for his daughter, he could have cared less. He didn't care who was gawking. He didn't care about the crowds. He only wanted a photograph of his beloved daughter. For me it spoke of an unconditional love." Inspired, Burson, who already had begun working with images of deformed children, decided to create a series of photographs of children with rare congenital conditions. Soon she began contacting and getting to know families.

Weeks before Burson was to begin her photographic series, her friend Jeanne McDermott gave birth to a baby boy who had Apert's syndrome, and at the age of twenty-one days Nathaniel became Burson's first subject. Apert's syndrome is a random genetic condition affecting one child in 125,000, causing webbed fingers and toes, asymmetrical skull, and a sunken face. "My love from the beginning for Nathaniel's extraordinary face," wrote McDermott in the book *Faces*, "was linked inextricably to knowing Nancy. He is the child we wanted and love, but never expected, never imagined."

Nathaniel attended the galley opening of *Faces* along with many of the other children whose images graced the walls of the gallery. Burson, who for twenty years had been developing a computer-simulated morphing machine (now used by the FBI to track missing children), included one in the show. Gallery visitors could sit in front of a computer and, by using a simple program, morph their own face to resemble any one of six facial conditions like those of the children on the walls. One little girl climbed eagerly into the morphing station and with the help of her father began manipulating her own face, giving herself smaller, more closely set eyes, a less pronounced nose, an asymmetrical chin, a larger skull. When her face looked like the kids on the wall, she glanced around the room and smiled.

Parents of a child with craniofacial conditions sat in the station and morphed their faces to resemble their own child's, and the children morphed their faces to be "normal" like their parents.

"No one," Burson believes, "who was in the gallery on those days will ever look at deformity in the same way."

Young British artist Gillian Wearing, winner of the 1998 prestigious Turner Prize presented by the London Tate Museum, trains her camera on Londoners' urban documentary style. Wearing is interested in humanizing people on the fringe, some of whom initially might be judged as "gender confused." In a series entitled *Take Off Your Top*, Wearing was photographed with three different transsexuals in various phases of their sex change. At home, relaxed in their own beds, with Wearing beside them also modestly draped in bed sheets with her top off, they appeared happy and serene.

Artist Harriet Casdin-Silver, a pioneer in art and technology since the 1960s and a premier artist of holography, focuses on "humanizing all of the 'others.' " In 1994 she made an eight- by ten-foot hologram of a woman with breasts and a penis and a man with a vagina. The reflective holograms appear on darkened metal plates reminiscent of large-format X rays mounted vertically on the wall. Each figure is sectioned into three pieces—head and chest, midsection, and lower legs—then reassembled again. Their naked bodies glow in shades of green and brown. Nothing seems extraordinary, only beautiful. In another piece, *The Renee Wall* (1993), which uses the same materials, Casdin-Silver made a hologram of an obese hermaphrodite named Renee, whom she met while working in Belgium. "It's a big goal of mine to reach the spectator," says Casdin-Silver. "I'm trying to show that people like Renee or anybody, the mentally ill, homeless (there are so many), are human. I'm not just showing flesh or the form."

Interested in issues of beauty, strangeness, and fear, photographer Zoë Leonard was shocked and angered at the sight of a late nineteenth-century bearded woman's head left forgotten and dusty on top of a file cabinet in the corner of an obscure private museum in Paris. What was disturbing to Leonard was the decapitation, the bell jar, the pedestal, and the specimen identification card. A short post holds the head aloft from the base of the large bell jar. "Who put this woman's head in a jar and called it science?" Leonard asks. "She isn't honored. None of our recognized rituals of honoring the dead are bestowed on her. No name, no grave, no plaque, just dismemberment and obscurity."

Leonard created a show of five black-and-white photographs of the specimen titled *Preserved Head of a Bearded Woman* (1991), in which the head looks out at the viewer through the glass of the domed jar, her eyes following you as you walk past. Curiously, Leonard notes, the scientists who stuck her head in the jar failed to include the identifying feature of breasts. "This series of photographs to me," said Leonard, "is less about her, a woman with a beard, than it is about us, a society torn up over difference."

Not wanting to exploit this woman, Leonard sought out the help of Jennifer Miller, a popular performance artist who herself is a bearded woman. Leonard and Miller also collaborated on a series of photographs of Miller as a pin-up girl and issued a calendar.

Joel-Peter Witkin's subjects include pre-op transsexuals as beautiful as Frida Kahlo, and he photographs them in such classical poses as *The Graces*. Their beauty is compelling, and after a while the blending of genders seems commonplace. Witkin reinterpreted the ancient sculpture *Venus de Milo* and, by manipulating the image, he makes his living goddess also armless against the dark backdrop. His *Venus Genetrix*, whose body resembles the original sculpture almost identically, is not draped as modestly, revealing her male parts.

In addition to portraying people whose gender is ambiguous, specimen artists are presenting humans with severed or lifeless limbs, often in a classical style. In one piece Witkin placed a voluptuous nude woman with a beautiful face and Lady Godiva-like blond locks delicately upon a pedestal table. Against an enchanted forest backdrop she appears like a princess—with legs amputated at the knees. In actuality, the woman suffered more than thirty operations in her lifetime and died recently at the age of thirty-eight. Witkin was careful to pose her in such a way as to conceal scars and other deformities. In another photograph, a man with a strong nose and the body of a Greek god stands like a statue before a landscaped painting of ocean, mountains, and billowing sky. In a classic pose, he is armless, but this time not by photographic manipulation.

Witkin met one of his favorite models at an art opening at the Whitney Museum in New York in 1985. He was struck by Jackie's Armenian beauty, her lips, and her outrageous blue feathered hat. A paraplegic, she was being pushed in a wheelchair by a companion. Wanting to meet her, Witkin chose to ride in the wheelchair-accessible elevator rather than take the stairs.

Months later Jackie agreed to be photographed by Witkin, but with certain conditions. In the discussions that followed, Witkin said he "felt like an Indian negotiating with Custer." Jackie agreed to be photographed only if it were in her own apartment, if she kept on her underwear (most of Witkin's models are nude), if he shot only one role of twelve exposures, and if she had final approval of the photograph. With characteristic understatement, Witkin says he "accepts limitations" and with a friend stayed up all night preparing for the shoot. His friend painted the fine backdrop of clouds and trees, they purchased heavy, tasscled drapery, and Witkin composed the shot in his mind. The next day from behind the camera, wanting a more perfect composition, Witkin asked Jackie to cross her legs. She reminded him that she could not move her legs, and then as if she were a still-life, he posed her in front of the staged set he'd created in her bedroom, adjusted her magnificent blue hat, crossed her legs, and over the next three hours "fell in love with Jackie as a friend." With all her imposed restrictions, the result was one of his strongest images. Witkin saw her astounding beauty, not her disability.

The latest work of artist Marc Quinn, one of the famed YBAs (Young British Artists), credited along with his friend Damien Hirst with sparking the British contemporary art movement in the late 1980s and early 1990s, reflects the same interest as Witkin. But as a trained sculptor, Quinn returned to the original material of marble. "Classical Greek sculpture of the past has been crippled [by losing limbs] in a way," he says about his decision to make classic marble sculptures of disabled people. His first pieces in this series are titled *Peter Hull* and *Jamie Gillespie*. Peter Hull, a para-Olympic gold medalist in swimming, was born with no legs and with stumps for arms. Gillespie, from Manchester, England, who lost part of one leg in a motorcycle accident while in the army, now makes prosthetic limbs. Quinn made a cast of their bodies, then sculpted the marble statues. In the summer of 1999, these works were shown in the German museum Hannover Kunstverein, and they will travel on to London, Milan, and the United States. Quinn notes that humans feel no discomfort in front of ancient dismembered statues but feel very uncomfortable when meeting someone who has no legs, half an arm, or some other disability.

For specimen artists, the classifications of normal and abnormal do not exist. To them what is real is far more interesting than cultural ideals. They want to shatter old classifications. Ugliness and beauty lie in the most unexpected places. "If looking at these images makes it any easier for us to look at the real faces of nature's mistakes," says photographer Nancy Burson, "then I will have increased our awareness that the real ugliness in the world comes from within us—not outside."

Someday genetic technologies may eliminate the "abnormal" proportions of a giant or dwarf. What will happen if we eradicate the less-than-perfect human "specimens" not only from view but from life itself? Genetic technology may allow us to "perfect" an idealized human form, but the illusion of perfection will be just that, an illusion. Perfection of form addresses nothing of the spirit. To "love the human spirit in whatever ephemeral package," as Jeanne Mc-Dermott has learned so well, may be difficult in a culture without disease or diversity.

The depth of the love of a parent like McDermott or of the father of the girl with cerebral palsy allows us all to see and feel life more clearly with less concern for the "ephemeral package." McDermott writes in *Faces:* "A period of grace accompanies birth. For a fleeting and sacred whisper of time, joy swaddles a newborn so tightly that those who love the child refuse to see, or imagine, that he is anything but perfect."

THE CORPOREAL BODY

The sight of blood makes some people faint. Nursing babies in public is offensive to others. Dirty gas station bathrooms can be really repulsive. Peep-show booths gross most people out.

Humans are messy. We bleed, we excrete, we flow.

Genetic technologies emphasize the human body as information and present it as something sterile. Meanwhile, specimen artists are demanding that we see the human body as corporeal. By using their own bodily fluids as their artistic medium, like paint or clay, they twist the context of material. Fluids that many people don't like to talk about, much less look at, and consider very private are now the stuff of art. Blood, semen, milk, urine, menstrual blood—specimen artists have reduced the human body to its essential plumbing.

Something magical happens when these universal fluids are focused on: Human difference is obliterated. Andres Serrano's huge photograph of blood (solid red and flat like wallpaper) or his photograph of urine (like a first coat of yellow paint on a bathroom wall) are universally human. Nothing is left to signify race, age, gender, appearance, cultural identity, or form. Body fluid art serves as a perfect metaphor for breaking old classifications of beauty and ugliness, normal and abnormal, real and ideal, and, most profoundly, race.

Serrano, who has explored the use of bodily fluids in art more fully than any other well-known artist, rose to fame in the late 1980s when Senator Jesse Helms (R.-N.C.) discovered with disgust that a National Endowment for the Arts recipient named Serrano submerged religious icons in urine to photograph them glowing under his studio lights as if in the light of God. "When I started the bodily fluids," Serrano says, "I didn't even think of it as provocative material. . . . I did it because—'damn, the colors would look good!' "

Serrano's *Madonna and Child II* (1989) could not be more tender. Submerged in urine, shadowed like a Rembrandt, the haloed glowing faces of the Madonna and child fill the frame. Catholic Sister Wendy Beckett, a beloved art critic for the British Broadcasting Company (BBC), takes no offense at Serrano's work. "I think people were rather quick to condemn that as blasphemous," says the nun. She goes a step further, calling Serrano's religious series "comforting art." Much of the controversy surrounding his work, which has been the subject of court cases in the United States, Australia, and the Netherlands, stems more from his titles than the process: *Piss Christ, Piss Pope, Piss Satan, Piss God.* Serrano, who believes that after his death he will be accepted as a religious artist, clearly takes pleasure in juxtaposing the sacred and the profane. His photographs suggest that humans exist as bodily material and as spiritual beings simultaneously. Neither exists in a vacuum, and one does not devalue the other. Serrano succinctly describes the general public's reaction to his work. People are "seduced by the beauty, offended by the context."

For the photograph *Crucifixion* (1987), Serrano immersed a

statuette of Jesus on the cross, with an apostle on either side, in a small vat of blood. The figures fade (though not unidentifiably), into a wavering black silhouette of the simplest of shapes, an anchor, against a solid glowing red background. It is one of Serrano's most powerful images, yet little controversy surrounded it because without blood in the title, the general audience did not know that blood was used. And perhaps the association of blood with Christ is less difficult to stomach than urine.

Ron Judish, owner of a Denver gallery, exhibits Serrano's work and wonders at all the controversy. "My own view is that we give so much attention to this dime-store plastic statue of what we assume to be the deity, yet the bodily fluids essential to our very existence are considered dirty and to be avoided at all costs."

Serrano also experimented with reducing the image of blood, urine, and milk to pure color, very similar to minimalist modern paintings. Like his flat-yellow *Piss* photograph and his flat-red *Blood* photograph, Serrano highlighted the uniquely feminine fluids of milk and blood in a piece simply titled *Milk, Blood.* The five- by four-foot image was split in the middle vertically, milk (pure white) on the left, blood (pure red) on the right. In a more graphic and raw representation of menstrual blood, titled *Red River #2* (1989), Serrano photographed a close-up of one of his wife's sanitary pads and blew the image up enormously. His representation of the uniquely male fluid was more dynamic. Titled *Untitled X (Ejaculate in Trajectory)* (1989), Serrano's photograph of semen resembles a piece of luminous rope stretched across a pitch-black background, its life-force undeniable.

Flow

The total volume of blood in the human body is nine pints, and during a period of four months in 1991 British artist Marc Quinn drew, froze, and stored his own blood until he had accumulated nine pints. He then cast the likeness of his head in his frozen blood. Quinn made *Self* look nothing like a globulous mass you might expect. The slatelike surface, the exquisite detail of eyelashes, dimples, and creases create an extraordinary work of art.

"It's a happy coincidence," said Quinn, "that the volume of my head is the same as in the circulation system." Working with a refrigerator engineer, Quinn created a meticulously crafted freezer. The elegant five-foot-tall base of stainless steel is topped by a two-foot-tall clear box. In the box, the dark-red head sits on a flat wooden pedestal, putting it at a height equal to a man about six feet tall. The stainless steel base reflects only the body of whoever stands before the piece — but not the head. The viewer sees him- or herself with a blood head. "It's based on the assumption that the similarities between people are greater than the differences," said Quinn.

Quinn went on to make a series of heads. In one piece titled *Origin of the Species*, Quinn cast his head out of frozen milk, a reference to the life-giving force of mother's milk. He made a second blood head in 1996, with plans to make one every five years until he dies, using an updated cast of his aging face each time. Jay Jopling, founder of White Cube Gallery, which represents Damien Hirst and Marc Quinn says, "The *Blood Head* is a very fragile sculpture and requires quite a degree of commitment on the part of the collector. [The original *Self* is in the renowned Saatchi Collection in London.] That sculpture in a very clear way expresses the fragility between life and death; the sculptural form of *Self* (literally its sculptural life) would be nonexistent if one were to pull the plug out. A lot of people are horrified by the idea of it but . . . it is remarkably serene. The eyes are closed; the mouth slightly open. I think it's a very significant work of art." The piece is also reminiscent of cryonics, a science that has moved away from storing whole bodies to storing heads. Both the cryonic heads and Quinn's blood heads must be kept "alive" by a machine that keeps them frozen. Quinn's pieces also reference medical life support systems that keep patients alive by a machine plugged into a wall. Unplug, you die.

In 1998, over the course of nine months, Iñigo Manglano-Ovalle and two other artists collected their own body fluids (mostly urine, but also a little blood, a little semen) to create a piece called

Fountain. After collecting all this fluid and keeping them separate, explains Manglano-Ovalle, the fluids "went through a process of distillation and purification until they became distilled water with no minerals, with no other deposits. The fluids became clean, super, super clean." It was exhibited as a pristine modernist water cooler with three ten-gallon glass dispensers containing the purified body fluids and labeled Figure 1, Figure 2, and Figure 3.

Anyone was welcome to help himself to a drink. More people drank the water in Brazil than in New York, Manglano-Ovalle noted. "It was about this idea that all these fountains were the same. There was no more information left in them, literally, no information left that could source or even depict or identify one individual from another." The artists had obliterated any differences among themselves and in the process returned less seemly human fluids to pure water—the dominant fluid in the human body. (Water makes up 50 to 70 percent of the human body, depending on the health and age of the body.)

Art made with body fluids is devoid of faces and bodies. Our humanity does not depend on apparent distinctions or visible differences but rather on our shared characteristics. The universal flow of blood, urine, milk, rivers, tides. One body, one earth, one universe.

DEATH

The most powerful theme of Specimen Art is death, which is replacing sex as America's greatest taboo. The artwork shatters our sensibilities and fascinates as it repulses. Unmistakable images of death— a photograph of a decapitated corpse, a dead head on a plate, a video of suicide jumps—provoke an almost perverse joy in being alive. But these images also raise the question of why so many specimen artists are intensely focused on death. What is it that our modern culture is missing when it comes to death?

Life here on earth has become our number-one obsession. Eat right, exercise, take loads of supplements, and go to the doctor regularly for checkups and maintenance. The more importance attached to life on earth and the more paramount life becomes, the more we fear death. Death was once God's will. You lived, you died. It was your time. There was some solace that God "called her home."

We are unconsciously creating a new Faustian bargain: Give your soul to technology for more time on earth (replacing the old Faustian bargain of giving your soul to the devil for knowledge and power). Liver transplant—three years. Tubes and oxygen—three more weeks. What happens when genetic technologies promise three more *decades* of a healthy life? What's not to like?

"I think we get carried away because of our fear of death. I saw this with my own father when he died," said Anne Pasternak, director of Creative Time. "He was brave enough to say 'Enough is enough. It's not going to get better. Take me home.' All my friends who have had parents die couldn't have them at home. They had to keep their parents in the hospital because they were so afraid of death. We have such an incredible institutionalized fear of death. And medicine promises to keep us living longer. I don't know if longevity should really be the focus."

We need to become reflective consumers when it comes to our use of technology in death as in life. No matter how much technology we employ to live, we will all die. The question is, do you want to relinquish death to technology?

Specimen Art reminds us that death is a core part of the human condition. It is inevitable and necessary. Specimen artists evoke the spiritual implications of death as distinct from the scientific pursuit to prolong life and suggest that death is profoundly important to the human experience of life. Specimen artists challenge us to love death as we love life. They challenge us not to blindly surrender death to technology and thereby lose the soul, the spirit, and the connection to all of life.

To love death means to know when to accept it, not fear it; to be willing to forgo technical fixes to hold someone in your arms and love them as they die. To love death means to accept that you can't prevent the death of a friend or parent and to question if surrendering them to medical technologies and physicians who will do everything in their power to keep the person alive another day, or week, or month is the right thing to do.

Animal Death in Specimen Art

"We have a problem with death," believes artist Damien Hirst, who made a medicine cabinet as art and called it *God*. "I don't think we can handle it, which is a bit of a mistake with all the medical advances. Death is the most inevitable thing in our lives and we run away from it." Hirst went on to explain why he made the work (which sold for more than $5 million at Christie's in London in April 1998), "People believe science but they don't believe art, which to me is kind of stupid. There's a massive confidence which comes with pharmaceuticals. . . . That's what made me put the medicine cabinets in the gallery, because I remembered being in the chemist in a bad part of London and seeing all these people that looked like shit, queuing up in the pharmacy to get these pills. Everything looks clean and perfect, except the people."

Labeled "Mr. Death" by some or an "Artful Butcher" by others, Damien Hirst uses dead animals as a metaphor for human death and titles his pieces so the connections are clear. He wants to make people face their own mortality in the presence of so much dead flesh. He began his famous dead zoo formaldehyde series—whole, sawed, or quartered animals displayed in glass Smithsonian-like display boxes—just as the Natural History Museum of London began replacing old-fashioned stuffed animal dioramas with simulated computer graphics.

In 1991 Hirst suspended a fourteen-foot tiger shark in an enormous tank of formaldehyde, its jaws open, so people would feel as if it might eat them. He called it *The Physical Impossibility of Death in the Mind of Someone Living*. Hirst had placed a want ad for a tiger shark in Australia, not thinking that the shark might be killed for his art. "After that, I've never killed anything for art," Hirst said. "Everything comes dead. It's easier."

According to Hirst, Mark Chambers, who works in "a knackers' yard in Guildford" cut the cows for his piece *Some Comfort Gained from the Acceptance of the Inherent Lies in Everything* (1996). "He cuts all the hard bone areas first, like the head, the sternum, and the pelvis. Then he ties it back together, freezes it solid for over two days, and chainsaws the rest of it. Then he delivers it to us at the studio where the dirty work starts: We have to inject it constantly for around a week (before it decays) in a swimming pool–size tank of formaldehyde, wearing wet suits and masks. We have to take all the shit out of its stomach. The liquid has turned brown and we are up to our knees in it." He went on to say that "it's a complete nightmare. But it's a great relief when it gets all summed up in Plexi and back to the right place."

Twelve tall slender tanks, trimmed in thick white wood in one long line, encase Hirst's twelve cow sections of two beasts crisply sandwiched between the Plexiglas plates in no particular order, but all at the appropriate height for a cow. The tall tanks are set a couple feet apart so people can walk in and out of the cubed cow and think of dinner, as the sausagelike slabs stare back at them. They are beautiful. Hirst says cows are the most slaughtered animal in the world, and he particularly likes working with them.

When we asked him about his well-known preoccupation with death, Hirst said, "I think I'm preoccupied with life. I get kind of a humorous kick out of death, and you can say that's morbid. But why can't people face it? It's obvious that there is nothing to be worried about because it's so inevitable. I say, life and death are like black and white. It's trying to understand black when you have only been given white."

Hirst, perhaps the most famous living British artist focusing on death, has sparked disgust or dismissal among critics. His work, like Serrano's, has come under attack. In the London Serpentine Gallery in 1994, Hirst's pickled lamb called *Away from the Flock* was damaged when an enraged man poured black ink into the case. But Hirst's work actually is among the more palatable of the Specimen Art addressing death. Hirst concedes, "At the end of the day, you just want to brighten up people's walls."

Human Death in Speciman Art

The Bureau of Inverse Technology, which calls itself "a multinational corporation," is an alias under which a group of artists and scientists have collaborated for eight years. This group went straight to human death itself—to the San Francisco Golden Gate Bridge, the most popular suicide spot in America. For 100 days, a video camera was aimed at the bridge, rigged to record any vertical motion. From a considerable distance, the camera captured seventeen suicide jumps, all of which looked very much the same, like flapping black dots.

The result of their observation efforts was a video called *SUICIDEBOX*, a spoof on information collection and data comparisons that was included in the 1997 Whitney Museum Biennial. The video explains that the fall from the bridge is 240 feet, the duration of the descent only four seconds, the velocity of the hit 75 mph, and that twenty-four people have survived the jump since the bridge was opened in 1937. Hannah Reich survived the fall—twice. The San Francisco Police Department stopped counting the number of suicides on June 5, 1995, after the 997th jump, for fear they would encourage the 1,000th. As an attempt to stem the rising tide of suicides, crisis hot line phones were installed on the bridge, but to this day no one has ever used the phones. Even though 82 percent of those who jump do so facing the city from the east side of the bridge, the authorities declined a suggestion to erect a barrier because it would mar the city's most attractive feature.

Death was the chosen subject of the Bureau of Inverse Technology's investigation into the political nature of information, and the suicide video became art in a museum.

Suicide victims usually spend time in a morgue, a place where nonforensic photographers are now looking for new models. *Death by Drowning* and *Rat Poison Suicide* are two pieces in Andres Serrano's *The Morgue* series (1992). "I like to make pictures where it seems you can hear a pin drop, as if there is total silence," says Serrano. Using state-of-the-art Cibachrome color film, Serrano created a serene portrait of death. Indeed, the poignancy of death conveyed by his images almost demands silence. Zoomed-in photographs of a hand or torso maintain the dignity and privacy of the dead. There is nothing exploitative in his images. This time critics all agreed and controversy was laid to rest: "Undeniably beautiful photographs"; "Tremendous directness"; "A very aesthetically coherent, kind experience."

Serrano's photographs, crisp and minimalist, are beautifully lit body parts against a dark, flat background. In *Death by Drowning*, the most abstract of the images in *The Morgue* series, the bluish flesh looks more like a landscape than an arm. The face of the woman who died by *Rat Poison Suicide* is shrouded in a black cloth, and over her torso perch her crossed arms, slightly raised as if rigor mortis is just setting in. Her flesh, covered in tiny goosebumps, appears chilled, and you wonder why she killed herself. Saddest of all is *Fatal Meningitis*. The tiny plump feet and ankles of a baby whose socks must have just been removed, for the impressions are still clear, is tagged with a soft white ribbon and manila card tied around the ankle. From a distance it could be a ballerina pose. Serrano filled the frame of two photographs with the hands and wrists of a murder victim, *Knifed to Death*, fingers inked from fingerprinting and cut wrists bearing marks like stigmata. His images are so empathic, so unthreatening, they could be your neighbor.

"I saw Andres's morgue series about a week after my father died," Anne Pasternak told us, "and I was with my father when he died. It was very beautiful and empowering and an incredibly tough experience. Andres always deals with taboo subject matter. Never before, other than Victorian death portraits, had I seen death—death. Public death. It was shocking and unbelievable, and people couldn't talk about it. We don't look at dead bodies. It's not something that we do, you know? We have such an unhealthy approach to death."

Photographer Joel-Peter Witkin looks at death all the time. As his friend artist Nancy Burson says, "There's a guy who knows his morgues." Witkin has cultivated a relationship with morgues and hospitals around the world and has his own unique wait list. Physicians and morticians call him when they get something interesting, which isn't often because Witkin will work only with "unclaimed bodies." He also makes it clear that he works "within the code of medical ethics." He has photographed the dead human specimen more than any artist. Being able to work with cadavers in his New Mexico studio is a luxury. Usually he sets up tableaus in the morgue itself, coming prepared with props, and has doctors and technicians "breathing down his throat." Many of his shots bear the telltale sign of white tiled floors typical of morgues.

In one photograph Witkin has arranged a skull, a leg (cut off below the knee), and an arm (cut off below the elbow) in a kind of skull and crossbones still-life. He explained that in one morgue in Mexico he could choose from a vat of body parts stewing in a brown liquid "like a soup." In another photograph, titled *Feast of Fools, New Mexico* (1990), Witkin mimicked the classic still-life *Cornucopia,* but replaced the pheasant with a baby (eyes shielded) and the meats with feet and hands tangled in a mass of gourds, grapes, shrimp, and octopus. Witkin set up another traditional still-life casually using a head (the top right quarter of which had been cut away) as a vase for lilies, tulips, and nosegay. In another photograph, he created the illusion of a man's head on a plate as if being served as the only course of a sparse dinner, set upon a clothed table.

"He looked like my father," says Witkin of one of his most startling images, a headless corpse propped up in the corner of the morgue, stark naked except for black socks. He sits so casually and comfortably, big belly draped upon his thighs, soft fleshy chest, hands relaxed, it's as if he's at a bathhouse. Witkin explains how he set up the shot. "My idea was to have him sitting on a chair. Now, I know the hospital well enough to pick the chair I wanted and when we got him onto it, luckily he was still pliable. After about five minutes he was telling me he was in balance. It was like primordial communication. Had the guy not had socks on, it would have been a scene of torture. But here he was, a sedentary guy, with beautiful hands, a human being."

Witkin prides himself on the love and respect he pays every human being and every human or animal specimen he works with. He also takes pride in the fact that he himself prints every one of his photographs, which he modifies laboriously by hand on old paper stock he hunts up wherever he can. For a man who says he didn't know there was night until he was five years old, he is very comfortable with the dark. "I want to die printing," said Witkin. "There is nothing like it. I will die in the dark. I will die happy."

Specimen Art is not limited to the West. On May 5, 1999, the *Wall Street Journal's* Ian Johnson filed this story from Beijing:

Illuminated by a single bright bulb, one of China's new-wave artworks dominates a bare concrete room: A wrought-iron bed frame, supporting a mattress of ice that encases a cadaver.

Only the grayish face of the sixty-something man is visible; at his lips, whispering in his right ear, is a human fetus, stillborn at about eight months and, along with the cadaver, "borrowed" from a hospital without permission from next of kin. The work's name: "Honey."

Across the Universe

British artist Marc Quinn's conceptual death *Across the Universe* is the most poetic of all the pieces described here. His 1998 work speaks directly to our reliance on technology in death and the isolation it causes. It also offers an idea of a noble death and a oneness with the universe.

A life-size man made of ice, dressed in garb similar to that of St. Francis of Assisi, stands nobly trapped in a massive glass refrigeration box that chills a room like an open supermarket freezer. The man's gaze is upward. His body is luminescent and waxy. But the ice man's life span is only three or four months due to a "melting" technique discovered by Quinn. Anyone who stands before the sculpture breathes in his essence as it spreads out into the gallery.

The ice man was cast from a mold of Quinn's robed body. Over time his figure softens, diminishes, and ceases to exist. He is plugged into the wall through a machine, but he dies anyway. He is protected and surrounded by gleaming stainless steel and professional technology, but inevitably he will vaporize slowly into the air, his figure washing away like an old tombstone, the shape of which becomes barely recognizable.

No matter how much we rely on technology we will die. Quinn's piece is a cautionary tale: Are we acknowledging the spirit in death? Or are we bargaining with technology for time?

His death is noble. He looks to the spirit and becomes one with the universe. Dust to dust, ashes to ashes, the gallery has an empty box.

epilogue

We began this project without knowing where it would end. It started with a nagging sense, a persistent glimpse, and uncomfortable hunch that America had somehow gotten out of balance. Though all of us— John, Nana, and Douglas—are profoundly different individuals with different ages, backgrounds, careers, and lifestyles, we shared a suspicion that all was not right with the world of technology and our cultural relationship with it. The problems we explored in *HIGH TECH · high touch* are complex. Many of the subjects are horrifying. Eugenics ... DNA discrimination ... Children who kill ... For the last year as we wrote the book we ended many of our days upset, sad, and depressed—feelings that come from recognizing that our culture is overwhelmed by technology.

Having researched and written this book, we will never see the world in the same way again.

In the summer of 1998, Nana's children, ages eight, ten, and fourteen, cursed this book and, specifically, the research conducted for the Military-Nintendo Complex chapter. Suddenly their mother was a radical about media violence, policing what they could watch. They were tired of her turning off the TV in the middle of such shows as *Celebrity Death Match*, and one tearful, frustrated night they begged her to understand that it was just TV, that there was nothing wrong with it, that she was exaggerating and downright wrong. Then she took away the TV altogether.

Two months later each child admitted that life was better without the TV. Evenings passed with Lily playing the violin, Jake doing math problems, and Rory reading, and there was plenty of time to do homework and play cards. For the first time in her life, Nana sometimes lay on the couch (which got used more as a hurdle to clear than a place to sit) doing absolutely nothing. There was no rush to leave the dinner table for a certain TV program, no refrains of "I'm bored," nothing measuring the passage of an evening except one small clock out of view. The kids drifted early upstairs for bed with a book as they got tired. Once hectic and tense, home life became peaceful.

Nana saw the effects of the Technologically Intoxicated Zone even in small-town Telluride. Jake's good friend, Jesse, had a Nintendo set at home and daily played Zelda (the story of a medieval boy who must slay dragons to survive). His mother, Robin, complained one day that Jesse and his six-year-old brother fought over the game, and it was driving her crazy. Nana mentioned the Military-Nintendo Complex chapter, which Robin asked to read. She and her husband then decided to put the set and the games (over $500 worth) in storage. Within weeks, her son Jesse had stopped having persistent nightmares and stopped compulsively chewing his shirts. Robin also began plans to hold a Lion and Lamb–style violent toy trade-in and an accompanying parade through town.

For Nana, raised an agnostic, the opportunity to speak with religious leaders like Donald Shriver, John Selover, and Abdulaziz

Sachedina transformed forever her idea about God and the place religion has in people's lives. Until she met them Nana was vaguely suspicious of religion and never understood its communal purpose or its transformative power. Their goodness touched her.

Nana, who began this project a near Luddite, now sees technology as a necessary constant in human life. She no longer has a knee-jerk reaction against technology, becoming more reflective about its appropriate benefits. For years she avoided computers, not wanting to introduce one more screen she didn't like into her life. But in spring of 1999, just two years after first using a computer, she bought an iMac for its simplicity, economy, and retro design. Now she is more facile than John or Douglas, who have worked on computers for fifteen years.

Among the three of us, John began with the most faith in the positive cultural effects of technology (although he was the least technologically inclined). He is now more reflective about technology's unintended consequences. He is consciously downscaling, simplifying his life. He's trading in for a much smaller house, cutting back on an extremely hectic travel schedule, and staying in one place longer. (No more a city-a-day travel.) He's giving up the idea of a mobile phone, preferring to be on his agenda rather than on the agenda of anyone who might call. He is turning off his home phones (which are also his office phones) for long periods of time, sorting through phone messages at a time convenient to him. John realized that he could shape the way he lives in time. On the other hand, he's giving up his 1986 Mac to get a new iMac and wants to take lessons to use all the features and be more efficient in Word. He might even start answering his e-mail himself.

John's initial presentations on the subject of High Tech · high touch were punctuated with images—photographs, illustrations, film and television clips—projected from a PowerBook onto giant screens before large audiences. As he spoke, he clicked from image to image or paused to run a film short. Few people had seen anything quite like it, but something was wrong with the presentation. John slowly realized that the high-tech presentation distanced him from the audience and distracted them from his message. He dropped the dazzling display of technology and went back to the old-fashioned way: looking at his audience, talking with them, and connecting.

John spent most of 1998–99 in Telluride working with Nana and Douglas on this book. It provided him an opportunity to really get to know Nana's three children, his grandchildren, and he realized that taking pictures of them, or videotaping them was no substitute for being with them.

Douglas began *HIGH TECH • high touch* having just finished the largest and most recognized art show of his career. Entitled *(HOME)*, it was an exploration of community. It featured sixty-nine Rembrandt-like mug shots of his friends and neighborhood regulars, fifty-six teddy bears trapped in translucent amber resin, and seventy small diagrammatic photographs of Douglas as kung fu instructor. It was, without question, Specimen Art—although he certainly didn't know it at the time. In fact, all he knew was that as the show closed, he was exhausted, sick of the city, and coughing incessantly from inhaling resin fumes.

Before *HIGH TECH • high touch*, Douglas had never considered writing a nonfiction book. He had always used his sensibility and his communications skills to create art—paintings, sculptures, installations, and performances—that were, at their heart, intensely personal and occasionally esoteric. He had grown accustomed to being "the outsider." As part of the *HIGH TECH • high touch* team, he was asked to work in a group, to function as both artist and antenna, to intuit what was going on in the culture, to portray it for the team, and to interview artists and scientists all over the world. In the process, he made a powerful discovery: that he was not alone.

For Douglas, talking to artists like Vito Acconci, Damien Hirst, Nancy Burson, and Marc Quinn and scientists like Nancy Kedersha and Terry Erwin helped him tap into a global community of artists and scientists who are struggling with the same issues, working on the same ideas, heading in similar directions. Most of them, like

Douglas, were working in isolation. Today he sees himself in a larger context, as working within the "school" of Specimen Art.

With the heightened sensibility he gained during the few last years, he can now see shades of Specimen Art and the symptoms of technological intoxication in the most unlikely arenas of popular culture: The bars of amber soap with RugRats characters suspended inside are Specimen Art; every issue of Martha Stewart *Living* displaying plants and flowers perfectly classified, like insects pinned to a scientist's tray. Airport X ray machines, with their heat-sensing images, are reminiscent of Justine Cooper's MRI self-portraits.

The questions and problems we've addressed are frightening and the implications profound. The conscious and unconscious choices we are making will shape our humanity and, indeed, the future of our planet. Some people are panicked by technology, moving to Montana and stockpiling food. Others are belligerent radicals, engaging in extreme protests. We believe there are less drastic ways to seed change. The problems are difficult and the answers are not easy, but we hope this book is a beginning, a primer for change.

Appendix A
Methodology

More than thirty years ago, in 1967, John Naisbitt left high-tech IBM, where white shirts and conservative ties were mandatory, to set out on his own, starting a small company in Chicago called Urban Research Corporation. It was a company of about fifty people that typically had more women than men, more blacks than whites, and plenty of students, including his own children. It was there that John honed a process called "content analysis," which culminated in his seminal work, *Megatrends*. But it was John's work at the White House that led him to this process.

His Washington experience began when President John F. Kennedy appointed him assistant secretary of education in 1963, and in time he became a special assistant to President Lyndon Johnson during the period of "Great Society" legislation. At the ripe old age of thirty-five, John was asked to get a sense of what impact this massive legislation would have on the country. John discovered that no one knew how to evaluate the present systematically, let alone predict what changes our vast and diversified country would undergo as a result of the Great Society legislation. It was one report he couldn't deliver.

Later, while at IBM, the question still plagued him: How could you systematically monitor what was going on in the United States? In 1967 he had an epiphany at a newspaper kiosk in Chicago. A headline in the Seattle *Times* caught his eye. It was about an educational experiment being launched in the local school system. Impulsively he bought a copy and a copy of every other out-of-town newspaper in the kiosk. During the next twenty-four hours, he read more than fifty local newspapers and was stunned by what he learned about America.

Having found his methodology, he quit his job at IBM. With his last paycheck he started Urban Research Corporation. Everyone told him he was crazy, especially his wife, the mother of their five children. He was giving up a good steady income to chase after his dream and her nightmare. In the late 1960s IBM was golden, and John worked with Tom Watson, the chairman. But it was also a time American cities were burning. Martin Luther King, Jr., and Bobby Kennedy were assassinated, students were rioting. To many Americans, revolution seemed imminent. It was a terrible time. There was widespread concern about why this was happening and what would happen next. American companies as well as individuals were fearful of the unrest. John wanted to try to understand social upheaval in American cities by systematically monitoring local American newspapers.

Long before the Internet and affordable computers, Urban Research categorized, formatted, indexed, and analyzed 200 local newspapers each day, 6,000 each month using the methodology of content analysis. The company collected information about what was going on locally and looked for patterns. With daily exposure to the ebb and flow of local events in cities and towns across the United

States, the staff was able to identify and evaluate emerging new patterns. They wrote reports about what was happening in America, particularly in the cities, and sold them to companies. Soon IBM, AT&T, General Motors, and others relied on Urban Research's *Urban Crisis Monitor* and later its *Trend Report* to keep current on broad social issues, patterns, and trends. Libraries bought the company's cataloged, microfilmed articles in the form of a monthly service called *Newsbank* (which most libraries around the country still receive). Since that day at the newsstand, John has long concluded that significant change is local, bottom-up. And as cynical as many of us may be about today's reporting, nothing chronicles local change like newspapers. Urban Research Corporation's *Trend Reports* were the genesis of *Megatrends*.

In 1967, when John started Urban Research, Nana Naisbitt was only ten, but she made it clear to her father that she wanted to work. Climbing into the front seat of a '62 red Volkswagen Beetle with her dad on Saturday morning on the way to his nearby office, Nana would routinely flip through his pile of unpaid orange parking tickets in the glove compartment. John gave her a sharp pair of scissors and clear tape to trim and paste newsprint to clean white pieces of paper so they looked centered. These pages eventually became microfilm in *Newsbank*. Nana worked with her father through grade school, high school, and in her first year at the University of Chicago. Her responsibilities grew as she got older, and John used to tell his colleagues, "It will be Nana who takes over the business." That was twenty-five years ago.

Much like the original *Megatrends*, the ideas for HIGH TECH• *high touch* emerged through a comprehensive process. The process is essentially a systematic search for patterns, followed by a detailed analysis of what those patterns reveal and imply for America. Our research methods for HIGH TECH • *high touch* included elements of content analysis used in the original *Megatrends* but were expanded to include the monitoring of popular culture through television, film, the Internet, trade journals, and particularly magazines. Print is the easiest to capture, and magazines offer a rich medium to study images and content. For each chapter, hundreds of back issues of relevant publications were collected. Clear patterns emerged from the content and the advertisements—from the messages as well as the images. Among the many publications chosen for "Death, Sex, and the Body: the New Specimen Art Movement," for example, were *Art Forum, Art in America, Doubletake, Art News, Art & Antiques, New Art Examiner, Discover, Science, American Scientist, Scientific American,* and *Popular Science.*

We discovered cultural patterns through "immersive" installations created by coauthor Douglas Philips, a business partner in the Nana & Doug Corporation and an artist who has been interpreting popular culture through art installations and exhibitions for more than ten years. As each chapter developed, the office filled with hundreds of images clustered in patterns on eight- by four-foot movable panels, revealing trends that served as the principal springboard for chapter concepts and the six symptoms of a Technologically Intoxicated Zone. Douglas brought art and an artist's visceral sensibility to the project and consistently generated conceptual breakthroughs. We came to think of him as the project's "antenna" for sensing cultural tremors.

Three research assistants, Allison Johnson, Kelly Hearn, and Joy Van Elderen, cast a wide secondary research net for each chapter. With this secondary and popular culture research as a basis, the team of authors and researchers held marathon sessions to capture and identify cultural patterns. From there additional targeted research of books, articles, the Internet, and trade magazines were conducted.

Once the chapter framework was developed, the next critical phase of the research began. We conducted scores of extensive interviews with experts: General Norman Schwarzkopf, documentary film director Ken Burns, bioethicist Arthur Caplan, entrepreneur and scientist Michael West, and artist Damien Hirst, to name a few.* (In the back of this book you'll find biographies of the community

---

* Any quotes not sourced in the endnotes come from interviews with the authors.

of individuals who shared their thoughts with us.) Red flags, jarring ideas, and recurrent themes bubbled up from the interviews, which again revealed patterns from which we drew hypotheses. For "Galileo→Darwin→DNA," for instance, we interviewed some of America's leading scientists, bioethicists, and theologians. Repeated references to Darwin and Galileo gave us pause. What was the significance of this pattern? It became clear that radical new developments in genetics were as discordant with religious thought as a heliocentric universe and the theory of evolution. Theologians and scientists alike also made repeated comparisons to the atomic bomb. Again, we wondered at this comparison, and we began to realize the power these technologies held in reality and in the minds of man. In the formation of "The New Specimen Art Movement," numerous unexpected references to the universe, death, and to AIDS could not be ignored. The interviews consistently sparked breakthroughs and further honed the structure of each chapter.

The research methods came after a long period of frustration. In 1997, when Douglas overheard two young art students in a bohemian coffeeshop in Chicago discussing the relevance of "this idea of High Tech • high touch in this book *Megatrends*," the seed of the present book was planted. John agreed to embark on a project with Nana and Douglas, but creating a means by which three people could write a book together was not easy. For more than two years John personally monitored a dozen daily newspapers and other publications, creating his own specialized *Newsbank* of High Tech • high touch. Part of his daily ritual always has been the creation of notebooks that evolve into a vision of his published books. John made fifty-five notebooks, each 160 pages, 8,800 pages total, for *HIGH TECH • high touch*. His books are personal and purposely serendipitous and consequently not easily shareable with coauthors. He collected anything in print that seemed to be a manifestation of High Tech • high touch and FedExed thousands of articles to Nana and Douglas in Chicago to read and analyze. Meanwhile, Nana and Douglas collected videos, images, books, advertisements, studied television and radio, and noted anything that they felt was an example of High Tech • high touch. But just as in the days of Urban

Research, when John and his team of researchers created ten relevant categories into which they organized an unprecedented number of articles, it was necessary to create a relevant structure for the beginning stages of this work.

Nana, writer, artist, entrepreneur, and mother, played a critically important role in the formation of the structure. She also knew that John's books could no longer be strictly informational. Information comes too easily, too fast, and too frequently today for most of us to desire any more of it. In an effort to discover a structure, Nana asked the initial question: What does it mean to be human? In a society that is no longer a survival economy, we as Americans have the luxury of thinking beyond food, clothing, and shelter. We celebrate our humanity through play, religion, art, story, music, dance, and the appreciation of time and nature. The next essential question was: What is technology? The authors came to understand technology in its various aspects—information technology, manufacturing technology, life sciences technology, consumer technology, engineering technology, science technology, space technology, and war technology.

In a room above Nana's garage in Chicago, the three shuffled, tacked, and retacked these high-touch and high-tech words to unfinished walls as they tried to make sense of High Tech · high touch. A structure began to reveal itself: There was a natural consilience between high touch and high tech. No longer are high-touch activities simply a balance to the high technology in our lives. High touch is becoming the human lens by which we must understand technology. We came to realize that consumer technologies could best be understood through the human lens of play and time and that genetic technologies could best be understood through the human lens of religion and art.

In the spring of 1998, it became apparent that we authors had to work in the same location. Nana, her three children, and Douglas moved to Telluride, Colorado, to work with John in his home office (a converted living room). Nana rented an old house one block south from John and Douglas rented an old miner's cabin a block to the west, forming a triangle that would represent their collaboration.

HIGH TECH · high touch indeed became a collaborative effort, although it was Nana who wrote the lion's share of the words. After countless passionate discussions (a.k.a. revisions), John, Douglas, and Nana collectively created the ideas, concepts, outlines, and conclusions of each chapter. What's the story? What's the message? What's the sequence? became the mantra of the team.

Some days the team also included Nana's children. Rory Sullivan, fourteen, came to the office daily for home schooling. When deadlines neared, Rory willingly dropped his schoolwork to research, read the manuscript, or simply help with copying and running errands. Rory, Lily, ten, and Jake, eight, shared their impressions of Douglas's installations in the early stages of the writing, and their ideas are sprinkled throughout this book. And although they got sick of the project ("Don't you ever talk about anything other than the book?"), they regularly added their ideas about media violence, designer babies, and Specimen Art. The local school in Telluride heard about the "immersive spaces" and requested class visits to the office. Groups of twenty to thirty children, from third grade through high school, came to John's home office to add their interpretation of the visual patterns. The kids took an immediate interest. The discussions were charged, serious, and lively. Their contributions are also sprinkled throughout the text.

In their research, the importance of multiple generations working together became viscerally apparent. With the shift from an agricultural society to an industrial society, work was removed from America's homes and families. Today, however, information technologies are increasingly bringing work and home back together again and present an opportunity to work with our children, albeit in a very different way. The presence of children can mean interruptions, distractions, demands, silliness, and wonder at their fresh way of looking at the world. We have drawn together four generations in the creation of this book, and our lives were immeasurably enriched in the process.

JOHN NAISBITT
NANA NAISBITT
DOUGLAS PHILIPS

Appendix B
profiles of
interviewees

ACCONCI, VITO. Acconci was born in 1940 in the Bronx, New York, and
graduated from Holy Cross in 1962 with a degree in literature. As a
premier artist, Acconci has held scores of solo and international
group exhibitions, including those at the Barbara Gladstone Gallery
in New York, the Klosterfelde Gallery in Berlin, and the James
Corcoran Gallery in Los Angeles. Acconci has produced almost
thirty works of public art in locations from New York and Japan to
Colorado and the Netherlands. Acconci has received several awards,
including four National Endowment for the Arts fellowships, a
John Simon Guggenheim Memorial Foundation Fellowship, and
an American Academy in Rome Collaborations Grant and since
1968 has taught at various universities, including Yale University
and the School of Visual Arts in New York. He can be reached

through the Barbara Gladstone Gallery at www.gladstonegallery.com or (212) 206-9300.

ALEXANDER, MELISSA. Alexander works at the Exploratorium, San Francisco's Museum of Science, Art and Human Perception. She joined the Exploratorium in 1989 and was appointed manager of public programs in 1997. Alexander runs the Artist-in-Residence Program, coordinating the Exploratorium's Osher Fellowship Program for visiting scholars and artists, and the Exhibit Development Staff Training Project, a program that brought thirty-six exhibit developers from national and international science centers to work with the Exploratorium's artists and scientists over a two-year period. She is currently project director for "Revealing Ourselves," an exhibition scheduled to open in March of 2000, which examines the social and cultural implications of medical and scientific representations of the human body. She can be reached through the Exploratorium at (415) 561-0324.

BOOKCHIN, NATALIE. Bookchin is an artist working in new and old media. She currently lives in Los Angeles, where she is a member of the faculty in the School of Art and the Graduate Department of Integrated Media at the California Institute of the Arts. She does not have her own domain but can often be found squatting on others. She exhibits her work and lectures widely in the States, in Europe, and in cyberspace. Her work has been written about in such publications as *ArtForum* and the *New York Times*. Her most recent project is a computer game based on a short story by Jorge Luis Borges entitled "The Intruder" that can be found at http://calarts.edu/~bookchin/intruder.

BRANDT, BARBARA. Brandt is the author of *Whole Life Economics: Revaluing Your Daily Life* and is a longtime social activist from the Boston area. Since 1989 she has worked as a staff person for the Shorter Work-Time Group, which challenges our workaholic culture and proposes shorter work-hour policies in the workplace and through government legislation. For more information, contact the Shorter Work-Time Group at (617) 628-5558 or visit their website at www.swt.org.

BREED, ANN. Breed is currently the head of the lower school at Francis W. Parker School in Chicago. Prior to this, she taught for twenty-three years—thirteen of them in kindergarten. She is an avid reader, cook, and gardener whose passion always has been children, their growth and development, and music. She can be reached at the Francis W. Parker School at (773) 549-0172.

BUBENDORFER, THOMAS. Bubendorfer is one of the dominating personalities of alpine solo climbing. In 1983 at the age of twenty-one, he set a yet-to-be-broken record climb on the Eiger North Face in Switzerland, the most difficult face in the Alps. Bubendorfer has authored four bestselling books in Germany, including *The Quality of the Next Step* and *Conquest of the Invisible*. He gives speeches at companies ranging from IBM and Mercedes to Lufthansa and Swissair, and he is a well-known media personality in Europe. Bubendorfer, who speaks four languages, lives in Monte Carlo, Monaco. He can be reached by email at: th.bub@mcn.mc.

BURNS, KEN. Burns was born in Brooklyn, New York, in 1953 and has been making documentary films for more than twenty years. He has produced and directed many award-winning films. His latest works have included the highly praised 1998 film *Frank Lloyd Wright*, 1997's *Lewis and Clark: The Journey of the Corps of Discovery*, and the public television eighteen-and-a-half-hour series *Baseball*, which Burns directed, produced, cowrote, and for which he served as chief cinematographer, music director, and executive producer. His series *The Civil War* has been honored with more than forty major film and television awards, including two Emmy Awards and two Grammy Awards. His next film, which is a continuation of his film *Thomas Jefferson*, will air in the fall of 1999 and is called *Not for Ourselves Alone: The Story of Elizabeth Cady Stanton and Susan B. Anthony*. Burns currently resides in Walpole, New Hampshire.

BURSON, NANCY. Burson is best known for her contribution to computer technology, which resulted in face compositing and "morphing" techniques that have enabled law enforcement officials to age missing children and adults. She has been making pictures of faces for twenty years, and her earliest computer-generated images of children were published in *COMPOSITES* in 1986. Her later black-and-white images were featured in *Faces* in 1993. In 1995 and 1996 the images she produced were portraits of individuals who have dramatic facial anomalies resulting from genetic disorders, burns, or cancer. These are Burson's intimates as well as her heroes, for they have overcome the challenge of self-acceptance. She can be contacted through the Jan Kesner Gallery in Los Angeles at (323) 938-6834.

CAPLAN, ARTHUR LEONARD. Dr. Caplan is director of the Center for Bioethics and the Trustee Professor of Bioethics at the University of Pennsylvania. He also is a professor of molecular and cellular engineering, professor of philosophy, and chief of the Division of Bioethics at the University of Pennsylvania Medical Center. As the preeminent expert on bioethics, Caplan has written more than 400 articles and reviews in professional journals and published nine books on the subject in this decade alone. Caplan has lectured widely in the United States and is a frequent commentator in the media as well. He is the chairman on the Advisory Committee to the Department of Health and Human Services, Centers for Disease Control, and Food and Drug Administration on Blood Safety and Availability. He can be contacted through the University of Pennsylvania at (215) 898-7136 or through his website at www.med.upenn.edu/bioethic.

CASDIN-SILVER, HARRIET. Casdin-Silver is America's foremost art holographer and a pioneer of the art-and-technology movement of the second half of the twentieth century. Her career in the visual arts began in the 1960s after having worked in theater, radio, and television, and her works have been exhibited internationally in such venues as the Brooklyn Museum of Art, the Royal College of Art in London, and the University of Ghent in Belgium. She has had more than eighteen solo exhibitions and contributed to more than sixty-five group exhibits. She has either published or been featured in a variety of publications and books, including *Holosphere 15* and *The New York*

Observer. Casdin-Silver was educated at the University of Vermont, Columbia University, and the Cambridge-Goddard Graduate School. Her posts have ranged from assistant professor of physics at Brown University to artist in residence at the Academy of Sciences in the Ukraine. She has received several awards, including the Lifetime Achievement Award from the International Symposium of the Art of Holography and two Rockefeller Foundation Fellowships. Casdin-Silver can be reached through the Gallery NANA Fine Art, Inc., at (617) 267-9060.

CONKELTON, SHERYL. Conkelton is the senior curator at the Henry Art Gallery at the University of Washington in Seattle. She holds an M.A. in the History of Art from Rutgers University and has received several awards, including three National Endowment for the Arts fellowships, travel grants from the Ministry of Foreign Affairs in France, and the Peter Norton Family Foundation Curator's Grant. Prior to working for the Henry Art Gallery, Conkelton was the associate curator in the photography department at the Museum of Modern Art. Conkelton has organized seventeen exhibits, including the 1999 *Coming to Life: The Figure in American Art, 1955–1965* at the Henry Art Gallery in New York. She has lectured at the University of California and California State University and has contributed to or written seven publications, including "The Deceptive Play of the Individual, or, In the Archive," which appeared in *Deep Storage, Arsenal of Memory.* She can be reached through the Henry Art Gallery at (206) 543-2281.

COSCI, GIANLUCA. Cosci was born in Sant 'Elpidio a Mare, in the province of Ascoli Piceno, Italy, in 1970. Since 1989 Cosci has lived in Bologna, where he attended the University of Bologna's Academy of Fine Arts for painting under Professor Concetto Pozzati. In 1990 he contributed to the Gaya Mater Studiorum foundation, a homosexual student collective at the University of Bologna. In 1993 he was selected for the Erasmus Exchange Project in Rotterdam for a period of three months. He obtained his degree in the Fine Arts at the Academy in 1994 with a thesis on Eva Marisaldi. In 1996 he was invited by a foreign museum to participate in an international exhibition *Prospect '96*, at the Frankfurter Kunstverein. In 1997 he presented his work in a conference at the Fine Arts Academy in Turin. In the same year he participated in the series of conferences called "Come spiegare a mia madre che cio che faccio serve a qualchecosa" (or How to explain to your mother that what you are doing is of some use), care of the Link Project in Bologna. In 1998 he was hired by the Higher Institute for Fine Arts—Flanders in Anvers as an external tutor of painting. His e-mail is NOL3040@iperbole. bologna.it.

COX, DONNA. Cox has authored many papers and monographs on computer graphics, information design, education, and scientific visualization. In 1987 she developed the concept of "Renaissance Teams" and has given more than 100 invited presentations of her academic research. They include keynote addresses in Australia, Finland, Japan, and Austria for institutions such as MIT, Princeton, and Kodak. Her work has been reviewed, published, or cited in more than 100 publications, including the *New York Times* and *National Geographic*, and she has appeared on international television, including CNN and *NBC Nightly News*. Cox was the associate producer for scientific visualization and art director of the IMAX film *Cosmic Voyage*, which was nominated for an Academy Award in 1997. She also was appointed to the National Research Council, Committee on Modeling and Simulation: Opportunities for Collaboration Between the Defense and Entertainment Research Communities. Currently she is serving as an elected council member on the University Corporation for Advanced Internet Development Strategic Council, Internet 2 Commission.

DEMERS, JOHN. New Orleans native John DeMers is the author of seventeen published books, most about food and wine, and the globetrotting former food editor of United Press International. After eating his way through more than ninety countries, he's almost surprised to find himself back home in New Orleans. He appears each week discussing food on the WYES-TV's *Steppin' Out* and also serves as food editor of *New Orleans Magazine*. He also is editor and publisher of *EasyFood*, a local food and wine magazine and host of *The Bayou Food Show* each Saturday morning on WBYU.

DILCHER, DAVID. Dr. Dilcher was raised in Minnesota and received his Ph.D. from Yale University, where he focused on the leaves of flowering plants preserved in clay and the fungi that lived on these leaves. He completed a postdoctoral National Science Foundation fellowship in Germany and then went on to teach at Indiana University for twenty-four years. For the past nine years Dilcher has been at the Florida Museum of Natural History and is a graduate research professor with the University of Florida. Much of Dilcher's research has centered on the search to find the world's first flower. He has found many fossil flowers, fruits, seeds, and plants in digs that have taken him from Kansas and Nebraska to foreign countries, including Chile, New Zealand, China, and England. Dr. Dilcher has published nearly 150 papers on his research and written or edited six books. He has received two Guggenheim Fellowships among various awards, is a member of the National Academy of Sciences, and serves as a board member of the Smithsonian National Museum of Natural History and the National Science Foundation. He can be reached by phone at (352) 392-6560 or by e-mail at dilcher@flmnh.ufl.edu.

DION, MARK. Dion was born in New Bedford, Massachusetts, and graduated from the School of Visual Arts in New York. Dion has exhibited his work solo and in groups for many international venues, including the American Fine Arts Museum in Soho, New York, the Museum of Modern Art in New York City, and the Galleria Emi Fontana in Milan, Italy. His works also have appeared in various catalogs ranging from the Weatherspoon Art Gallery in North Carolina to the Nordic Pavillion for the Venice Biennial. He has produced several books and articles, including *Concrete Jungle* and *Mark Dion (Contemporary Artists)*. He currently works and lives in Pennsylvania and can be reached through the American Fine Arts Company at (212) 941-0401.

DOERFLINGER, RICHARD M. Doerflinger is associate director for policy development at the Secretariat for Pro-Life Activities, National Conference of Catholic Bishops, where he has worked for over eighteen years, and adjunct fellow in bioethics and public policy at the National Catholic Bioethics Center. He has presented testimony on human embryo research before Congress, National Institutes of Health advisory groups, and the National Bioethics Advisory Commission. Since 1991 Mr. Doerflinger has edited the monthly newsletter *Life at Risk: A Chronicle of Euthanasia Trends in America* and has coordinated efforts against physician-assisted suicide for the bishops' conference. He has also published widely on this and other issues. He holds B.A. and M.A. degrees in Divinity from the University of Chicago and has conducted doctoral studies in theology at the Catholic University of America. He can be reached at (202) 541-3070.

EAGEN, JOHN. Dr. Eagen has been senior pastor of Regional Grace Church in Edina, Minnesota, since 1987 and is the founder of Home Inspirational Studies Ministries, an evangelical Bible study ministry. Before coming to Grace Church, Dr. Eagen served as president of Crown College. He holds a Ph.D. in education from Texas Tech University and has addressed audiences throughout North America and around the world. He has authored or edited several publications, including *The Pulpit Series* and *The Bible College in American Higher Education*. Dr. Eagen is a member of the Phi Kappa Phi National Honor Society, and he serves as a board member or advisor to various civic, religious, and legislative organizations, such as the Board of Reference for the Association of Church Missions Committees. He can be reached at (612) 926-1884 or through the church website at gracechurch-mn.org.

EWING, WILLIAM A. Ewing is director of the Musée de L'Elysée in Lausanne, Switzerland, and is a recognized authority in the field of photography. He has published seven books including the 1996 *Inside Information: Imaging the Human Body* and the 1991 *Flora Photographica: Masterpieces of Photography from 1835 to the Present*. His exhibitions have been shown in numerous international venues including the Museum of Modern Art in New York, the Centre Pompidou in Paris, the National Museum of American Art in Washington, D.C., and the Palazzo Fortuny in Venice. He can be reached in Lausanne at (011) 41-21-617-0786.

ERWIN, TERRY. Dr. Erwin is a research entomologist and curator in the Department of Entomology at the Smithsonian Institution in Washington, D.C. He received his Ph.D. in entomology at the University of Alberta in Canada and finished postdoctorals at Harvard University and the Lund University of Sweden. His interests and areas of expertise range from biodiversity to biogeography and conservation biology, and he has spoken internationally on these subjects. Erwin also has received numerous grants to pursue his work from organizations such as BIOLAT, NLRP, and INBio, from which he received a 1998 grant for $250,000 to inventory Costa Rican beetles. Erwin is a fellow of the California Academy of Sciences in San Francisco and the Museum of Comparative Zoology at Harvard and is on the editorial board of *Neotropical Fauna and Environment* and *Biodiversity and Conservation*. He can be reached via e-mail at erwin.terry@nmnh.si.edu or by phone at (202) 357-2209.

FAUST, DOUG. Faust is currently the publisher of *PlayStation Magazine (PSM)*, which has a monthly readership of 250,000 and is the fastest-growing magazine in the history of the video games industry. Faust entered the games industry in 1993 as an independent advertising sales representative for GP Publications and then moved on to *Electronic Gaming Monthly (EGM)*. In 1994 he moved to Imagine Publishing where he helped launch the magazine *Next Generation*. Faust is thirty-nine years old and considers himself "one of the older ones" in the business. He can be reached at Imagine Media or through their website at www.imaginemedia.com.

FITZGERALD, KEVIN T. Dr. Fitzgerald is a Jesuit priest and a research associate in hematology/oncology and in medical humanities at the Loyola University Medical Center in Chicago. He received a Ph.D. in molecular genetics from Georgetown University and is currently completing a doctorate in bioethics at Georgetown. His principal research areas at Loyola are the investigation of abnormal gene regulation in leukemia and research on ethical issues in human genetics. He can be reached at kfitzge@luc.edu.

FRANKEL, FELICE. Felice Frankel is artist in residence in science and technology and research scientist at MIT. Working in collaboration with scientists, Frankel creates images for journal submissions and publications for general audiences. Her most extensive collaboration, *On the Surface of Things, Images of the Extraordinary in Science*, with George M. Whitesides, is now in its second printing. The book has received rave reviews in diverse publications ranging from *The New Yorker*, to *Wired*, to *Scientific American*, and Frankel's work has been broadly profiled in the media, including on NPR's *All Things Considered* and in *The Christian Science Monitor*. Frankel has received numerous grants, including those from the Guggenheim Foundation, the National Science Foundation, the National Endowment for the Arts, and the Graham Foundation for Advanced Studies in the Fine Arts. She was a Loeb Fellow at Harvard University. She can be reached by phone at (617) 253-5604, through her website at web.mit.edu/edgerton/felice/felice.html or via e-mail at felicef@MIT.EDU.

GERSTEIN, DAN. Mr. Gerstein has worked for Senator Joseph Lieberman since 1994 and he currently serves as the legislative/press assistant. His main areas of expertise are the media influences on society and children, and he was involved in writing the V-Chip law. Prior to working for Senator Lieberman, Gerstein held positions as the communications director to Congressman Gerald Kleeczka and as a staff writer for *The Hartford Courant*. In 1989, he graduated *cum laude* from Harvard University with a B.A. in history and a specialization in American politics. He can be reached at (202) 224-4041.

GOOKIN, KIRBY. Gookin is an art historian, critic, curator, and public artist. He received his B.A., M.A., and M.Phil. degrees in art history at Columbia University. He is a staff critic for *Artforum* magazine and also has written articles and reviews on twentieth-century art for *Artscribe* and *Arts* magazine as well as for gallery and museum publications. He has produced public art projects in association with Expo '92 in Seville, Spain, and is currently developing a public art project for Frederick Douglas Circle in New York City. Gookin is on the Board of Directors of White Columns and teaches Critical Studies in the Department of Art at New York University. He recently curated an exhibition with Robin Kahn titled *Disappearing Act* at Bound and Unbound and Leslie Tonkonow Art + Projects in New York. He is preparing a book on the parallels between nineteenth-century aesthetics and the advent of modern genetic science tentatively titled *The Idealized Human Body: Francis Galton and The Aesthetic Foundations of Genetics*, to be published by G+B Arts International in early 2000. He can be reached through the Critical Studies Department at New York University.

GREENBERG, IRVING. Rabbi Irving (Yitz) Greenberg is the President of the Jewish Life Network, a Judy and Michael Steinhardt Foundation. An ordained Orthodox rabbi and scholar with a Harvard Ph.D., Rabbi Greenberg has been a seminal thinker in confronting the Holocaust as an historical transforming event and Israel as the Jewish assumption of power and the beginning of a third era in Jewish history. Greenberg has published numerous articles and monographs on Jewish thought and religion, and several books including his newest, *Living in the Image of God: Jewish Teachings to Perfect the World*. He sits on several scholarly boards, including the Religious and Theological Sub-Committee for the International Council of Christians and Jews, and is a member of many religious committees and professional organizations, such as the American Academy of Religion. Greenberg served for many years as the founding president of the National Jewish Center for Learning and Leadership, and before that he was a professor at Yeshiva University and City University of New York.

GROSSMAN, DAVID. An internationally recognized scholar, author, soldier, and speaker, Lieutenant Colonel Grossman is a retired Airborn Ranger Infantry Officer and prior sergeant and paratrooper with more than twenty-three years experience of leadership in the military. Grossman, who is a West Point professor of psychology, is one of the foremost experts in the field of human aggression, the roots of violence, and violent crime and has developed a new field of scientific endeavor called "Killology." Author of *On Killing: The Psychological Cost of Learning to Kill in War and Society*, Grossman has testified before the U.S. Congress on such subjects and served as an expert witness or consultant in such cases as *United States v. McVeigh*. He has been widely featured in the print and television media. Grossman's latest book is his 1999 release called *Stop Teaching Our Kids to Kill: A Call to Action Against TV, Movie, and Video Game Violence*. He can be reached at LtColDave@aol.com or at (870) 931-5172.

HAYEK, NICHOLAS G. Hayek is the cofounder, chairman of the board of directors, and Chief Executive Officer of the Swatch Group. The strategies he developed in the early 1980s led to the success of the entire Swiss watch industry and helped it to regain its leading position worldwide, which it has maintained since 1984. He holds two honorary degrees from the University of Bologna and the University of Switzerland and was appointed by German Chancellor Helmut Kohl to the Council for Research, Technology, and Innovation in 1995. Hayek also is founder, chairman of the board, and CEO of Hayek Engineering, which undertakes projects in engineering, project-management, and consulting, among other opportunities. He can be reached at (201) 271-1400 or through www.swatch.com.

HEALY, JANE. Dr. Healy has been an educational psychologist and professional educator for more than thirty-five years. A graduate of Smith College, Healy received her Ph.D. in educational psychology from Case Western Reserve University. Her educational experiences have included working as a classroom teacher, college professor, reading and learning specialist, and elementary school administrator. Healy has authored three books, including the award-winning *Endangered Minds: Why Children Don't Think—and What We Can Do About It*, and her most recent book *Failure to Connect: How Computers Affect Our Children's Minds—For Better or Worse*. She is a frequent guest on NPR's *Parent's Journal* and has been twice named "Educator of the Year" by Delta Kappa Gamma. Healey lectures and consults to public and private schools and parent groups and lives in Vail, Colorado.

HIRST, DAMIEN. Hirst was born in Bristol, England, in 1965. He attended Goldsmith's College of London and then curated a series of exhibitions of work by his contemporaries that culminated in the highly acclaimed FREEZE exhibition in 1988, which helped to reignite the British Contemporary Art scene. Museums and galleries around the world have since exhibited and collected his paintings, sculptures, and installations. In 1994 Hirst received the DAAD fellowship of Berlin, and in 1995 he won the Tate Gallery's prestigious Turner Prize. In 1997 he published a landmark book of his work to date, entitled *I Want to Spend the Rest of My Life Everywhere, with Everyone. One to One. Always. Forever. Now.* His renowned Pharmacy Restaurant & Bar, which opened in London in 1998, was designed and conceived by the artist as a functioning artwork. Currently he is working with Larry Gagosian on his biggest show to date, scheduled to take place in Los Angeles and New York City in the autumn of 1999. Hirst can be reached through Science Ltd. at (011) 44-171-637-3994.

JENTZSCH, HEBER C. The Reverend Jentzsch has been president of the Church of Scientology International since 1982 and an active, ordained minister of the church for more than twenty years. He is the leading spokesperson for the Church of Scientology International and has been featured widely both in the press and on television shows, including *Larry King Live* and *60 Minutes*. The Reverend Jentzsch has lectured on Scientology internationally and is a member of the Executive Board of the American Conference on Religious Movements. He received his education at Weber State University in Utah and was schooled in various Eastern faiths at the University of Utah. In 1986 he received an honorary degree from St. Martin's College and Seminary for his work to end drug abuse among young people and expose psychiatric abuses among minorities. In Los Angeles he worked closely with other religious leaders including The Gathering, a coalition of 350 ministers committed to civil and human rights issues and to the resolution of drug abuse and illiteracy. He can be reached at (323) 960-3500, through the website www.scientology.org, or via e-mail at PresCSI@scientology.org.

JEREMIJENKO, NATALIE. Jeremijenko, 1999 Rockefeller Fellow, is a design engineer and internationally renowned technoartist. Her work includes digital, electromechanical, and interactive systems in addition to biotechnological works that have recently been included in the Whitney Biennial '97, Documenta '97, and the Arts Electronic prix '96. Jeremijenko has presented at the Museum of Modern Art in New York and at the Media Lab of the Massachusetts Institute of Technology and has a forthcoming retrospective at the Museum of Contemporary Art in Australia. While working toward her Ph.D. in design engineering at Stanford, Jeremijenko also teaches engineering in the Yale Design Studio. She has worked in research positions including several years at Xerox PARC in the computer science lab and in the Advanced Computer Graphics Lab and has been faculty in digital media and computer art at the School of Visual Arts, New York, and the San Francisco Art Institute. She is known to work for the Bureau of Inverse Technology.

JOHNSON, RANDY. Johnson is the editor of United Airlines' award-winning *Hemispheres* magazine. Prior to working for *Hemispheres*, he conducted backcountry research for the U.S. Forest Service and the Appalachian Mountain Club. He also has written and spoken widely on trail management and use fees. His articles and photos on travel, skiing, and environmental topics have appeared in numerous publications, including the *Boston Globe*, *Backpacker*, and the *Atlanta Journal-Constitution*. Johnson is a member of the Society of American Travel Writers and the North American Ski Journalists Association and a winner of a North Carolina Press Association Award. More information on *Hemispheres* can be found at www.hemispheresmagazine.com.

JOHNSON, ROGER N. Dr. Johnson, who received his Ph.D. from the University of Connecticut, has been a professor of psychology at

Ramapo College in New Jersey for almost thirty years. He serves on the executive council of the International Society for Research on Aggression, where he is editor of the North American ISRA bulletin. Dr. Johnson has published and presented many academic articles and papers on topics ranging from higher education, to nuclear war, to television news coverage. He has published a book, *Aggression in Man and Animals,* and serves as an editorial reviewer and consultant for several academic journals and publishers. Dr. Johnson's honors and grants include a Senior Fulbright-Hays Fellowship, a H.K. Guggenheim Foundation Grant, and three research grants from the National Institute of Mental Health. He can be reached through www.israsociety.com or at (201) 529-7755.

KATZ, WARREN. In 1990 Katz cofounded MÄK Technologies, the world's leading supplier of simulation networking software to the defense and commercial communities. Currently Katz serves as chief operating officer, where one of his areas of expertise involves the collaboration between the defense and video game industries in the 3-D real-time simulation area. He has authored articles and lectured on the subject and pioneered the first "dual-use" video games between a commercial company and the Department of Defense. Prior to founding MÄK Technologies, Katz worked for Bolt, Beranek and Newman on the SIMNET project. He holds dual B.A.'s in mechanical and electrical engineering from MIT. More information on MÄK Technologies is available online at www.mak.com.

KEDERSHA, NANCY. Dr. Kedersha was born in New Jersey and meandered into a highly illustrated (not to mention illustrious) career in science. She obtained her Ph.D. from Rutgers University in 1983 and then spent five years at UCLA in the laboratory of Dr. Leonard Rome. During that time she discovered vaults, mysterious new cellular organelles found in organisms as divergent as humans and slime molds, but whose function is still unknown They are currently the subject of active research in several labs. She perfected a technique of staining and photographing cells in order to reveal their inner structures and organization, which began her collection of "bio art" images. Subsequently she worked for ImmunoGen, Inc., a small biotech company in Cambridge, Massachusetts, where her studies of many different types of cancer cells greatly expanded her collection. These images have been seen in *Discover, Time, Newsweek*, and *Le Figaro* as well as in many textbooks and museum exhibits. She is currently a member of the Harvard Medical School faculty at the Brigham and Women's Hospital.

KEENAN, JAMES F. Father Keenan is a professor of moral theology at the Weston Jesuit School of Theology in Cambridge, Massachusetts. He was educated at the Gregorian University in Rome (S.T.D.), the Weston Jesuit School of Theology (M.Div.), and Fordam University (B.A.) in the Bronx, New York. He has published, edited, or been featured in several books, including his 1999's *Commandments of Compassion* and 1996's *Virtues for Ordinary Christians*. He has published academic articles and essays in journals such as *The International Philosophical Quarterly* and the *Catholic Medical Quarterly* and has received several awards and grants, including a fellowship from the Institute for Advanced Studies in the Humanities and the Center of Theological Inquiry. His professional services include acting as consultant to the New York State Transplant Council and chair of the Catholic Theological Coalition on HIV/AIDS. His interests range from casuistry and virtue ethics to Aquinas, the history of moral theology and bioethics. He can be reached through the Weston Jesuit School of Theology at (617) 492-1960 or by e-mail at jfkweston@aol.com.

KLINE, STEPHEN. Dr. Kline is a professor of communications and the director of the Media Analysis Laboratory at Simon Fraser University in British Columbia. His main interests are children's media, promotional communication, and nonbroadcast video design. Kline has published several studies and papers, including the 1998 "Video Game Culture: Leisure and Play Preferences of B.C. Teens" and the 1996 "Virtual Toys: Video Games and Postmodern Play" published in the International Toy Researchers Association Conference Proceedings. Since 1995 he has written six book chapters for publications ranging from *In Front of the Children* to *Toy Marketing: It's*

Child's Play. He has given many presentations at conferences, including the World Summit on Children and Television in Melbourne, Australia, the German Historical Society, and the Smithsonian Institution Conference in 1995 and has made more than seventy media appearances as an advocate for children's cultural rights. Currently Kline is working on a new book that will be published in 2000 by Columbia University Press called *The End of Play.* He can be reached at (604) 291-3520.

LAND, RICHARD D. Dr. Land is a sixth-generation Texan. He has been the president and Chief Executive Officer of the Southern Baptist Ethics and Religious Liberty Commission since 1988. He not only speaks publicly around the country concerning issues facing American society and cohosts a weekday radio show heard on 196 stations in thirty-four states. Land has published articles in journals and popular periodicals and served as contributing editor to a number of books. He is an ordained Southern Baptist minister. He can be reached at (615) 244-2495.

LEONARD, ZOË. Leonard was born in Liberty, New York, and has exhibited extensively at such venues as the Paula Cooper Gallery in New York, the Gallery Anadiel in Jerusalem, Israel, and the Galerija Dante in Umag, Croatia. Leonard has held twenty-nine solo exhibits and participated in more than 100 group exhibits. She has participated in numerous films, including *The Watermelon Woman,* which was shown at the Berlin Film Festival, the Los Angeles Gay and Film Festival, and the Toronto Film Festival. Her photographs or set designs have been used in theater productions such as the 1996 *Naked Angels Takes on Women,* and her work is housed in the public collections of seventeen museums, including the Museum of Modern Art, the Philadelphia Museum of Art, and the Groninger Museum in the Netherlands. She can be reached through the Paula Cooper Gallery at (212) 255-5156.

LIEBERMAN, JOSEPH. Senator Lieberman (D.-Connecticut) received both his bachelor's degree and law degree from Yale University. He was elected to the Connecticut State Senate in 1970, after which he served as Connecticut's attorney general. In 1988 he was elected to the U.S. Senate, where he is currently serving his second term. Author of four books, Senator Lieberman has been a vocal advocate for keeping media violence out of the hands of children and helped foster a rating system for video games and a V-chip law. He can be reached through his website www.senate.gov/~lieberman.

MANGLANO-OVALLE, IÑIGO. Manglano-Ovalle was born in Spain in 1961 and received an M.F.A. in sculpture from the School of the Art Institute of Chicago in 1989. He has had more than seventeen one-person exhibits, including *The Garden of Delights* at the Max Protetch Gallery in New York in 1998 and *Flora and Fauna* at the Rhona Hoffman Gallery in Chicago in 1997, and more than forty group exhibitions. Manglano-Ovalle has been awarded numerous honors, including the PACE Foundation International Artists Residency Fellowship, the National Endowment for the Arts Visual Artist Fellowship, and the Illinois Arts Council Special Projects Award. He has been featured in publications that range from the *Los Angeles Times* to *Art in America*. He can be reached through the Max Protetch Gallery in New York.

METZGER, KAREN. Metzger is a mountain-dwelling freelance writer, editor, and connoisseur of part-time jobs who strives to live her convictions — that work should be fun, nature must be respected, life is adventurous, and simplicity is the key to happiness.

MONTGOMERY, LISA. An editor of *Electronic House* magazine for ten years, Montgomery has covered every aspect of the home technology industry, from entertainment systems to complete home automation systems. She has interviewed hundreds of homeowners, top technology developers, and system designers and installers, and has visited and reported on dozens of automated homes throughout the nation. Her reporting style and experience make her one of the most respected technology journalists in the industry. She can be reached at (219) 287 6849 or through the *Electronic House* website at www.electronichouse.com.

MURI, SCOTT. Muri is a leader and innovator in education and currently works as the instructional technology specialist at Celebration School in Celebration, Florida. Muri has been involved in various education initiatives and has received numerous awards, including the Apple Distinguished Educator, the NCAE Human Relations Award, the Computerworld Smithsonian Award, and has been named one of America's first National Board Certified teachers. Currently Muri also serves as a consultant to the University of Central Florida and with schools across the nation on issues of technology integration. He also serves as the minister of youth at the Celebration Community Church.

PASTERNAK, ANNE R. Pasternak is executive director of Creative Time, a twenty-five-year-old alternative arts organization that brings cultural expression to urban landscapes while introducing the public to cutting-edge contemporary art practices. Before coming to Creative Time in the fall of 1994, Pasternak was the cofounder and director of BRAT, an arts organization committed to bringing innovative works of artistic merit to the public realm and cultivating new and expanded audiences. She has worked as an independent curator and writer, served as a curator for Hartford's Real Art Ways, where she organized gallery exhibitions and public art programs of emerging and under-represented artists, and was director of the Stux Gallery in New York City and Boston. She curated the traveling exhibition *Garbage*, and has published articles in the *Columbia Journal of American Studies* and the *Journal of Contemporary Art*, and essays in select exhibition catalogues. She is a board member of Art Table and the journal *Lusitania* and can be reached at www.creativetime.org or by phone at (212) 206-6674.

POBER, ARTHUR I. Dr. Pober is the executive director of the Entertainment Software Rating Board (ESRB), the organization that rates all video games and interactive software. Prior to establishing the ESRB, Dr. Pober was vice president and director of the self-regulated Children's Advertising Review Unit for the Council for the Better Business Bureaus. He also has held various positions in the field of education, including principal of Hunter College

Elementary School, director of special programs for the Board of Education in New York City, and director of gifted and talented, New York City. Pober has lectured throughout the world on topics ranging from education to intelligence training and arts education. He serves as a consultant for ABC's *One Saturday Morning*, *Squigglevision*, and Channel One. He received his doctorate in educational psychology and organizational development from Yeshiva University. Dr. Pober can be reached through the ESRB's website at www.esrb.org or at (800) 771-3772.

PUETT, J. MORGAN. Puett received her B.A. and M.F.A. from the School of the Art Institute of Chicago. Her artistic career has taken her from costume design in Telluride, Colorado, to exhibits and installation collaborations with artists such as Mark Dion, to her own venture projects—J. Morgan Puett Inc., a design and wholesale manufacturing business that focuses on handmade textile products. Puett has been featured extensively in the media, including *New York Magazine*, *Vogue*, and *Art Forum* and has received several awards: a Loeb Fellowship Nominee for design and architecture from Harvard, an Excellence in Design Award for best catalog design, and *Design and Merchandising* magazine's "Best Stores in Manhattan." Her latest venture product, Shack Inc., is a small retail business in New York that is an agency for her designs, environmental installations, and art projects. She currently lives in Pennsylvania and can be reached through Shack Inc. at (212) 267-8004.

QUINN, MARC. Quinn was born in London and graduated from Cambridge University in 1986. He held his first solo show in 1988 at the Jay Jopling/Otis Gallery in London. Since then he has shown his work in several venues, including at the Sydney Biennale in 1992, the Saatchi Gallery in 1993, the Tate Gallery in 1995, the Museum of Modern Art in 1996, and at the South London Gallery, Camberwell, in 1998. Quinn, along with artist Damien Hirst, is often cited as one of the founding figures of the 1990's British contemporary art movement and prefers to use his own body as a primary source for his work, as it is free from the associations of implied relationships.

RAO, K. L. SESHAGIRI. Dr. Rao is professor emeritus in the Department of Religious Studies at the University of Virginia, where he worked for nearly twenty-five years as a full professor. Rao has authored numerous articles and four books, has edited four volumes on *Religious Traditions of the World,* and is editor-in-chief of the forthcoming eighteen-volume *Encyclopedia of Hinduism.* His areas of specialization are Indic religions, Gandhian studies, and interreligious dialogue. He is the recipient of many distinctions and awards including the Hall of Fame "Anim Award" and the Ecumenical Studies Award, Dr. Rao can be reached at 937 Assembly Street, Suite 1018, Columbia, South Carolina, 29208.

READER, PERRY. Reader is vice president and general manager of the Celebration Company. A veteran architect/planner and real estate executive, Reader oversees business operations and development in Celebration, the master-planned community created by The Walt Disney Company in Central Florida. Formerly Reader was the vice president and general manager of Atlantic Gulf Communities in Orlando. A registered architect, Reader is a member of the Urban Land Institute and holds a master's degree in architecture from the University of Florida. He has served as the co-chair of the American Institute of the Architects' National Committee on Internship and is a member of the University of Florida Real Estate Advisory Board.

RICHARD, MARIO. Richard is a thirty-three-year-old who was born in Quebec City, Canada. His first skydive was in 1988, and he's since completed more than 2,000 dives. His first B.A.S.E. jump came in 1991. As B.A.S.E. jumper number 320, he's since completed more than 730 jumps. Richard is also an avid rock climber, paraglider, pilot, scuba diver, and nature lover. He works in research and development for Vertigo Base Outfitters.

RIFKIN, JEREMY. Rifkin is the author of fourteen books on the impact of scientific and technological changes on the economy, the workforce, society, and the environment, including his latest bestseller, *The Biotech Century: Harnessing the Gene and Remaking the World.* He has testified before numerous congressional committees and lectured at more than 500 universities in some twenty countries in the past twenty-five years. Rifkin, who was educated at the University of Pennsylvania and Tufts University, acts as a consultant to heads of state and government officials around the world and is founder and president of the Foundation on Economic Trends in Washington, D.C. He can be reached at (202) 466-2823 or through his website at www.biotechcentury.org.

ROSENBLOOTH, TOM. Rosenblooth is currently the director of admissions and financial aid at Francis W. Parker School in Chicago. He also teaches a high school course called "Adolescence in America." Rosenblooth was the director of the middle school at Holland Hall School in Tulsa, Oklahoma, from 1992 to 1997. Prior to that he taught seventh-grade English at Francis W. Parker and was the coordinator of the middle school. He has taught third and fifth grade and likes to write about middle school life, passionate teachers, and physics.

SACHEDINA, ABDULAZIZ. Dr. Sachedina was born in Lindi, Tanzania. He received his B.S. in biology and his Ph.D. in Middle Eastern and Islamic studies at the University of Toronto in Canada. Currently he teaches at the University of Virginia as a professor of Islamic studies and has focused his interests on Islamic medical ethics and Islamic roots of democratic pluralism. Dr. Sachedina also has been a visiting professor to several other institutions, including Haverford College and the University of Jordan. He has lectured internationally and either published or presented several papers and studies on Islamic theology and law. He is a senior associate, Preventative Diplomacy, at the Center for Strategic and International Studies, where he is a key contributor to the program's efforts to link religion to universal human needs and values in the service of peacebuilding. He can be contacted by email at aas@virginia.edu or by phone at (804) 924-6725.

SCHNEIDER, GARY. Schneider was born in South Africa and received his B.F.A. from the University of Cape Town and his M.F.A. from the Pratt Institute in Brooklyn, New York. He currently teaches at

Cooper Union in New York and has had fourteen solo exhibitions ranging from *Botanicals* and *From Life* at the P.P.O.W Gallery in New York at to *Genetic Self Portrait* at the Musée de L'Elysée in Lausanne, Switzerland. Schneider also has participated in more than fifty group exhibitions, and his works are housed in the public collections of various museums, including the Art Institute of Chicago, the Fogg Museum of Art in Cambridge, Massachusetts, the Metropolitan Museum of Art, and the National Gallery of Canada in Ottawa, Ontario. Schneider has an extensive bibliography and has been featured in magazines and newspapers, including the *New York Times*, *World Art*, and *Art on Paper*. He can be reached through the P.P.O.W Gallery in New York at (212) 941-8642 or by e-mail at ppow@juno.com.

SCHWARZKOPF, H. NORMAN. General Schwarzkopf, a graduate of West Point Academy, has had a distinguished military career that culminated with his success as Commander in Chief of the United States Central Command and Commander of Operations Desert Shield and Desert Storm. An overnight national hero, Schwarzkopf retired in 1991. He has received the Presidential Medal of Freedom among many other honors that include four honorary doctorates and the Ambassador of Hope Award in 1998. Since retiring, "Stormin' Norman" has written a bestselling autobiography and worked for many causes including The Nature Conservancy, STARBRIGHT, the Boggy Creak Gang, and Cap CURE.

SEEMAN, NADRIAN C. Dr. Seeman was born in Chicago and received his Ph.D. from the Department of Crystallography at the University of Pittsburgh. Seeman was a research associate in molecular graphics at Columbia University from 1970 to 1972 and was successively a Damon Runyon and a NIH postdoctoral fellow in nucleic acid crystallography at MIT from 1972 to 1977. After eleven years on the Department of Biological Sciences faculty at SUNY/Albany, he joined the Department of Chemistry at New York University as professor of chemistry in 1988. He has served as director of graduate studies in chemistry since 1991. Seeman has been the recipient of several awards, including a Basil O'Connor Fellowship, a Research Career Development Award from the National Institute of Health, and a *Popular Science* award in science and technology for the construction of a DNA cube. For the past fifteen years, Dr. Seeman's interests have centered on stable DNA branched junction molecules, and he has published several papers concerning this subject. He can be reached through New York University.

SELOVER, JOHN. Selover has been a member of the Christian Science Board of Directors for more than fourteen years and concurrently serves as the manager of The Christian Science Publishing Society, which publishes *The Christian Science Monitor, Journal, Sentinel, Herald*, and *Quarterly*. Before working for the Christian Science Church, Selover's career was in marketing, advertising, and publishing in the San Francisco and Silicon Valley area. He can be reached by email at seloverj@csps.com.

SERRANO, ANDRES. Serrano was born in New York and educated at the Brooklyn Museum Art School. Since 1985 Serrano, who focuses on photography, has had more than seventy individual exhibits, including A *History of Sex*, which showed at the Paula Cooper Gallery in New York, as well as internationally in Milan, Stockholm, and Paris, and *The Morgue*, which showed at the Museum of Contemporary Art in Montreal and also in Stockholm, Paris, and New York. Serrano also has contributed to more than 250 group exhibits internationally. He has received several grants and awards, including a New York State Council on the Arts sponsorship, a grant from the Louis Comfort Tiffany Foundation, two awards from Art Matters, Inc., and a National Endowment for the Arts fellowship. He can be reached through the Paula Cooper Gallery in New York at (212) 255-1105.

SHRIVER, DONALD W., JR. A native of Norfolk, Virginia, Dr. Shriver is an ordained minister who holds degrees from Davidson University, Union Theological Seminary in Virginia, Yale University Divinity School, and Harvard University. Shriver was president of Union Theological Seminary in New York for fifteen years and also has served as a Presbyterian pastor in North Carolina and an ethics professor at Emory University. He also has held numerous adjunct teaching appointments. Author of twelve books, including *An Ethic for Enemies: Forgiveness in Politics*, Dr. Shriver is a member of the Council of Foreign Relations and of the Advisory Committee for Social Witness Policy of the Presbyterian Church. He can be reached at dwshriver@aol.com or at (212) 222-5112.

SILVER, LEE M. Dr. Silver is a professor at Princeton University in the departments of molecular biology, ecology and evolutionary biology, and neuroscience. Silver authored *Remaking Eden: How Genetic Engineering and Cloning Will Transform the American Family*, and serves as the coeditor-in-chief of the international journal *Cloning, Science and Policy* and of the journal *Mammalian Genome*. Silver has published more than 150 scientific articles, was elected fellow of the American Association for the Advancement of Science in 1993, and received a ten-year National Institutes of Health MERIT award in 1995. He has spoken about reproductive technologies before Congress and in the national media. Dr. Silver can be reached through the Department of Molecular Biology at Princeton University or by phone at (609) 258-5976.

SLY, RANDOLPH. The Most Reverend Archbishop Sly, who has been in the ministry for more than twenty-seven years, is Archbishop of the Eastern Province of the International Communion of the Charismatic Episcopal Church, Diocese of the Potomac, and Rector of the Church of Holy Trinity in Washington, D.C. In addition to his work in the ministry, Archbishop Sly is a published author who has more than thirty multimedia and film scripts and more than 100 commercials to his credit. He had been named three times as one of the "Outstanding Young Men in America" and has appeared in *Who's Who in Religion* and *Who's Who in the Midwest*. He can be reached by phone at (703) 404-0754, by e-mail at abpsly@iccec.org, or through his website at www.iccec.org.

SPITZER, VICTOR. Dr. Spitzer is the director of the Center for Human Simulation and associate professor in the Department of Cellular and Structural Biology and Radiology at the University of Colorado School of Medicine. Spitzer received a B.A. in chemistry and a B.S. in math-physics from the University of Southern California. He received both his master's of science in nuclear engineering and his Ph.D. in physical chemistry from the University of Illinois in Champaign and then went on to do postdoctoral work at the University of Colorado Health Sciences Center. In 1991, along with David Whitlock, Dr. Spitzer was awarded a contract from the National Library of Medicine's Visible Human Project to be the principal investigator. His e-mail is vic.spitzer@uchsc.edu.

STRASBURGER, VICTOR. Dr. Strasburger is currently chief of the Division of Adolescent Medicine, professor of pediatrics, and professor of family and community medicine in Albuquerque, New Mexico. He has been featured nationally in the media and authored more than 120 articles and eight books on adolescent medicine and the effects of television on children and adolescents, including *Adolescents and the Media*. He is a consultant to the American Academy of Pediatrics' Committee on Communications, immediate past chair of the Academy's section on adolescent health, and has served as a consultant to the National PTA and the American Medical Association on the subject of children and television. He can be reached through the University of New Mexico.

TERRANOVA, J. T. First Lieutenant Terranova served in the U.S. Army's 2d Armored Cavalry Regiment and in the Gulf War in 1991. A graduate of the University of Oregon, Terranova compiled his experiences in the Gulf War into a book and a video, both called *Mirage, The Soldier's Story of Desert Storm*. Currently Terranova lives in Telluride, Colorado, and is working on a new book called *The Conchies, The Men Who Dared*, which looks at conscientious objectors in England during World War I.

THURMAN, ROBERT. Professor of Indo-Tibetan studies at Columbia University, Dr. Thurman is an internationally recognized scholar, translator, and author of books about Buddhism and Tibet. He is considered the leading American expert on Tibetan Buddhism and has published several books, including *Inner Revolution: Life, Liberty and the Pursuit of Real Happiness*. In 1989 he cofounded the non-profit cultural center Tibet House New York, which is dedicated to preserving Tibetan culture. Co-curator of an international traveling exhibit of Tibetan art, Dr. Thurman, who received his B.A., M.A., and Ph.D. from Harvard, was named one of *Time* magazine's most influential Americans in 1997. He can be reached at the Columbia University Center for Buddhist Studies at (212) 854-3218.

TSIARAS, ALEXANDER. Tsiaras is president and CEO of Anatomical Travelogue. He has more than twenty years of experience in the fields of medicine, research, and art and has won world recognition as a photojournalist, artist, and writer. His work has been featured on the covers of *Life*, the *New York Times Magazine*, and *Discovery*, among others. The Anatomical Travelogue has created a medical/technological space of the future from its penthouse perch in midtown Manhattan with 270-degree panoramic views of the entire city. The Anatomical Travelogue can be contacted at (212) 302-8188 or at travel@anatomicaltravel.com.

VON HAGENS, GUNTHER. Dr. von Hagens was born in Alt-Skalden, Germany, and pursued medical studies at the Friedrick-Schiller University in Jena, Germany. Between 1977 and 1995 von Hagens invented and perfected the process of plastination and gave lectures on it in more than twenty-five countries. Between 1984 and 1996 he participated as the main lecturer at eight international plastination conferences, and in 1995 he founded the Center for Plastination at the State Academy at Bischkek, Kirgisia, and at the Medical University at Dalian, China. Currently Dr. von Hagens is a profes-sor in anatomy at the University of Heidelberg School of Medicine. His 1997 show *Worlds of the Body* drew spectacular crowds and attention from the press. He can be reached at the Institute for Plastination in Heidelberg, Germany, at (011-49) 6221-3311-0.

WADE, NICHOLAS. Wade was born in Aylesbury, England, in 1942 and was educated at Eton and King's College, Cambridge. He became science editor at the *New York Times* in November 1990. Wade had served on the editorial board of the newspaper since February of 1982, concentrating on issues of defense, space, science, medicine, technology, environment, and public policy. Formerly a reporter with *Science* magazine, Wade also was Washington correspondent and deputy editor of *Nature*. He is the author of several books and has contributed articles to many other publications. He can be reached through the *New York Times* offices.

WADE, NIGEL. Born in Adelaide, South Australia, Wade now holds British and Australian nationality. Wade has been editor-in-chief of the Chicago *Sun-Times* since 1996 and was formerly the assistant editor and foreign affairs editor of Britain's leading newspaper, the *Daily Telegraph*. A journalist since 1964, Wade is an award-winning foreign correspondent who reported from Washington during Watergate and who was the first reporter to tell the outside world about the arrest of Madame Mao and her "Gang of Four" from Beijing, for which he won the prestigious Britain "What the Papers Say" Reporter of the Year Award in 1976. He can be reached through the offices of the Chicago *Sun-Times*.

WALSH, DAVID. Dr. Walsh is the president and founder of the National Institute on Media and the Family. Psychologist, educator, author, speaker, and parent of three teenagers, Dr. Walsh has emerged as one of the leading authorities in North America on family life, parenting, and the impact of media on children. Walsh has written five books, including the award-winning *Selling Out America's Children*, and authored the American Medical Association's *Physician Guide to Media Violence*. He has received numerous awards, including the 1995 Minnesota Medical Association's "Stop the Violence" Award, and has been featured as an expert on the effects of media violence in the print and television media. He can be contacted through the National Institute on Media and the Family at (612) 672-5437 or www.mediafamily.org.

WEIL, ANDREW. Dr. Weil was born in Philadelphia in 1942 and received a B.A. degree from Harvard and a M.D. from Harvard Medical School. He currently is director of the program in integrative medicine at the College of Medicine, University of Arizona, and has a general practice in Tucson, Arizona. He is the founder of the Foundation for Integrative Medicine in Tucson and editor-in-chief of the journal *Integrative Medicine*. Weil has authored many scientific and popular articles and seven books while also appearing as a frequent lecturer and guest on talk shows. He is an internationally recognized expert on drugs and addiction, medicinal plants, alternative medicine, and the reform of medical education. He can be reached through his website at www.drweil.com.

WEST, MICHAEL. Dr. West is the Chief Executive Officer of Advanced Cell Technology of Worcester, Massachusetts, a company focused on the medical applications of nuclear transfer technologies. He received his Ph.D. from Baylor College of Medicine in Texas and has focused his academic and business career on the application of developmental biology to age-related degenerative disease. From 1990 to 1998, West was founder, director, and vice president of Geron Corporation, where he initiated and managed programs in telomerase diagnostics, telomerase inhibition, telomerase-mediated therapy, and human embryonic stem cells. In 1998 he cofounded Origen Therapeutics, a company developing transgenic technology in commercial poultry. Advanced Cell Technology is located on the Web at www.advancedcell.com.

WHITE, DAPHNE. White is the founder and executive director of the Lion and Lamb Project, a national grass-roots parents' organization working to stop the merchandising of violence to children. The group has developed a Parent Action Kit, a resource guide that includes information about dealing with violence in the media, selecting nonviolent toys and games, and resolving family conflicts peacefully at home and on the playground. Lion and Lamb also cosponsors Violent Toy Trade-Ins around the country and offers parenting workshops nationwide. Lion and Lamb can be reached at (301) 654-3091 or on the Internet at www.lionlamb.org.

WHITLOCK, DAVID. Dr. Whitlock is a former chair of the Departments of Anatomy at the Upstate Medical Center of the State University of

New York in Syracuse and the University of Colorado School of Medicine in Denver. He is a past president of the Association of Anatomy Chairmen, a former member of the Neurology Study Sections of the National Institute of Neurological Diseases and Stroke, U.S. Public Health Services, a former NASA ATS-6 experimentor, a past member of the National Board of Medical Examiners, and a participant on the Radiological Society of North America's Task Force for cross-sectional anatomy. He is author or coauthor of sixty-four scientific publications on brain research and has published numerous articles, books, and computer-generated videodiscs on three-dimensional human anatomy. With Victor M. Spitzer, he is a principal investigator for the National Library of Medicine's Visible Human Project.

WITKIN, JOEL-PETER. Witkin was born in Brooklyn, New York, in 1939. Since 1969 he has held eighty-four individual exhibits at venues such as the PaceWildensteinMacGill Gallery in New York and Los Angeles and the Fotology Gallery in Milan, Italy, and participated in forty-eight group exhibitions internationally. He has been featured in *Vogue* and *World Art* and has either published, edited, or been featured in numerous books, including his latest, *The Bone House* and *Joel-Peter Witkin: A Retrospective*. Witkin's photography is in twenty-two permanent collections, including at the Metropolitan Museum of Art in New York, the Museum of Fine Art in Boston, and the Bibliotheque Nationale in Paris. He has received many awards, including the Augustus Saint-Garudens Medal from the Cooper Union School of Art in 1996, four National Endowment for the Arts photography fellowships, and the International Center for Photography Fourth Annual Award in Visual Arts. He can be reached through the PaceWildenstein MacGill Gallery at (212) 759-8964.

acknowledgments

As with most creative projects, *HIGH TECH • high touch* depended upon
the efforts of a larger team, most especially our researchers Allison
Johnson, a fiction writer known to us as "the supreme goddess of the
universe" for her unfailing efforts to do whatever, whenever for the
book; Kelly Hearn, a journalist by trade who whispered "genetics"
long enough for us to hear; and Joy Van Elderen, John's veteran
researcher who worked her usual magic by finding manifestations of
High Tech • high touch in the press.

Henry King, an I.T. specialist, played a critical role early in the
project, helping us establish a conceptual framework for the research
and answer to the question, what is technology? And Professor Bradd
Shore, chairman of the anthropology department of Emory
College, played an equally important role in guiding us in our question, what does it mean to be human? Special thanks to our readers,

Daphne White, Michael West, Arthur Caplan, Robin Hope, and Joe Gee for reading various chapters and generously sharing their comments and insights, and especially to Stephen Rhinesmith, who read the entire manuscript. And Foong Wai Fong, not only for thoughtfully reading the manuscript, but for arranging the translation of this book into Chinese.

Our appreciation goes to Larry Keeley and everyone at the Doblin Group who listened to our ideas in their earliest form and generously welcomed us into their Chicago office whenever we needed a place to work in the city.

Reading early drafts, Patricia Aburdene, who co-authored many books with John, gave us encouragement to keep going and offered insights that led us in the right direction as we laid siege to the kitchen, living room, dining room, and spare bedrooms of her home in Telluride—covering every horizontal and vertical surface with our work. Marsha Bailey, who has the energy of an angel, kept the refrigerator full of food, the cupboards full of drinks, and the whole infrastructure running.

Our dear friend Peggy Firestone not only provided the breakthrough we needed for understanding the Technologically Intoxicated Zone, but had undying faith in us and the same belief in truth. Dear thanks to Joan Childs and Jerry Zaret, who shared their friendship, their ideas, and their home as an escape when most needed. We also wish to thank our friend, writer and film critic Ray Pride, whose e-mail response time to our numerous inquiries was frighteningly fast and always witty; Sol Trujilo, CEO of U.S. West, who arranged for us to get an ISDN line in a week rather than in months in our remote location; Ken Olson, our computer doctor, who never failed to make us and our computers happy; Janice Clark, Toby Zallman, Jonathan Hahn, and William Potter, who early in the life of HIGH TECH • *high touch* so beautifully designed or brilliantly programmed various presentations and put up with three very visually opinionated writers; Sandy Grubar and Brian Gorman, who consistently and creatively problem-solved production processes for many of those early presentations; John DeMers, a writer and gentleman, for personally showing us his city of New Orleans; Lewis Branscomb, for sharing his incredible intelligence and experience with us as we mined his mind; enormous thanks to everyone who so generously granted us lengthy, earnest, and lively interviews, and whose thoughts were critical to the formation of this book, even if their words did not find their way into these pages; and the galleries, which graciously sent large portfolios about the artists they represent and which made the interviews with the artists possible.

Bill Leigh and Wesley Neff, our agents, patiently worked with not one, but three authors over the years as the book organically unfolded; and John would especially like to thank Suzanne Oaks, our editor, for taking more care with this manuscript than any editor he has ever worked with. We must also extend a word of thanks to our publishers, Nicholas Braeley, in the United Kingdom, for his early involvement and support; Bill Shinker, who signed on at the Frankfurt Book Fair in September of 1998, and his successor, Bob Asahina. We especially wish to thank our German language publisher, Doris Dinklage, for believing in the book first, offering helpful advice throughout the project, taking the photograph that became our publicity shot, and embracing us as a team of three.

Nana is most grateful to her sweet children, Rory, Lily, and Jake, who understood why she was working so hard, and to bright Molly Taylor, whose care and love made the lives of the children and Nana immeasurably better during the long project. Rory deserves a special thanks for thoughtfully reading and intelligently annotating the entire manuscript.

Douglas is most grateful to his family for their love and support, and especially to his brother Bob Philips, who kept in close touch despite the distance. Douglas is also indebted to Master Jian Hua Guo, of the Championship Martial Arts Academy of Chicago, for his patience, understanding, and continued mentorship, again, despite Douglas's absence.

The town of Telluride deserves a big thank-you for listening to our never-ending refrain "Still working on the book" in answer to all queries of "What's up?" We owe thanks to the staff of the Great

Room at the Peaks in Mountain Village for actually liking the fact that we periodically camped out there with computers and piles of papers, desperately needing a change of scenery. To the folks at Rustico, for opening their doors on their day off to provide a venue for the first reading of this book. We cannot forget to thank Dan Hanley from the Bean, who is an uncommonly good reader of popular culture, and DJ Harry for making our dancing feet happy at the Moon.

Warm thanks to all our friends and family, who forgave us for disappearing into the book vacuum and reemerging only years later.

But the one person who deserves our deepest gratitude is Joe Crump. He brought the team back together when we were falling apart by helping us define our roles in the complicated collaboration of three authors. He had confidence in us when we didn't. He had love for us when we needed it. He was willing to let any and every conversation shift at some point to the book. He insightfully commented on early drafts and half-done chapters, read and edited the final manuscript, making brilliant changes. He wrote for each of us these words, which we kept posted on our computers: "Wouldn't it be amazing if you can keep coming from a place where you help each other be great?" We can't say we accomplished that.

But we thank you, Joe.